Right
from
the
Horse's
Mouth!

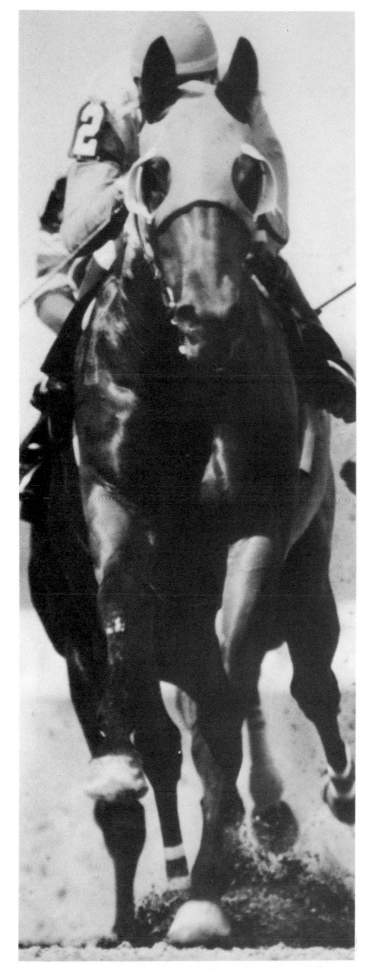

Right from the Horse's Mouth!

The Lives and Races of
America's Great Thoroughbreds
as told in their own words

John Devaney

Howard Liss

CROWN PUBLISHERS, INC., NEW YORK

Grateful acknowledgment is given for permission to reprint the following:

Photographs on pages 4, 7, 11, 12, 21, 24, 30, 35, 37, 38, 54, 55, 56 by Keeneland-Cook.
Photographs on pages 14, 33, 49, 59, 63, 81 by J. C. Skeets Meadors.
Photographs on pages 16, 22, 27, 28, 36, 42, 44, 47, 48, 50, 57, 60, 64, 67, 79, 83, 84, 86 by Keeneland-Morgan.
Photographs on pages 90, 92, 93, 94, 97, 99, 100, 104, 107, 109, 112, 117, 119, 120, 122, 126, 127, 130, 132, 136, 137, 139, 141, 143, 144, 148, 150, 151, 153, 154, 156, 161, 162, 163, 168, 174, 175 (2), 177, 178 by Bob Coglianese.
Photographs on pages 70, 73, 75 from *The Blood-Horse* magazine.
Photograph on page 167 by World Wide Racing Photos.

Published by Crown Publishers, Inc., 225 Park Avenue South, New York, New York 10003, and represented in Canada by the Canadian MANDA Group

CROWN is a trademark of Crown Publishers, Inc.

Manufactured in the United States of America

Library of Congress Cataloging-in-Publication Data

Devaney, John.
  Right from the horse's mouth!

  1. Race horses—United States—Biography.
2. Thoroughbred horse—Biography. 3. Horse-racing—
United States. I. Liss, Howard. II. Title.
SF338.M3   1987   636.1′2   86-19882
ISBN 0-517-56517-X

10 9 8 7 6 5 4 3 2 1
First Edition

For Robert Seth Fox,
with thanks for your suggestions and advice

CONTENTS

Right from the Horse's Mouth!

INTRODUCTION: SLIPS

From time to time sportswriters meet unusual people, rare birds, each one of a kind, with a certain quality that sets them apart from the ordinary. Such a person was Edward Jeremiah Madigan, born October 23, 1908, in the town of Manorhamilton, County Leitrim, Ireland; gone to God on November 15, 1985. Eddie was known to his horseplaying peers as "Slips." He was like no other Thoroughbred devotee we have ever encountered.

Slips was not at ease in any world other than the one at the racetrack. Whenever he spoke to anyone—and it was not that often—it was usually to respond to a question. Only when the topic was horses did he open up. On that subject his knowledge far exceeded the encyclopedia.

For instance, at a moment's notice Slips could tell you who won the fifth race at Hollywood Park on August 12, 1963, and while he was at it Slips would recite the win-place-show payoff and the name of the winning jockey. He knew the genealogy of every Kentucky Derby entry up through sire, grandfather, and great-grandfather.

Although Slips did play the horses, he was also gainfully employed writing a twice-weekly racing column for a small news syndicate that serviced a number of midwestern papers. In his columns Slips never predicted the winner of any particular race, pointing out that not even the horses themselves knew the outcome. Slips's approach was to make the reader know the horse, see the animal through Slips's eyes, understand the uniqueness of the Thoroughbred horse. To this slender, polite, soft-spoken Irishman, the racehorse was the only animal species—mankind included—that truly mattered to him. Horses were something of an obsession. Most other racing writers kidded Slips about his passion for colts and fillies, but we never did. We liked Slips, we respected him. Perhaps this mutual affection explains what happened later.

Slips traveled a lot through the length and breadth of the United States. He would be gone for a couple of weeks at a time, visiting the tracks and farms in Kentucky, Virginia, Texas, California, and Florida. Evidently he was always welcomed by the various owners, trainers, grooms, and stableboys, for he returned to those haunts again and again. He was free to wander through the paddock areas without hindrance, even free to enter the inner sanctum of the individual stall.

We ran into Slips occasionally at Belmont, Monmouth Park, or Aqueduct, the tracks in the Greater New York area. It was easy to spot him, a slim figure in a tweed jacket and battered hat, which he wore in all weather except on the most humid summer afternoons. We always gave him a big hello, and Slips seemed genuinely glad to see us. But he rarely smiled. The expression on his face was usually the same, not exactly mournful but rather wistful, like the look of a little kid standing outside a bakery with seventy cents in his pocket, knowing he had promised his mother to return with a quart of milk instead of the jelly doughnuts he really craved.

Slips Madigan acquired his nickname from the contents of his pockets. They were crammed to overflowing with slips of paper. That meant *all* his pockets, including those at the sides of his jacket, the inside breast pockets, the handkerchief pocket, and the pockets of his pants on both hips. Some of the slips were torn out of a schoolboy's copybook, others were once sheets of ruled notebook paper carefully cut into even lengths

This snapshot of Slips, taken at a place and time unknown, was found by the authors in one of the shoeboxes.

1

and widths. Words were penciled on both sides of each scrap of paper, but we didn't know what was written on them, at least not at the time.

Those slips of paper changed Slips's body contours as a day at the track progressed. Before the start of the first race Madigan would be as thin as a wire hanger, because the papers were stacked neatly on his person. Then, between races, he would excuse himself and head off toward the paddocks. He wasn't gone long, and when he returned that wistful, thoughtful look was etched even deeper on his face, blending into the wrinkles around his eyes and throat. Also, he had jammed into various pockets those slips of paper on which he had written, so that by the end of the eighth race, with his pockets bulging, Slips began to resemble a stuffed acorn squash.

As a horseplayer Slips had his share of winners, although he admitted that at times his choices ran out of the money, indicating that he was not quite in the superman class as a handicapper. Still, if asked, he would give us an occasional tip. Speaking in his own argot he would say, "Put down a couple of Washingtons or maybe even a Lincoln on Straw Hat in the sixth." We took his advice and often won.

We never saw Slips place a bet at the track he attended. He was too busy moving between the paddock and his grandstand seat. However, Slips usually took care of that detail in the morning before he went to the track. For instance, if we happened to meet him at Saratoga, he had already phoned his friendly neighborhood bookie earlier to place his wagers at Hialeah or Rockingham. Sometimes, when the mood was upon him, Slips might even risk some bucks whimsically on "those horses who ran funny"—the pacers and trotters entered at Yonkers or Monticello raceways. He recognized the qualities of the gaited horse that pulled a sulky, the bloodlines, the training. He called them "different kinds of Thoroughbreds." Praise indeed.

It was shortly before the end of November 1985 when we got a call from a lady named Elizabeth Neary O'Neill, who identified herself as a niece of Slips Madigan, the daughter of his sis-

ter. Sadly she informed us that her beloved uncle had gone to that great racetrack in the sky, and would undoubtedly spend eternity in the company of those creatures he loved best, Thoroughbred racehorses. After we had expressed our condolences, she told us that she had something for us, a gift from Uncle Slips. We agreed to meet with her and pick up the legacy of Slips Madigan at Parnell's, which is a friendly bar over on First Avenue in Manhattan.

The lady arrived carrying two plastic shopping bags containing more than a dozen shoe boxes, each box stuffed with the slips of paper accumulated by Mr. Madigan over the years. We thanked her kindly, shared a few rounds of bourbon with her, and took our leave.

It took a long time to sort and decipher those thousands of slips of paper amassed by Slips Madigan, and often we wondered why we bothered. It was a frustrating process, comparable to fitting together scattered pieces of a meaningless jigsaw puzzle. A couple of months went by as we desultorily worked on the contents of those shoe boxes. It wasn't an everyday task, because to have persisted would have driven us around the bend. Slowly, from the welter of scraps of paper, a pattern began to emerge, and the story of the repeated visits of Slips Madigan to the paddocks of American racetracks became clear.

These were diaries of horses! No, not the histories of horses—*diaries!*

When the slips of paper had been organized into sets, they took the form of an autobiography, full of quotes, written in *first person singular*. Like, "*I* won the Derby by three lengths . . . *my* jockey went to the whip at the sixteenth pole . . . *I* had to carry 135 pounds in that race."

We didn't know what to make of it. Had the late Mr. Madigan been suffering from periodic hallucinations? Perhaps these were the delusions of a lonely man, sitting in a chair late at night with a whiskey bottle at his elbow, ruminating and fantasizing a horseplayer's dream of getting the tip straight from the horse's mouth.

Yet there was in Slips Madigan's spidery scrawlings a certain ring of authenticity. He certainly did know about racehorses—he had been around them all his life. We recalled a few conversations we'd had with Slips in the past, when he told us he'd been a stableboy back in the Old Country at the age of ten, and how he got a job as an exercise rider when he immigrated to the United States. In that case, was it possible that perhaps Slips Madigan "heard" things the rest of us do not hear, because his ear was tuned toward those things and away from everything else?

There was still more to do after Slips Madigan's papers had been arranged and read. We had to check his "horse diaries." As writers, we learned long ago that flimsy rumors and coincidences do not make the solid bricks of fact. We were thorough, spending long hours researching the files of the *Morning Telegraph*, a newspaper that is to horseplayers what *Variety* is to people in show business.

Everything Slips Madigan wrote down was ac-curate. He was right on the money with every horse, every race. The pile of evidence made our ultimate verdict inescapable.

Somehow, perhaps through translating the neighs and whinnies, the stomping of a hoof, the pricking up of ears, the nodding of a head, the flaring nostrils, Slips Madigan had managed to grasp the vocal and body languages of Thoroughbred horses. If that didn't explain it, what else could?

This volume, then, is our final salute, a last tip of the hat to Mr. Edward Jeremiah "Slips" Madigan, biographer of Thoroughbred racehorses, "the Boswell of the bangtails," as it were. We miss him. But we are certain that somewhere in the lush meadows, where the air is clean and the clover is sweet, retired stallions and mares will pass on to their foals the story of the man who understood them.

MAN O' WAR

Dates on Slips's scraps of paper indicate that he visited Big Red, as Man o' War was known to his grooms and almost everyone else in racing, on at least a half-dozen occasions from about 1935 to 1943, at the Faraway Farm near Lexington, Kentucky, where Big Red lived in retirement.

People come here—they come here by the thousands each year—and they ask Willie Harbut [his groom] for a good story about me. Willie tells them lots of stories, not all of them true. I wish he'd tell them my favorite.

You know Sam Riddle. He's my owner. Sam loves a dollar—I hear he was a shrewd businessman, making things like blankets and suits. He saw me standing in a barn and paid $5,000 for me just because he liked the way my shiny red coat glimmered in the afternoon sun. He liked me better when he saw me run. And why not? I always liked what that writer [Joe Palmer] once put down in a newspaper about me. He wrote—I think I got this right—that I "was as near to a living flame as horses get."

Anyway, two years after Sam bought me and I was winning races by as much as a hundred lengths, a Texas millionaire came to Sam and offered to pay a million dollars for me.

Sam said no. The Texan handed Sam a blank check and told him to fill in the price he wanted.

I can never forget what Sam said. One reason

His number appropriate, Man o' War proudly struts to the starting line, eyes fixed even then on the horizon. Clarence Kummer is in the saddle for what, with one exception, was always a gallop to the winner's circle.

I can't forget is because Sam is always telling people what he said when he brings them around to look at me. Sam said, "You go to France and bring back the Tomb of Napoleon. You go to India and buy the Taj Mahal. Then I'll put a price on Man o' War."

I never heard of Tomb of Napoleon or Taj Mahal, but they sure must have been some horses.

People asked Sam why I was so good. He told them to look at how I was built. I stood about sixteen and a half hands, which meant I was rangier than most of the horses of my time. I heard a doctor, after examining me, tell my trainer that few horses have a cannon bone—that's the bone between the knee and the ankle—that measures 9 inches. Mine measures 10. Most big horses have a chest of around 75 inches, he said. Mine ran almost 80 inches. With that big a chest, the doctor said, I had to have a pair of boilers for lungs. Those lungs gave me the strength to run a mile and a half carrying 20 pounds more than any other horse in the race. And my size—I weighed about 1,150 pounds, which was 50 to 100 pounds more than other horses—gave me the weight in my hindquarters for speed. "Speed and stamina," Sam always said. "God never gave so much of each to any other horse."

Well, maybe. But there was another reason why I ran so fast. I don't know if I should tell you what it was. You might think I'm crazy. In fact, when I talk to myself about it, I often tell myself, "Big Red, you *are* crazy."

Let's get back to more pleasant subjects. Like my coat. When the sun strikes it on a late afternoon, people have said that it shines like gold. A lady, one of the thousands who came here each year, once stared at my coat and said, "Oh, I wish my hair would look like that." Willie heard her and said, laughing, "Lady, it would if you got all the care and brushing that Big Red gets."

It's true; Mr. Riddle sees to it that I get the best of care since he took me out of racing way back in 1920. I was only three years old. I had won every race I started except one, and I'll tell you later why I should have won that. I had lots of running left in me. But Sam pulled me off the track. Even when I was racing, he seldom let me go all out. Once I heard him say to a friend, "We never lifted a jockey to his back that we didn't tell him to hold the horse down, so as not to win by too wide a margin."

Why? you ask. Well, for one thing, he didn't want to wreck the morale of the other owners and horses by my winning too big. Sam was always talking about "improving the breed" and making racing what he called "The Sport of Kings." And what king wants to bet on a horse that goes off at odds of one to a hundred? Those were the odds in three of the eleven races I raced in my last year. Still, some people were so positive that I'd win that they slapped down a hundred-dollar bill to get back one dollar. In fact, I have heard that someone named "Chicago" O'Brien once bet $100,000 on me to get back $1,000, which is what I call confidence.

Sam took me out of racing for another reason. He winced every time he saw the weight the handicappers put on my back. They put 130 pounds on me when I was two, and that's the most weight a two-year-old is allowed to carry. When I was three, I had to carry 138. Sam worried that I'd break down carrying that weight in the longer races of a mile and a half that I'd run as a four-year-old.

But I loved to run, still do. When my exercise boy, Will Harbut, takes me out for a morning run these days, he has to pull on the reins. He leans over in the saddle and says to me, "Easy, Big Red, we're just galloping, we ain't racing."

In most of my races—except for the two famous ones I know you want to hear about—I finished eased up. You look at the charts, you'll see that it's so. In most of them, I ran hard for no more than a furlong or maybe two. Then the jock, like Sam told him, held me down so I didn't win too big and scare away horses for my next race.

Eased up or not, I set records. I set records for the mile, the mile and an eighth, the mile and three-eighths, the mile and a half, and the mile and five-eighths. Those records might still be on the books if I hadn't been reined in for most of my races.

Sometimes they couldn't hold me back. I won a race at Belmont—it was the Realization Stakes in 1920—by almost a hundred lengths over the second-place horse. That horse's name was Hoodwink, and he was the only other horse in the race. All the other owners, when I entered the race, took out their horses. It cost an owner maybe a hundred dollars to start, and they knew they were throwing their money away against me.

Before I tell you about the two races where I really had to go all out, let me answer the question that most tourists ask when they come here to visit. Do you know that I'm just about the single biggest tourist attraction in Kentucky? I don't know how many people come here each year [about forty thousand], but there are lots. And the one question I hear most is: "How did Man o' War get his name?"

What surprises them is that Man o' War wasn't the first name given to me. Let me explain. You know that I was foaled on March 29, 1917, at the Nursery Stud not far from here [in Lexington, Kentucky]. My sire was Fair Play. I've heard it said that he could have been a big winner, but that he sulked when he should have been running. He got the bad temper from his sire, Hastings, my grandfather, who was a real mental case. As he ran by horses during a race, he took a bite out of them.

My dam was Mahubah, who was tall and rangy. I got my size from her. Yearlings, as you know, are taken from their dams after weaning,

Two views of the solidly built machine that was as appropriately named as any champion could be.

so I don't remember much about her, but I'm told she was of a sweet disposition. When they mixed Mahubah's sweetness with Fair Play's sulkiness, they got a horse that bites its hooves the way some of you humans bite your fingernails. Which is one of the reasons why I think I'm crazy like my grandfather, although at least when I passed horses I didn't bite.

When I was a yearling my owner was Mr. Belmont [August Belmont II, a financier whose father was one of the first owners of American Thoroughbreds]. In 1918 Mr. Belmont was Major Belmont. He had joined the army even though he was past sixty-five. He went to France to fight in a war going on over there. His wife was so proud of her soldier that she decided to name one of his horses after him. She picked me and named me "My Man o' War." When I was registered, though, the first word was dropped and I became Man o' War.

Busy being a soldier, Mr. Belmont put all of his yearlings up for sale at the Saratoga auction. Sam Riddle, who had made millions in the clothing business, had decided to buy a few horses. When he saw me, it was love at first sight. I was standing in the sunlight, my coat gleaming gold. Later I heard him say, "He simply bowled me over. I couldn't think of anything but the colt."

He paid $5,000, cheap even then, and turned me over to trainer Louis Feustel. He brought in a tough little guy named Harry Vitotoe, who had the smashed-up face of someone who had swan-dived into a empty pool. Harry was a horse-breaker. He got me used to wearing a saddle and having someone sit on my back. If you think horses just naturally like people sitting on their backs, get down on all fours and have a child sit on your back with a stick in his hand. You'd be a little skittish. So are horses.

I don't know what *you* would do, but a horse bucks forward and rears backward to throw that unfamiliar weight—the saddle and the human—off his back. Harry knew how to cure a horse of rearing. When I reared, he pulled sharply on the reins. I had to stare upward at the sky, front hooves pawing the air. Since I couldn't see what

was below me, I had the frightening notion that there'd be nothing solid under me when I put those hooves down.

When my hooves did come down onto solid ground, I didn't want to rear again. And bucking didn't seem like such a good idea either, since I feared Harry would tug at those reins and make me look upward where I couldn't see anything. I was, as they say, broken.

Or so they thought. An hour later, along came little Johnny Loftus, who would be my jockey. Johnny got on my back. I threw him about forty feet.

Harry came running. He leaped on top of me and jerked at the reins. I got the idea. When he got off and Johnny got on, I trotted as gently as a lady's carriage horse. Later I heard Harry tell Sam, "Tossing Johnny was the last bad move Man o' War ever made." Indeed, whatever my mental quirks, I was always a gentleman.

I ran my first race, now a two-year-old, at Belmont on June 6, 1919. It was a five-furlong race for maidens. As Johnny boarded me, Feustel told him to take his time leaving the starting line. "Wait until the other horses get out of your way, Johnny," Feustel said, "then let him go after them."

Right from my first race, you see, they were holding me back—me, who loved to run!

We broke from the starting line—in those days a tape barrier was lifted—and I watched six horses scamper away from me. I caught the leader about a hundred yards from the start and won by five lengths. The next day's paper said I had made the other two-year-olds look like $200 horses. The grooms picked that up and I caught some nasty glares from the other stalls, but I thought the newspaper told it the way it was.

Now let me get to the first of the two races where I had to go all out. This is the race everyone talks about—the only one I lost, to Upset. Upset by Upset, you might say. Let me tell you what really happened and you decide who lost—me or my jockey.

It happened in Saratoga in August of 1919. By then I had won my first six races as a two-year-old. The handicapper put 130 pounds on me, and Sam was cross. He swore a blue streak about no two-year-old having to carry that much weight. Most of the other horses carried less than 120. Upset carried only 115.

As we lined up for the start, my legs trembled, my heart thumped. Starts were always hard on me. I felt this urge to bolt away from the other horses and keep as much distance between me and them as I could. That was all right on a racetrack—it was *good* on a racetrack. Trouble was, I got that anxious urge to bolt when I was in a stall. I wanted to run away from anything that was horse. Since I couldn't run away, I'd lie down in my stall and bite my hooves. Do you wonder why I think I may have picked up more than a little of Hastings's madness?

Anyway, I'm lunging at the barrier for this race at Saratoga, the Sanford Memorial. The other horses wheeled and turned, trying to form a straight line behind the tape barrier. The jockey on Upset was Willie Knapp. He shouted at Johnny Loftus, "Johnny, let's back up this time and maybe we can get a start."

Johnny, Mr. Good Fellow, turns me around to back me up. Wise Willie doesn't turn Upset around, and he backs up only a couple of steps.

Up flies the barrier. The jocks whoop and spur their horses off the line. I'm facing the wrong way. I turn around to see a line of horses disappearing into a cloud of dust.

I bounded down that track, frantic. I had never been so far behind, and I always had this nutty feeling I just had to escape from anything horsey.

I caught up with two horses, The Swimmer and Captain Alcock, as they swerved inside toward the rail. They cut me off. I had to pull up and go outside. Now I was even more crazed because I could see the two leaders, Golden Broom and Upset, go into the curve and pull even farther away from me.

Johnny wasn't holding me back this time. He knew he'd been tricked by Willie and that we had a lot of catching up to do.

As we turned for home, Golden Broom and

Upset led me by about five lengths. Golden Broom clung to the rail, Upset galloping outside, a big hole between them.

I charged for the hole. Willie heard me coming. He turned to look.

"Move over, Willie!" Johnny shouted. "I'm coming through!"

"Take off, you bum!" Willie yelled over his shoulder. "Or I'll put you through the rail."

He swerved Upset inside to close the hole. If Johnny had kept quiet, I would have shot through that hole before Willie could close it.

Johnny hesitated, then swung me outside. That meant going sideways while Golden Broom and Upset were going straight ahead. We lost more ground.

I saw only a hundred yards between me and the wire. I tried to cover that hundred yards in one long bound. I didn't, of course, but I swept by Golden Broom and, seconds later, came up to Upset and flew by him.

And even as I did, I know I was too late. We had gone under the finish. Upset ahead by less than a length.

I couldn't sleep most of that night. The race kept running in my mind—over and over. Finally, when I did drop off to sleep just before dawn, I had this dream. I saw Upset in front of me. I'd charge right up to him. Something held me back. I couldn't pass him. I charged again—and again some pressure forced me back. I woke up to the sound of hammering. I realized I had been kicking at the stall, the grooms staring at me, mouths wide with fright.

Almost every night, for the next few weeks, I had the same dream. Then, in my next race, I left Upset in the ruck with the rest of the pack. In the Hopeful Stakes at Saratoga, I flew by him and everyone else. He and I went to the Futurity at Belmont.

"You're two wins and one loss against me," he said when we met one morning after our workouts. "This next time I'll even us up."

He'd been listening to his trainer, who was telling people that Man o' War wasn't the horse of all time, as people had been saying. "Man o'

War can be taken," he told reporters. "We proved it in Saratoga, we'll prove it here."

I paid no attention to Upset or his trainer. I knew what had happened at Saratoga—and, I think, so did Upset.

I won the Futurity, and Upset wasn't even close. I heard no more from Upset or his trainer. And I stopped having that dream.

That victory ended my racing as a two-year-old. I had nine firsts, one second, in ten starts. People said I was a shoo-in to win the three-year-old Triple Crown in 1920, just as Sir Barton had won the three big races in 1919. But Sam Riddle once again wouldn't let me run. Sam said he didn't believe that three-year-olds were strong enough in early May to run a mile and an eighth.

What a hoot! Big Red couldn't run a mile and an eighth? What did he think I was—one of those runty little sprinters?

Sam did let me run in the Preakness. I won easily. One of the horses who ate my dust was Upset, which didn't make me feel bad at all.

I won everything I entered that summer. After my races, I would listen to the grooms reading the *Daily Racing Form* charts. The charts said things like "Man o' War won easily" or "won cantering" or "won eased up."

But I didn't finish eased up in the Dwyer Stakes at Aqueduct that July. That was the second of the two tough races of my career. Only one horse entered the race against me—a little sprinter named John P. Grier. The newspapers said he was fast enough to build up a lead in a mile-and-an-eighth race that I couldn't close—especially since he'd be hauling 108 pounds and I had 126 on me.

The biggest crowd in the track's history up to that time came out to see the race. By now, Man o' War was as famous as Ty Cobb or Babe Ruth or any of those baseball players. Today, you know, the 1920s are called "The Golden Age of Sport" because there were so many heroes. But I heard Sam Riddle say more than once that the first hero of that Golden Age was Man o' War.

He knew that John P. Grier had only one way of beating me: by running his race. His trainer figured I'd stick close to John P. no matter how

fast he sprinted—he knew I couldn't let any horse get too far ahead of me. Sprinting wasn't my game. It figured that I'd be more exhausted than John P. when we turned for home.

We streaked off the starting line, me on the inside, John P. at my flank. We flew over the first half mile in 46 seconds, a track record. We went by the five-furlong mark in :57²/₅, another record. We passed the three-quarter pole in 1:09³/₅, a third record. We ran by the mile mark like we were glued together, the time 1:36 flat, still another record.

We thundered side by side down the stretch. My head was filled with a tremendous dull roar, and when I saw John P. move slightly ahead of me, head thrusting, I knew my eyes had to look like his—bugged out.

I stretched my thirty-foot stride, trying to catch up. Eddie Ambrose, atop John P., felt the little sprinter stagger. Eddie sensed his horse was almost through. As he said later, he knew his only chance was to lure us into a trap.

He let John P. drift a few feet outside. He wanted me to charge by on the rail. Then he'd swing inside and cut me off. My jock, Clarence Kummer, would have to pull up and go outside. There wasn't enough ground, maybe a hundred yards, for me to stop, come around, and try to catch even a staggering John P.

I saw Ambrose swerve John P. toward the inside. Clarence wasn't holding me back this one time—we were behind.

I blew by John P. as fast as I have ever run in my life. Eddie watched me go through the space he had tried to slam shut. Later I heard him say, "He went by me like a red flash." I won by about five lengths.

John P. Grier never again raced with the speed and confidence he had shown before our race. Once, I heard a trainer tell Sam: "Something went out of John P. when Big Red flew by him. It was like he had seen something that wasn't of this world."

One of the other big names of the Golden Age was Earl Sande. What was it that the writer Grantland Rice wrote about Sande? Something about "Give me a handy guy like Sande, bootin'

In his hardest-fought victory, Man o' War flashes by John P. Grier in the 1920 Dwyer Stakes at Aqueduct. Minutes later his hide was still so hot that clouds of steam billowed around him as handlers hosed him with water.

those winners home.'' Something like that. Sande rode me in one race at Saratoga. Later, in the winner's circle, he told reporters that my stride was longer than the stride of any horse he had ever seen. He said I ran so smoothly it was like I wasn't running at all. Lots of people said that when they put their binoculars on me, I seemed to be running in slow motion, I was so smooth. It was only when they put their glasses down—and saw how I was pulling away from the field—that they realized how fast I was running. Sande said I was the greatest horse he had ever ridden.

That opinion probably cost Earl a ride on Sir Barton in what some newspapers in 1920 called "The Match Race of the Century." A Canadian track in Ontario challenged Sam to race me against Sir Barton, the 1919 Triple Crown winner, for $75,000. Sam accepted.

Everyone wanted to read about the race. Newspapers printed rumors, under huge black headlines, that gamblers might try to drug me or even kill me. Sam hired private detectives to guard me twenty-four hours a day. When we took the train to Ontario, Sam brought along his own cooks to make my meals.

In one of his last races, Man o' War overtakes Damask near the finish to win the 1920 Jockey Club Gold Cup at Belmont. The Belmont course was then a left-handed one, the horses running clockwise.

12

Sir Barton had the speed of a sprinter like John P. Grier—but a lot more stamina. His people, we learned later, believed he could beat me to the top of the stretch by at least five lengths, enough space for him to hold off any charge I might be able to make in the last few yards of the mile-and-a-quarter run.

Trainers are always coming up with strategies like that. I never paid much heed to all that talk about laying back or "taking the track," which is a favorite expression of trainers, meaning to take the lead. Now, when I get a chance to talk to my sons and grandsons, like that Seabiscuit, who is going to be something, I say: Don't worry about the tricks that trainers come up with. Speed and stamina will win out over tricks. Just run the race.

The race was held on a bright, sunny day in front of a tremendous crowd in Windsor, just across the border from Detroit. I trembled under Clarence Kummer as we stood at the starting line, jittery as usual. Earl Sande had been supposed to ride Sir Barton, but at the last minute another jock took his place. Sir Barton's owner had his revenge for that remark about my being the greatest.

The tape barrier dropped. We went off as a pair—me on the inside, Sir Barton at my side. Together, jaw to jaw, we ran the first furlong in the fastest time ever recorded at the track.

Sir Barton crept ahead to take the lead. Clarence held me back. He thought no one could run as fast as we'd been going at the start of a mile-and-a-quarter race. I thought I could—but Clarence wouldn't let me.

We came out of the first turn and into the backstretch. I pounded along at Sir Barton's heels. I kept my head bobbing forward, trying to give Clarence a message. Finally the message got through.

Clarence let go. With three or four strides I shot by Sir Barton and opened up a two-length lead. It was three lengths at the turn, four halfway through the turn, and six as I entered the homestretch. Halfway down the stretch, Clarence looked back. He saw Sir Barton sucking for air. Clarence rose in the stirrups to wave his stick at the cheering crowd. We crossed the finish line

some eight lengths ahead. We had smashed the Canadian record for the mile and a quarter by a full six seconds.

And that, as the grooms say, was all she wrote for me. Sam announced I would never race again.

I would begin to raise a family. Stud duty is the racing man's term, which always seemed a kind of brutal way of defining the task. Sam said that I "would improve the breed."

But I still wanted to run.

I'd run only twenty-one times in two years. In those days I could have run every week. I'd won twenty races, finished second in my only defeat, to Upset, a horse I beat the next four times we raced each other. You would think that with a record like that, I would have been allowed to compete at least one more year as a four-year-old. But Sam had spoken. I was washed up, finished, through—and disgusted.

Of course, I have no gripes about life here at the Faraway Farm. I am up at five for a six-mile jaunt. My exercise boy, Bobby, holds me back or I'd run like in the old days. Well, almost like in the old days.

After my jaunt there's a washing down, plus good food—six pounds of oats, bran, and carrots—and the chance to meet all the people who came to see me.

I like to pose for pictures. A friend of mine, Major Trent, an old steeplechaser, taught me how to pose. I always stand straight and still, my head raised high as if I am trying to gaze at something just beyond the horizon. Major Trent said that the pose got him into the society pages of Sunday newspapers. People love a horse to look like that, I don't know why.

Will Harbut always gives a little spiel when he shows me off. He takes the tourists to the other stalls and then he stops at mine. He says—I know it by heart—"Ladies and gentlemen, this horse owes nobody nothin'. He raced ten times as a two-year-old and eleven times as a three-year-old and nobody beat him."

Somebody in the crowd, of course, asks about Upset. With a sly smile, Will says, "I didn't see it, mister, so I still say it's a lie."

That gets a big laugh and it's my entrance cue.

13

I come forward out of my stall as Will turns and says, "Ladies and gentlemen, the mostest horse in the world. Come on out, Big Red!"

Man o' War sired 386 foals. Some 220 were winners and 61 won stakes races on flat tracks. The most famous was War Admiral, but the most successful probably was Battleship. He won steeplechasing's biggest race, England's Grand National, in 1938.

Man o' War celebrated his thirtieth birthday in 1947. The equivalent of a ninety-year-old man, he was still frisky with his grooms, tall and distinguished when he stood before the tourists who flocked to see him year after year. In some thirty years, it was estimated by people on the farm, more than three million came to his stall.

He leads me out. They applaud. I begin to canter. The applause grows louder. But oh, gee, I wish they could have seen me when.

On November 1, 1947, a heart attack killed Big Red in his sleep. Some two thousand people came to the funeral service. A jockey trumpeted a last call to the post. *Blood-Horse* magazine wrote this tribute: "The horsemen who came from all over the world to see him in his prime at Faraway will remember him vividly—the massive body, the wide sweeps of muscle, the great chest and abnormally wide spacing between the forelegs, the die-cut perfection of his legs and feet, the slight dip of the back, the high head, the imperial air, the feel of power and mastery. They will not look to see another like him."

In retirement in 1937, Man o' War is led by Willie Harbut on a morning stroll. Thousands came each year to Lexington to view what was, and still is, a legend.

SEABISCUIT

Let me tell you what it was like for me that early part of 1940. I was seven years old. I was fat after a summer on a farm up in the California hills. They wanted me to beat the best young horses in the country—three-year-olds and four-year-olds—and grab the richest purse in racing, a purse I had missed winning twice by a nose. No way, people said. If I heard it once, I heard it a dozen times during that winter of 1940: "They never come back."

I had broken down in 1939—and no wonder. My first trainer—you know him, "Sunny" Jim Fitzsimmons—said, way back when I was two years old, that I had a trick front knee that could splinter under me at any time. But that didn't stop Sunny Jim from racing me until my rib bones stuck out from my sides. I ran thirty-five races as a two-year-old—more than most horses run during a career today [circa 1950, according to Slips's notes]. I ran seventeen times before I finally won. Of those thirty-five races, I won only five. My total earnings for that year came to about $12,000 [$12,510], which was about what Omaha made in an afternoon.

The grinning former cowboy, Tom Smith, leads a tired-looking Seabiscuit and an exultant Iceman, George Woolf, toward the winner's circle after the match race victory over War Admiral at Pimlico in 1938.

Sunny Jim and his people seemed amazed just to see me finish. They called me the Runt when I was a colt because I had to look up at most of my stablemates. When I began to race, they called me the Ugly Duckling—and I even heard that name just before my big match race against War Admiral. The Beauty and the Ugly Duckling, the reporters called us. My bucked knees bent outward. Sunny Jim once said that I ran like a duck swimming.

I fooled Sunny Jim. He got rid of me for $8,000 and I made more money for the man who bought me, Charles Howard, than any horse up to then except one. I won purses for Mr. Howard wherever a railroad track would take me. One year, I heard a groom say, Pumpkin and me covered fifty thousand miles in a railroad car, crisscrossing the United States from coast to coast about half a dozen times.

I guess you don't know about Pumpkin. He's gone now, got sick and died. He was a palomino, a cowboy pony, and he sure helped me fit in with Mr. Howard's stable. I didn't know what to expect and I acted standoffish when I met Pumpkin, who was a stable pony. Pumpkin said something like this to me:

"You Thoroughbreds are all alike. You think because your family goes back four hundred years, you can act like a prima donna. Look, little fella, my family first came to this country with the conquistadores of Spain. That was about four hundred years ago, and we were old then."

I may have acted like a big shot, but I sure

didn't feel like I was anything special when I came to Mr. Howard. I guess I had what you people call an inferiority complex—acting like a big shot on the outside, scared to death on the inside. Who could blame me? As long as I could remember, I had to look up to other horses and, for a long time, especially with Sunny Jim, I was just another small face in a big crowd.

Then came winning years for Mr. Howard, bucked knees and all, even though I couldn't win the Santa Anita Handicap, the richest race of them all. Running in a race during the summer of 1939, someone stuck a knife into my leg—or, at least, that's the way it felt. What had been predicted for me for five years had at last happened—I'd broken down.

Mr. Howard took me to his country farm, brought me lovely mares, and I began to make little Seabiscuits. Then came that try for a comeback to win the Handicap one last time.

You know what happened when I tried, of course, but I know you are here to find out *how* it happened.

After I was foaled back in 1933 on the Claiborne Farm in Kentucky, my dam, Swing On, liked to take me as a weanling on short walks around the farm. I can remember her saying that one day I'd be as tall and rangy as Gallant Fox, who lived there on the farm in retirement. I stared at the Fox. He seemed so big. Mom told me tales about my grandfather, Man o' War, and how I might be as big as Big Red.

I worried that I'd never be big. I knew the grooms called me the Runt. Most weanlings have straws for legs, but mine were reedier than the rest. Ribs stick out of a weanling's chest, but mine, I heard a stablehand say, "you could play like a banjo."

My sire was Hard Tack, who stood as big as his father, Big Red. I heard people say that when Hard Tack raced, he slashed his way through the field. But pop gave me my bucked knees. He had my kind of knees, bowed a tendon in his second year, and went to stud at Claiborne.

I left Claiborne in the fall of 1934, bought by Ogden Mills, whose trainer was Sunny Jim. People called him Sunny Jim because he nearly al-

ways had a sunny smile on his face. Whenever he looked at me, all I ever saw was a dark cloud.

Not that Sunny Jim looked at me very often. He looked most of the time at just two horses. One was Omaha, the champion horse of 1935. The other was Granville, who would be the champion of 1936. They were the stars. The rest of us were, to Sunny Jim, the supporting cast.

When Sunny Jim did talk about me, I heard things I didn't like. He talked about my left front knee being what he called "dangerously sprung," which meant it could collapse when I raced. He said I had what he called "a good early lick," meaning I got out of the gate fast. But he said that in workouts I had a bad habit of letting the other colts catch up with me.

Sunny Jim said I loafed. To me, it was just good horse sense to take it easy in the middle of a race, saving a burst for the end. But horses flew by me when I slowed down.

I went south to Florida for my first race that January of '35. In a three-eighths-of-a-mile sprint, I ran fourth. What I still recall about that day was that parade to the post. A woman pointed at me and said, "Oh, look at the funny-looking bay horse. He looks tired already."

As you can guess, I didn't come to racing bearing the stature of a champion.

I raced as often as twice a week that year of 1935 as a two-year-old. Sunny Jim must have decided that the more I ran, the less I might eat—but I ate a lot. The grooms kept a muzzle on me until chow time. Otherwise, I'd gobble up my straw bedding and have no place except the ground to sleep. That eating packed pounds onto my square frame. Once I heard a soldier say I was shaped like a tank.

I won a couple of races, the biggest the Ardsley at Aqueduct, but in those thirty-five starts, I finished in the money only seventeen times— five firsts, seven seconds, five thirds. I have often wondered whether the $12,000 I earned paid my train fare.

The next spring came deliverance from those dark-cloud looks Sunny Jim threw at me. Trotting to the post at Suffolk Downs, I saw a tall, thin railbird gazing at me. I stopped, for some reason, and met his eyes. I sensed we would meet again. We did.

The man was Tom Smith. Tom Smith had been a cowpuncher and a rodeo rider. He knew horses. A rich man in San Francisco, Charles S. Howard, hired him to build a stable of racehorses. He came east to look over three-year-olds like myself. My blocky build caught Tom Smith's eye at Suffolk. He liked me better when I won the race by a length and a half.

Tom went to Saratoga to meet Mr. Howard. Sunny Jim had sent me up there to run in the Mohawk Claiming Stakes. Minutes before the race started, Mr. and Mrs. Howard, just off a train from California, settled into their seats. Mrs. Howard watched me and a string of other three-year-olds canter down the track toward the start. "What about that little bay?" she said to her husband. "He's the blocky one with the black points running clear up his legs."

They looked at their program and saw my name was Seabiscuit. Mrs. Howard has told this story many times. She said to her husband, "I bet you a cool drink he doesn't win this."

He won the drink. I won by six lengths. Sipping his lemonade, Mr. Howard told Tom Smith that he thought I looked like too good a horse to race in cheap claimers. Tom said he liked the way I'd won my last two races, but that I'd been worn down from too much racing.

Mr. Howard offered Ogden Mills $8,000 for me. Sunny Jim growled that he didn't want to lose me after I'd started to win, but finally he agreed. I think he was sure my knees would give way.

Tom Smith watched me pace my stall one night. I couldn't sleep. From all that racing, I heard starting bells clang in my head. I heard pounding hooves come from behind to catch me. In short, I brought my races back with me to the stable, and who can sleep while still running a race—especially one that you lost?

Then Tom put Pumpkin in the stall next to me. He cut a window in the wall between our stalls. Pumpkin and me could do what the old cowpuncher called "visitin'."

At night I'd watch Pumpkin settle down in his straw bedding. He'd nibble at the straw. He'd grab a long straw between his teeth, let it dangle from his mouth. He dozed off. The straw slipped out of his mouth. He snatched it back.

I'd watch him for a half hour. He made me feel relaxed, no more bells or pounding in my ears, and I'd soon flop down and fall asleep. For the first time in almost two years, since I came to racing, I slept soundly.

I put on muscle, especially in my hindquarters, where a horse gets that breakaway speed. In workouts I know I was faster than I'd ever been. I could tell by the sparkle in Tom Smith's eyes as he gripped his stopwatch and stared at me when I came back to the barn.

He knew—I guess from Sunny Jim—that I slowed down after those lickety-split dashes from the gate. One day he brought a tall, skinny young jockey to my stall. His name, I soon learned, was John Pollard. Everyone called him "Red" because he had hair the color of carrots.

Staring at me, Tom said to Red: "This horse has more early speed than maybe any horse I've ever seen. But once he jumps out in front, he thinks it's all over unless you remind him that it isn't."

Red said he would remind me. You know, of course, about the time he didn't. But Red made that mistake only once.

Mr. Howard and Tom decided after about a month that I was rested enough and strong enough to race. They led me and Pumpkin into a railroad boxcar—boy, was I going to see a lot of it in the next few years—and off the train rolled to Detroit.

Tom Smith had heard from Sunny Jim that I slept hardly at all when I rode a train. That was true. A conductor on a train once told a man, while I was listening, that trains made a sound like this—*heinie-manush, heinie-manush*—that drove him crazy. Ever since, when I got on a train and tried to sleep, all I heard was *heinie-manush, heinie-manush*, and who could sleep with that sound in his ears all night?

I once heard a horse say that there is a real person named Heinie Manush, a baseball player, but I didn't believe that, do you?

Anyway, when I got on the train to Detroit—dreading the trip—Pumpkin came on after me. Right away he stretched out on a bed of straw, the straw between his teeth. That made me think—this is just like a regular stall except it's moving. I slept all the way to Detroit.

I won my first race at Detroit. Before we left I had earned at least twice the $8,000 Mr. Howard paid for me. By the end of 1936, I had won almost $30,000 [$28,995], most of it for Mr. Howard. I had raced twenty-three times, won nine, finished second once, third five times, and out of the money in only eight races.

At the start of 1937, Tom and Mr. Howard entered me in the world's richest race, the $100,000 Santa Anita Handicap, in which the winner gets better than $50,000. A year earlier I had been running in cheap claimers. Now I stood in the gate next to the best three- and four-year-olds in the nation.

Tom told Red Pollard to hold me back at the start. He didn't want me to get caught in the pack. He was afraid that someone might bang into that trick knee of mine.

We got off cleanly and I tucked in along the rail as we went by the grandstand the first time. I must have been maybe ninth or tenth in a sixteen-horse field. Two sprinters, Special Agent and Boxthorn, shared the lead, the rest of us trailing in a long string as we hit the backstretch.

Red let out the reins a notch. I knew what he wanted—one of those bursts of speed I had showed in my workouts.

Back went my ears, low went my body so I could lengthen my stride. My rear quarters felt like a pair of tightly coiled springs. I came up on Boxthorn and went by him, feeling as though he was standing still. I came around the far turn seeing only one horse in front of me—Special Agent. As I turned into the stretch, I came up on Special Agent, saw his frothing mouth and heard his gasping. I went by and knew he was through.

But something was happening behind us. One of the year's best four-year-olds, Rosemont, streaked by the other horses and came charging at me.

I can still hear the crowd's sudden roar as Rosemont came closer. But I thought the roaring was for me, and with the roaring, I didn't hear Rosemont coming up. Worse, I made an old mistake and thought, after passing Special Agent, that it was all over. Seeing the wire so close, I eased up.

Red had been warned not to let this happen—and now it happened. Rosemont suddenly popped up on my right, as big as a truck you don't see until it's too late.

The surprise gave me a jolt of energy. I leaped forward, the leap putting me ahead of Rosemont by half a length. But I came down awkwardly, my rear front foot hitting the turf first. I rebounded like a basketball that has no air in it. My next stride took me only half my usual length. Rosemont surged forward and the two of us swept under the wire as one.

The crowd's roar had faded to an anxious murmur as the two of us cantered toward the winner's circle. As we got close to the stands, I heard that distinct *whirr* as the photo came down the wire from the photo booth to the judge's stand. A minute later, the result flashed on the board. I was looking at Mr. Howard's face and I knew in a moment we had lost.

We'd lost by half a nose. Red jumped off me and his face looked redder than his hair by a couple of shades of scarlet. When Tom Smith got closer, Red's face could have passed for a stoplight. I turned away, knowing the loss was as much my fault as Red's.

When Tom calmed down in about a week, according to what I heard later from the scuttlebutt, he told Red: "Watch Biscuit's ears coming down the stretch. If they're pricked forward, remind him that this business isn't over yet. Cluck to him, tap his head, give his rear a couple of whacks. Make him know that something like Rosemont may be charging at him."

But Red never had to remind me that business was still to be done. Never again did I come down a stretch without seeing the name Rosemont flash across my brain.

Tom and Mr. Howard told each other that I'd win the Santa Anita the next year. They took me and Pumpkin to a freight car and this time we

Seabiscuit flies to the wire to take the 1937 Butler Handicap at Empire City. Seabiscuit, his fans said, "would go anywhere a railroad track took him" for a race.

His nearest pursuer, Jesting, swallows his dust as Seabiscuit wins the 1937 Yonkers Handicap at Empire City in New York. Then he stands dutifully in the winner's circle with Tom Smith and Red Pollard.

hand the winner by the length of his nose. I had lost two straight Santa Anitas by no more than a pair of noses.

I had celebrated my fifth birthday the previous January 1. I could try again to win the Santa Anita Handicap when I was six. But that's pretty old for someone competing against a lot of young and hungry horses for the world's richest race.

War Admiral, meanwhile, tore by horses in races back east. Belmont Park offered a pot of $100,000, winner take all, for a match race. Mr. Howard said yes. I got on a train that pulled our boxcar east for the race, which was scheduled for late May.

I came off the train woozy and then I trained even woozier. Mr. Howard asked that the "Race of the Twentieth Century," as the newspapers called it, be postponed. Of course, all the eastern people said we'd ducked away from War Admiral.

We rolled back west, toting up more railroad track mileage for the year. I won the Hollywood Gold Cup, carrying top weight, as usual, of 133 pounds. But the fun of winning was spoiled by the taunts from the East—that I could only beat the best of the West, not the East's best, War Admiral. When Pimlico, the Maryland track, offered $15,000, winner take all, for a match race, Mr. Howard quickly said yes to silence the taunts once and for all.

Back into my boxcar I trotted for the three-thousand-mile trip to the East. I didn't say anything to Pumpkin or the other horses in Mr. Howard's stable but I thought to myself: Why couldn't War Admiral come west by riding the rails for four or five days? Every horse should get to know *heinie-manush*.

At Pimlico I heard about the rules for the match race. Sam Riddle, who owned War Admiral, had made the rules. The distance: a mile and three-sixteenths. There would be a walk-up flag start, no starting gate. Each horse would carry 120 pounds. Winner took all.

Mr. Howard knew that the flag start might send War Admiral winging to the front. War Admiral often started slowly out of the gate.

Not surprisingly, I guess, the bettors picked War Admiral. You got one dollar for two dollars

The newsreel cameras of the day film Seabiscuit, with Red Pollard in the saddle, as the California horse goes to the post for a 1938 race at Belmont.

chugged east—all the way to the Atlantic. At Suffolk Downs I showed up for the $50,000 Massachusetts Handicap, at that time the richest race in the East. I gave away as much as thirty pounds and won while setting a track record.

By now, to the public, I was that California ugly duckling who made you wonder how he won—but he won. That was the way they talked about me from coast to coast by the end of 1937. My record for the year came to eleven wins in fifteen starts. I finished second twice, both by a nose, third once, out of the money once. I'd won more money than any horse that year [$168,580], a tad ahead of another grandson of Man o' War. That was three-year-old War Admiral, who had raced eight times and won all eight, including the Triple Crown.

Everyone wanted me to hook up with War Admiral in a match race. Mr. Howard said no—at least for the moment. He wanted me ready for the 1938 Santa Anita Handicap. It was still the richest race. It was still the race we lost last year when we should have won.

The handicappers gave me top weight of 130. When I saw the list of weights, I had a sinking feeling. Carrying only a hundred pounds was a horse a lot of people raved about. His name was Stagehand.

George Woolf—the "Iceman," as he was known—climbed aboard me for the race. Red Pollard sat in a hospital. He fell during a race and three horses ran over his body and face. He wouldn't ride me or anything else for a couple of years.

They gave me an outside position for the start. At the bell I stumbled and swerved into a horse on my left. He bounced me to the right and, like a punched fighter, I went down almost to my knees. George pitched forward out of the saddle. He hung on by throwing a wrestler's hold around my neck.

I came up even keel as George slid back into the saddle. I took off after a line of horses like a little kid chasing older boys and yelling, "Hey, wait for me!"

By the first turn, sprinting madly, I caught up with half the pack. I went by more horses as we

curled around the turn. Entering the backstretch I slipped into the rail in fourth place, running smoothly now and seeing the first-place horse no more than five lengths in front.

Plenty of track left to pick them off, one and two and three, I thought to myself. There's still better than half a mile to go in this mile-and-a-quarter race.

George wasn't as optimistic. That bad start had shaken him and, at least this once, the cool deserted him. He hadn't been aboard me before and so he didn't realize how much catch-up speed he had below him.

George told me to go get 'em—and I did. I sprinted the next half-mile in an unofficial clocking of around forty-four seconds, two seconds faster than the half-mile record. And I still had about a third of a mile to go.

The sprint catapulted me into the lead. As we leaned out of the last turn and straightened into the stretch, I saw nothing but a blurred brown track in front of me. The homestretch seemed to sway in the bright March sunshine. It looked like a long reddish brown snake.

I'd sprinted twice in this race—to catch up, then to go by everybody in that half-mile sprint—and the second sprint cost me so much that I was seeing things. Once I heard a trainer, who did a lot of long-distance running, say the same thing had happened to him in one of those marathon races that go on forever. As he got close to the finish, he said, he had used up so much oxygen that his brain told him to go left instead of straight ahead. He ran into a tree and knocked himself cold.

I tried to keep myself headed straight down that twisting stretch. I knew I had slowed up. And from my right I heard a growing rumble that sounded like summer thunder—Stagehand!

We flew head to head by the eighth pole. Roaring filled our tight little world—the roar of air blasting out of burning lungs. I don't recall the last hundred yards at all, but I know we shot under the wire together because I saw the photo in the next day's paper.

The picture, a second straight photo finish for me in the Santa Anita Handicap, showed Stage-

if you picked him, about three dollars to one dollar if you liked me.

The four-year-old War Admiral had won eleven of his last seventeen races. The reporters labeled him "fiery." They called me "the ugly duckling with the lame leg." They dwelled on how I had raced thirty-five times as a two-year-old and won only five races. They didn't total my record for Mr. Howard. Of my last twenty-five races in his colors, I had won sixteen, finished second six times and third twice—out of the money only once!

More than forty thousand showed up at Pimlico, the biggest crowd in the track's history. They saw George Woolf come out aboard me. Charley Kurtsinger, the regular rider, sat on War Admiral. We—the four of us—posed for pictures. I told War Admiral I was sorry our date in May had been postponed, but that the traveling had tuckered me out. He said he understood. He told me to pay no attention to all that drivel in the papers about my ducking away from a challenge. He said no grandson of Big Red would be scared of a race. I told him he should try to come to California, that he'd like the weather. He said he understood he would be retired to stud duty after this race. I said that didn't sound so bad, either.

It was that kind of friendly conversation. We'd let the race decide who was the fastest.

Tom and Mr. Howard had come up with a simple strategy—I had to take the track away from War Admiral, who liked to front-run. I was to jump out in front right at the start and make him challenge me if he wanted to take the track. That meant a lightning start.

Twice we walked up to the flag for the start, and twice we had to wheel around and go back, one of us a noggin ahead of the other.

On the third approach, we stood nose to nose, me on the outside. A bell rang, down swung the flag.

George gave me the message with a lash of the whip. I jumped like a tongue of flame had shot down from heaven and singed my rump. In two or three strides I opened up a length lead and as we went by the grandstand I opened up the gap to two lengths. By the first furlong I had enough

space behind me to cross in front and take the rail.

At the first turn I drew out from the rail. That forced War Admiral, running now on my flank, to go wider, which meant he had to cover more ground just to stay even with me.

We curled out of the turn and drove into the backstretch. War Admiral made his move to take the track. He came by me and forged in front by a head. I knew I had to hold the inside by staying in front. Then, on the final turn, I could again force War Admiral to cover more ground on the outside.

George was thinking right with me. He loosened his hold. I stretched out, ears pinned back, tail flying, body low. I pulled even.

We spun around the turn like one horse, stride for stride, head against head. Again, as in the first turn, we drew away from the rail, pushing War Admiral into a wider and longer arc.

We swung into the stretch with only my head and half my neck in front. I glanced at War Admiral. His eyes bugged wide and his head jerked back toward the jockey as it bobbed, a stiffening you'll nearly always see in a horse that's about to fade. In the stables they call it "tightening up." That extra distance had taken its cost. War Admiral was breaking.

I moved ahead by a length, then two. George tried to make me ease up as we came to the wire, but I was still moving away at the finish to win by four lengths. My time was 1:56³/₅, a track record.

Hundreds of people swarmed onto the track and mobbed me on the way to the winner's circle. They slapped me on the flanks, they shouted that I was the greatest. One young fellow shouted, "You are Man o' War's greatest." I wondered if Big Red had listened on the radio.

The Seabiscuit Special rolled back to California. My legs ached all the way home. Tom bandaged them and soaked them with a special liniment he made just for me. My left front leg, the bucked one, had taken a rap during a race earlier that year. After a race or even a workout, it ached so bad I limped.

Mr. Howard and Tom looked at me with worry

in their eyes. They feared, I knew, that I'd finally break down. But I knew how badly they wanted to win that race I'd lost twice by a nose—the Santa Anita Handicap.

Early in 1939—I was now six years old—I ran in a race at Santa Anita to prep for the Handicap. As I came around the far turn, pain knifed through my left front leg. I lurched toward the rail and stumbled.

George Woolf steadied me and somehow, trying to run on three legs, I got to the finish two lengths behind the winner. George slowed me, then jumped off. I saw Tom and Mr. Howard hurrying down the track toward us—on the run.

Back at the stable a doctor looked at the left front knee, which had puffed to the size of a human head. He said he didn't know how I had run down that stretch with a knee like that. He said the knee had finally given way. He said I would never run again.

Two days later Mr. Howard announced to a big press conference that my running days had ended. He said I would go to his farm in Ridgewood, in northen California, for a quiet life in stud.

I whinnied happily all the way to Ridgewood. I never wanted to run again if I had to worry that pain that fierce would strike me.

The farm looked like one of those picture-postcard places—green hills, blue lakes, white-topped mountains off in the distance. Chickens and pigs scampered around near my stall. Pumpkin stood next door. Horse vans brought mares to the farm—I recall Flying Belle and Lady Riaf in particular—and I began with relish to do what I thought would be the work of the rest of my life, making a tribe of junior Seabiscuits.

As you know, I have always liked my groceries. That summer of 1939 I packed on weight. I ballooned to almost thirteen hundred pounds, up from the eleven hundred of my racing days. I thought I looked better than the sleek, racing Seabiscuit—chestier in the front, solidly packed in the rear.

Mr. Howard and Tom came to the farm one day. I saw immediately that they didn't like my new shape.

Both looked surprised and pained. Then, as they talked, I got a surprise. They told each other that my leg seemed strong enough for me to go back to racing. They wanted me to try again for the victory that had eluded me—the Santa Anita Handicap.

That 1940 race was only six months away. I had grown fat and flabby. How did they know my leg was strong enough for racing? If it gave way under me, I could hit the ground and be trampled under a couple of tons of flying hooves. And, at seven years of age, what chance did I have against a bunch of three- and four-year-old swifties?

But no one asked me what I thought. An exercise boy rode me each morning up and down the nearby hills. As I puffed and panted up each one, they looked as high as the distant mountains. Even worse, Tom cut down on the carrots, apples, and other goodies the grooms had been tossing my way. That irritated me, and I kicked at my stall at the hour when I had been served my second meal. On one meal a day I dreamed half the day about food. One morning a pig wandered by my stall. I lunged at him. He ran away, squealing with fright. I could have eaten him right off the hoof.

The fat melted away. I felt my body hardening. And my comeback chances seemed brighter to me one afternoon when Red Pollard showed up at the farm. He'd been limping in and out of hospitals for the past two years while his broken bones mended. He looked at me and said, "The two old cripples are back together. We'll show 'em we still have one good year left in us."

And then I got another spur to push me toward the finish line at Santa Anita. I heard from Red that if I won the race, I would have won more money than any horse ever. I could go back to stud with the title of "The World's Richest Horse." I liked the ring of that.

Not many people thought I had a chance. When we arrived at Santa Anita early in 1940 to begin work on the track, I heard talk almost every day on the stable radio about my comeback. Most of the people on the radio said I should have been kept in retirement. One man said it would be a shame if the old champ came in last. And he repeated what I heard every day: "The old champs should stay retired. They never come back."

I raced in two tune-ups. I finished third in one, sixth in the other. Red didn't ask me to run all out in either race. He, Tom, and Mr. Howard wanted to be positive that my knee was strong.

The Santa Anita handicapper paid no attention to those tune-ups. He gave me 130 pounds, the top weight. Some strong, young horses would line up with me, the favorites being Whichcee and Kayak, who was also owned by Mr. Howard.

Then, suddenly, race day! After a year away

At last, after three straight near-wins, Seabiscuit comes home first in his last race to win the 1940 Santa Anita Handicap. Behind him is stablemate Kayak II.

from the starting gate, I stepped in nervously. Red sensed that I had a case of nerves—he kept patting me and saying, "One more time, old boy, one more time."

I went out smoothly enough and as Red swerved me in toward the rail, all the nervousness vanished. Running once more was a joy.

I moved up on the inside and tucked into second, behind Whichcee, as we leaned into the first turn.

We came into the backstretch and I heard nothing behind us. Whichcee's speed had pulled us away from the pack strung out behind us. But a voice within me kept repeating: Remember Rosemont!

Whichcee and I stayed one-two down the backstretch, around the turn, and into the homestretch. I heard nothing from behind us but I suddenly remembered something I had overheard in the shed row the night before. Kayak was speaking to another horse and he said, "I'll see him in the stretch." I figured he meant me. And I knew he was jealous of all the attention Tom Smith paid to me. I could understand that— I still burned when I remembered how Sunny Jim stared at Omaha and seldom looked at the rest of us.

My ears were pricked back, listening for hoofbeats, as I shot by a burned-out Whichcee. I saw we had about an eighth of a mile to go when I head that hard roar that five years of racing told me was not the roar of the crowd. And good horse sense told me that the hard roar came from the hooves of Kayak.

I still ran hard as I surged by Whichcee, my eyes now on an invisible wire 100 yards beyond the real one. I wouldn't stop running hard until I went under the wire that only I could see.

Kayak came closer, I could hear his bellowing, and then I heard his jockey screech—"Come on, come on"—as Kayak put his head even with my saddle.

He never drew closer. I heard the gurgling sound of exhausted horse and the *thumpety-thump* clatter of hooves fading away from me. I blew under the wire ahead by a length and a half. My time was 2:01$\frac{1}{5}$, a track record and the second fastest mile and a quarter in the history of American racing. I had taken a long time to win this race, but when I won it, I won it big.

The prize money raised my total winnings to $437,730, which was about $60,000 higher than the previous record [set by Sun Beau about ten years earlier]. In the winner's circle Mr. Howard gazed at me for a long time. I guessed he had to be thinking about the time he bought a tired bag of bones for $8,000.

That ended my racing career. Mr. Howard sent me back to the farm up in the California hills, where I am now, the ugly duckling with the limp.

Ready for retirement after a long and distinguished career, Seabiscuit perks up his ears for a portrait with Tom Smith. Seabiscuit passed away in 1947.

WHIRLAWAY

Once, when I was a two-year-old, I came back to my stall—we were at Saratoga—and I saw my trainer, Ben Jones, glare at me. I knew he was mad—and I knew why. A man came up to Ben and said, "I hear you have a half-witted horse, Ben."

Ben ran his hand through his thinning hair and shouted so loud I bet they heard him in the grandstands, "He's making a half-wit out of me!"

I knew why he was mad. During a race a few minutes earlier, I'd gone into the far turn and swung so wide I ran into the *outside* fence. Yes, the *outside* fence. By the time Johnny Longden, who was riding me that day, could get me on the right track, I was dead last. I heard later that when Ben Jones saw me crash into that outside fence, he swore a blue streak and the nicest thing he called me was a knucklehead.

I don't know why he got so mad. I won the race, catching the leader in the last twenty-five yards.

It was a typical race for me, at least during that part of my career—before Eddie Arcaro came into my life. I always took the turns wide, although never again *that* wide. I never liked to stick close to the inside rail. I dreaded the feeling

Ben Jones, no longer so scornful of Whirlaway's quirks, oversees the readying of his horse for a Hialeah race.

of being closed in by the other horses, like I was trapped. I always wanted to be on the outside, running free. Of course, that meant I had to run a longer distance than the horses that kept to the inside—maybe a yard and a half to every yard that they ran.

I didn't mind. I knew I had the strength and the speed to come from behind and catch all of them in the stretch. Most of the time, anyway. And even if I didn't catch them all, isn't that what horse races are all about—to find out if you can catch them, or you can't?

Ben Jones, of course, being the Calumet Farm trainer and being paid to win, got mad. He hated to see me doing what I loved best about racing—coming from behind. He'd scream at my jocks: "Can't you teach that fool horse that the shortest distance between two points is a straight line?"

I had to laugh at that because my mother was always telling me the same thing when I was a yearling. She was Dustwhirl and I think she was the first horse I ever raced against. I know I always wanted to race her when I was growing up here [at the Calumet Farm near Keeneland, Kentucky, according to Slips's notes]. I was a weanling when they let us out onto a field called Fiddler's Green, with all the other mares and their weanlings. There was a white fence, I remember, at the far end. I'd say to Mom, "I'll race you to that fence!" She'd say, "Now don't try to run too fast, your legs are still too thin."

She would never try to beat me, just run fast

enough so I could lope at her side. But when I was a yearling [in 1939]—I remember it was in February or March—I got to the fence before her and I could see that I had honestly beat her—she was puffing. She looked down at me with that proud look you see in the eyes of mares when they talk about their weanlings—that "isn't-he-just-the-greatest?" look. She said that I would be as famous as my pop, Blenheim II. She often told me how he had won the Epsom Derby, which is run in England, and how he had been brought here to make American racehorses like me. In fact, I was one of his first sons. She told me how he had gone into the stretch during the Epsom Derby and picked off one horse after another to come from behind and win. Maybe it was then, I'm not sure, that I began to like the idea that also drove Ben Jones crazy—starting slow, cruising along the backstretch, then turning on the speed in the far turn and coming from behind in the stretch to win.

I know I did get into the habit of zigzagging during the race when I raced with my mother on Fiddler's Green. Since I was beating her to the fence every time, I decided to make the races more interesting. I'd zigzag left or right, let her get ahead, then come on with a burst to catch her. Catching her was *easy* because she was *hee-hawing* so hard.

When I raced the other yearlings to the fence, I nearly always won. I started out zigzagging, then tried to catch them from behind. Sometimes I did, sometimes I didn't. I really didn't care who got to the fence first—it was the running *to* the fence that was the fun of it for me. But I remember losing one race and hearing my mother, who didn't like me to lose, remind me that the straight line is the shortest way to go from one place to another. I knew she was right, of course, but playing catch-up was, to me, a lot more fun than winning.

Most racehorses worry. I remember Our Boots, who gave me some tough races. He was a big worrier. He worried, he once told me, about what the trainer would say if he lost, what the jockey would say if he lost, what the owner would say if he lost. He even worried about what the other

horses would say if he got beat. During a race, he told me, he thought about alibis he could use back in the shed row to explain why he lost. That was no way, I thought, to run a race.

I told him that he should think only about the excitement of the race. That's why I like to cruise at the beginning. That made the race more exciting. When should I make a move? Will I catch the horse that's ahead of me? And the next one? And the next? Each horse I passed, it was a thrill.

And if I didn't catch them all, I had had my thrills, right? When I got beat and I met the horse that won, I'd say, "Welcome to the I Beat Whirlaway Club. It's a small club, so be proud to join it. It's got to be the smallest club in the world."

That pipsqueak Alsab—have you ever met him?—after our match race, he went around saying that anyone could beat Whirlaway. But he was only three years old and you know how those three-year-olds think they know everything.

I have always said that on any given day, any horse can beat any other horse. That's why they have horse races, right? You find out who is the best of that day. On another day, someone else might be better. If that wasn't so, then 100-to-1 horses would never win. And you and I know that 100-to-1 horses win almost *every day* at some track somewhere.

Not that I know much about being a 100-to-1 horse. In the first race I entered, I was the favorite. That was on June 3, 1940, at Lincoln Fields in Chicago. I had come up from Florida, where I had been training all spring with the other two-year-olds from the Calumet Farm. Other horses said we were snooty. Calumet horses weren't snooty. We were proud. We were proud because Calumet horses had won more Kentucky Derbys than anyone else. And that spring a lot of writers were saying that I'd win the 1941 Kentucky Derby.

I won my first race the same way I won nearly all my races. I took it easy at the start, not wearing myself out the way those nervous speed horses kill themselves off. I swung wide on the first turn so I wouldn't get that trapped feeling. I bolted down the backstretch and closed ground

Whirlaway, with his bushy tail at parade rest, shows off a shiny magnificence during a free moment at the Calumet Farm.

on the leaders. I swung wide on the far turn and I was on the outside of the leaders as we came to the head of the stretch. Then I ran them all down to win going away from the field.

I went to Saratoga and you know how those Saratoga people are. You would have to be the new Man o' War to get their attention, they've seen so many horses. But after the Saratoga Special, which then was the only winner-take-all race in the country, I got their attention.

That was the race—it was for three-quarters of a mile—that I swung so wide on the far turn that I ran into the outside fence. I was dead last com-

ing into the stretch. Someone said later that I passed horses in that stretch like they were pulling trucks. A magazine that Ben Jones likes to read [*Blood-Horse*] said that my stretch drive that day was the hardest driving that racing had seen since my pop came down the stretch to win the Epsom Derby in 1930. I was the first of his sons to win an American stakes race. I was told later that when he heard, he went around bragging about it to the other stallions.

I ended 1940 as the top money winner among the two-year-olds [$37,850]. I had raced sixteen times and won seven, including three of my last

33

four. I finished second twice, third four times, and I was out of the money only three times. I was the winter favorite to win the 1941 Derby.

The newsreel photographers came down to Florida in January of 1941 to take movie pictures of me and pretty soon I was as famous as that fellow Gable and any of those Hollywood stars. It was because of my tail, I guess, which was always longer than anybody else's. People around the Calumet stable called me Mr. Long-tail and the name stuck. A newsreel guy said he wished they could shoot me in color instead of black and white, which they used then, because he had never seen a chestnut horse with such a colorful tail. The newspaper reporters also began to write about me and my tail and I remember one wrote that the tail flashed like burnished gold in the sunlight, or something like that.

I always say: If you got it, flaunt it. So when the newsreel guys came around, I swished that tail right into a groom's face. Boy, the cameramen loved that, and I had to keep on doing it so they could get the look on the groom's face from different angles. I don't think the groom cared for being swatted in the face by a horse's tail, but all of us wanted everyone to know about Calumet. We wanted Ben Jones to be proud of us.

But when I finished third in a couple of races in Florida that spring, Ben was just plain mad at the Half-Wit, as he called me. I was still swinging wide on the turns. We went up to Keeneland [Kentucky] for the Blue Grass Stakes. I got hemmed in along the rail as we came to the final turn. I swung way outside, almost to the fence. By the time I straightened out, Our Boots was too far away to catch and he won by six lengths.

Ben Jones was ready to climb trees. He said I was a loafer who didn't run until the stretch even though, when I wanted to, he said, "Whirlaway can pass any horse that ever lived." He talked about the shortest distance between two points. But he couldn't look into my head and see that I was scared of being trapped along the rail.

We went to Churchill Downs, with the Kentucky Derby a week away. I ran in the one-mile Derby Trial. Again I steered myself wide of the pack as we rounded both turns and lost to a

nothing named Blue Pair. Ben stared at me with disgust splashed all over his face. I heard him say to the jockey that we had covered more ground than the German army, which, you remember, was covering lots of it at that time.

Ben didn't come near me for two days. Then, just a couple of nights before the Derby, he stomps into the shed row and stops in front of my stall. Next to him is a little fellow with a big, curving nose. I knew right away he was Eddie Arcaro, one of the best of the young jocks, or so I had heard the grooms say. Right away I knew two things about Eddie. One, he was strong. You could see that by the way he cocked that big head of his. Two, he was tough. He stared at me like I was one of those public enemies I heard about on the radio that those G-men were always chasing.

Ben told Eddie how I swung wide on those turns. He said he wanted Eddie to glue me to the turns even if he had to make me jump over the inside rail like I was one of those jumping horses. I thought he was also going to say I was a loafer, but he didn't. That made me think that Ben didn't mind my cruising starts as long as I gave him those Whirlaway finishes.

They left. I have a new jockey, I realized, and he's been told to be tough with me. That night I had a talk with myself—looking myself in the mirror, as some of the horses say.

Whirly, I said—Whirly is the name the grooms use and I like it—Whirly, you got to do something about this problem. So you get panicky near the rail, so what? You can take a few seconds of panic, can't you? So you don't have to run a mile and a half when everyone else in the race is running only a mile. And if that Arcaro is as good a rider as everyone says, you'll be trapped along the rail for only a few seconds until he can point you through a hole. And you know you've got the speed, as Ben says, to pass anything that's ever lived.

Still, I was very nervous, unusual for me, as we went out onto the track for the Derby. I knew Arcaro would keep me tight to the rail. I hoped I didn't get so panicky that I'd do something stupid, like really jumping over the rail and running

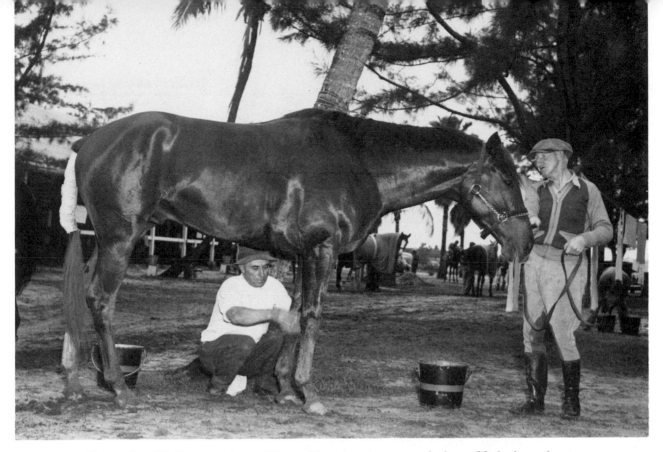

The pride of Calumet, tail taped for safekeeping, is groomed after a Hialeah workout.

like an idiot in the infield. I'd never be allowed to live that down—especially me, a *Calumet* horse.

The day was hot, the track dusty, and my tongue was dry as a bone as we stepped into the gate. The bell rang and off we went, eleven of us, and right away I feel Arcaro's strong hands pulling me to the inside. Ahead of me I see six or seven horses and my first thought is: If they begin to come back to me, I'll be trapped inside. I try to slow up, figuring to keep distance between me and those front-runners. But Eddie whacks me with the whip so I know I have to run.

Into the turn we go, the jockeys shouting with their shrill voices, our hooves on the hard track as noisy as a thunderstorm. I was still on the inside and I bet my eyes were popped halfway out of my head, I was so scared. I was thinking only of that flashing white rail on my left and what seemed like a mountain of brown and gray flesh on my right.

Finally—it seemed forever—we came to the end of the turn. I had been thinking about everything except racing, of course, so I wasn't surprised later on to learn that I was twelve lengths back as we went into the backstretch. There were six horses in front of me.

And I knew I was going to win. I knew because I came out of that first turn feeling full of run, fuller than I could ever remember. I knew why, of course. I had run as straight a line as possible between two points.

I stayed on the inside, the panic all gone—forever. I passed two horses and drew close to the four leaders, who were running together as a tight knot.

Later I heard Arcaro tell reporters that he'd been trying to hold me back along the backstretch. "I tried to lay back," he said, "but when he saw those horses in front, he wanted to run."

He was right. I caught them all at the top of the stretch, still on the inside. I think I saw the hole the same second that Eddie did. He hit me with the whip to let me know this was the time to run away from the four of them. I lanced between Our Boots and Dispose, and from the way they were panting I knew they were through. Later I told Our Boots that if you go running with speed horses at the beginning of a race, you're going to be hurting at the end.

We won by two and a half lengths. Rounders came from far back to take second and Attention caught the speed horses to take third. Ben Jones

35

pocketed a big check [$61,275]. That had to make him smile, of course, so I don't think he should have said what he did to Arcaro after the race. It hurt me more than a little: "Well, we finally got through to old Rockhead."

Rockhead! I thought to myself: Hey, horses have feelings too, you know.

A man on the radio the next day said that Ben had put together, with me and Arcaro, a winning combination. I thought he was right. Eddie let me have it my way by cruising through the first half of the race, I let Eddie have it his way by sticking to the rail on the turns.

We ran the Preakness as we had the Derby and won by five lengths ahead of King Cole and seven ahead of Our Boots. Poor Our Boots. The day after the race I had to convince him that his owner wouldn't send him to a farm in Tennessee to pull a plow. He said that happened to a friend of his. I told Our Boots that I didn't doubt that's what happened to his friend. But I told him, "Look, you finish second or third in a Triple Crown race, they keep you for stud duty." He felt better. I think he was always made more for stud duty than for racing, which, come to think of it, makes him the wiser of the two of us. Or, at least, the more normal.

Calumet had won a lot of Derbys. But it had never won the Triple Crown. You can imagine how excited I was, determined to be the first Calumet wearer of the Triple Crown.

Other owners said they didn't want to throw away entry fees just to lose to me. Only three horses showed up for the Belmont Stakes. They were Robert Morris, Yankee Chance, and Itabo. But they sprang a surprise on Eddie and me.

We went off smoothly enough. The other three horses took the track and I followed at their heels. As we came to the first turn, Eddie steered me to the inside, well behind, so I had no fears of being trapped.

Itabo had the lead. Suddenly he slowed down. So did the other two, Robert Morris and Yankee Chance. I almost ran right up the back of Yankee Chance and into the saddle of the jockey.

They were slowing the pace! They figured that they would save their energy and their speed.

They'd chance trying to outrun me in the stretch.

Eddie and I were having none of that. We went right around them, took the track, and by the three-quarter point of the race, we led by seven lengths. I cruised down the stretch to win by three. The time, of course, was slow, the 2:31 nearly three seconds off the track record.

Slow times or fast times, they made no difference to me. I always said that all I look at after my name on a chart is that big "1." Ben Jones gave me the same smile after a slow "1" that he gave me after a fast "1." And I knew why. He got paid for "1s." How fast or slow they were, that made no difference to Ben.

Only four horses before me had won the Tri-

Whirlaway seems ignored by the photographer after winning the 1941 Belmont Stakes and the Triple Crown. Hogging the scene are trainer Ben Jones and jockey Eddie Arcaro.

Whirlaway, all four hooves aloft, flies to the finish a length ahead of Market Wise to win the 1941 Dwyer Stakes at Aqueduct. A year later air raid warnings stood near the finish line.

ple Crown. They were Sir Barton, Gallant Fox, Omaha, and War Admiral. I didn't hear any more talk about a half-witted horse. Again, you get the "1s"—you're a genius.

That spring and summer, counting the Triple Crown, I won six straight races. The streak snapped when I finished second in a mile-and-a-quarter race at Arlington Park in Chicago. In the Narragansett Special I lost the mile-and-three sixteenths race to War Relic, who carried 107 pounds. I lugged 118. I finished off the year by winning the mile-and-five-eighths Lawrence Realization at Belmont and then came in second to Market Wise in the two-mile Jockey Club Gold Cup. I wasn't embarrassed by that loss—Market Wise had to set a new American record, 3:20⁴/₅, to beat me.

That was my twentieth, and last, race as a three-year-old. I had won thirteen, finished second five times, third twice, and I was never out of the money. I'd won around a quarter of a million dollars [$272,386]. In two years of racing I'd

won more money than any other racehorse except Sun Beau, who was second in all-time winnings, and Seabiscuit, who was first. Later I heard that someone [apparently Burt Clark Thayer, author of a book on Whirlaway] said that no horse since Gallant Fox had been greater than I was in three ways. One, showing I had speed; two, showing I could go distances; and three, showing I could win in any going.

I was happy about myself, especially since I didn't hear any more of that half-wit poppycock. I boarded a train for California, where I rested that winter, and I heard a groom say I looked as gay as a puppy dog jumping in for a ride in the family car.

I didn't race again for quite a while [about five months, until April 1942]. We went to Keeneland, here in Kentucky. By then, of course, the war was on. I saw lots of soldiers and sailors in the grandstands. They were let in free, you know. One day, as we trotted to the gate, I heard my jockey say to another as he pointed to a sign on

On the far outside, Mr. Longtail finishes a stride ahead of War Relic on the inside to win the 1941 Saranac Handicap at Saratoga.

the infield: "That's the new warning about air raids. If the air raid siren goes off, we're supposed to gallop the horses over to that shed and take cover."

Air raids! Take cover! I knew what air raids were. I'd been hearing on the radio in the stables how the Germans were blowing up Pop's country, raiding London and places like that. Now they had air raid signs posted at all the tracks on the East Coast, or so I heard. I expected the German planes to come over the track whenever I ran. The sound of a plane in the sky helped me to run faster.

My first big race of 1942 was the Dixie Handicap at Pimlico. Later I heard one old-timer [perhaps Burt Clark Thayer] say that he could not recall a race that was its equal.

There were four fast, strong handicap horses

in the field. One was Attention, who had beaten me the previous fall at Arlington. There were also Challedon, Best Seller, and Mioland. The handicapper must have mulled over our records all night. He assigned us weights that differed from top to bottom by only four pounds. Modesty forbids my telling you who carried the most.

The race was a mile and a sixteenth. At the half-mile I was eighth and dead last. But we were all so tightly packed that I was only two lengths behind Attention, who was fourth, and only four lengths behind Best Seller, the leader.

Near the far turn I did my thing, stomping on the gas pedal, as the grooms say. I couldn't believe what happened next—it had never happened to me before. Attention was moving away from me!

I hugged the rail as we curled around the far

turn. Even so, as we turned into the stretch, I had dropped to eight lengths behind Attention. His burst of speed—I had never seen so much speed so quick—had pitched him to the head of the pack.

I put down my head and dug as hard as I could to catch up. I collared three horses, one by one, but with no more than a furlong to go, my lungs bursting, Challedon, Mioland, and Attention pounded toward the wire ahead of me. You could have dropped my stall around them and corralled all three.

I came up to Challedon and Mioland. Both were blowing as hard as one of those locomotives chugging into a station. Challedon's eyes bugged wide in his head. Mioland weaved like a drunk on a Saturday night. Both slipped behind me.

I came up on Attention's neck with no more than fifty yards to go. I thrust my head in front and tried to keep it there. I kept my eyes on the wire straight ahead, but I could hear Attention panting and wheezing. My legs ached like I was carrying cannonballs in my shoes.

I went across the wire a half-length to the good. There was only a space of one and a half lengths between me and the fourth-place Challedon.

By the early summer I had passed Sun Beau's total winnings to stand second, behind Seabiscuit. We went up to Suffolk Downs for the mile-and-an-eighth Massachusetts Handicap, the richest race in the East. If I won the first prize of about $50,000, I'd go by Seabiscuit.

A crowd of almost thirty thousand, which was a record, I was told, for the track, came out and I knew they wanted me to top Seabiscuit. Seabiscuit was the California horse who had beaten the eastern champion War Admiral in their match race a few years earlier. And now I was the eastern champion, so this was a way of finally giving Seabiscuit his comeuppance. But I admired Seabiscuit because he went to races wherever a railroad track would take him, or so the grooms say. I agree with them: He was truly America's horse.

Anyway, back to the Massachusetts Handicap. Ben Jones said it was the best race I ever ran. As usual, I came into the stretch in the ruck, maybe seven or eight lengths behind Attention. Someone later said I went by horses as though they were frozen in aspic. I caught Attention three strides from the wire and went under it in the fastest time for nine furlongs in the history of American racing.

Attention was always a friendly loser. The next day, as we were both being walked, he said to me, "I just wish one thing."

"What's that?" I asked.

"That they'd make these homestretches about a couple of yards shorter. You'd never beat me."

I had now won almost half a million dollars [actually $454,336, compared to Seabiscuit's $437,617]. In ten races in 1942, I had five firsts, four seconds, one third. Ben Jones went around telling people he thought I was a very smart horse the way I took off slowly and came on with a rush. That's trainers for you—they're never wrong.

That summer Alsab was the talk of the three-year-old world, having won the Preakness and the Belmont Stakes. Talk began about a match race between us. When the Narragansett people offered a winner-take-all purse of $25,000 for a mile-and-a-sixteenth match race, Ben Jones said yes. Alsab, as you probably know, was as fresh as a three-year-old can get.

I met Alsab for the first time at Narragansett a few days before the race. I knew his story. He'd been bought for $800 and proved to be a jewel. He had a chip on his flank about that $800 price tag. I said to him, "You have come a long way since they thought you were worth only eight hundred dollars."

"I was worth a lot more than eight hundred dollars," he growled. "The people who had me, they didn't know a racehorse from an orangutan."

He stalked off. I shrugged. I knew why he was carrying that chip. He had an undistinguished—that's the polite word—ancestry. He knew who my sire was—the winner of the Epsom Derby. I knew he hungered to beat me. I heard that from the other horses.

"If he wins," I said, "he can join the I Beat

Whirlaway Club. It's a very exclusive membership.''

I heard later that Alsab told someone to tell me that I could join the I Beat Alsab Club, which was a lot smaller than mine.

See what I mean about being fresh?

Everyone knew that Alsab would try to take the track at the start and see if he could stave me off in the stretch. That was all right with us—Ben Jones, Eddie Arcaro, and me—because we figured I could run down anything in the stretch that I was reasonably close to.

On most days, anyway. But not on that day at Narragansett. I went into the stretch two lengths behind. I closed the gap and with a quarter of a mile to go, we raced head to head, eyeball to bulging eyeball. Alsab was panting like a beached fish and I was just as loud. I strained to get my head out in front, so did he. We went under the wire like one horse.

I pulled up on the first turn and cantered back. I knew who had won. In a photo finish, I think, the loser is always the first one to know who was second. But I kept my head up, knowing that if the race had been a few yards longer, I would have driven my snoot in front.

Alsab came alongside. He looked exhausted and worried. "You won," I said to him. "Welcome to the club."

We met again, as I had hoped, for the two-mile Jockey Club Gold Cup that fall of 1942. In spite of his victory over me in the match race, Alsab, being a three-year-old, had to carry only 117 pounds to my 124. I let him run his fool head off and he galloped ten lengths ahead of me along the backstretch. I made my move going around the far turn, caught him in the stretch, and this time I forged ahead to win by three-quarters of a length.

As we came back toward the winner's circle, I shouted at him, "There'll be no photo this time."

"Welcome to the club!" he shouted back.

You would think he could come up with his own lines.

That victory raised my total winnings to more than half a million dollars. One newspaper writer gave me a new nickname to go with Mr. Long-

tail. He called me Croesus Whirlaway.

Alsab and I hooked up with each other one last time. That was in the two-and-a-quarter-mile New York Handicap at Belmont. I don't like to alibi. You know that. I'll just give you the record. I had raced close to four and a half miles during the previous fourteen days, carrying as much as 132 pounds. The record also says that Alsab and I ran head to head for the first two miles. When we came to the stretch, for one of the few times in my life, I called on a finishing kick. It wasn't there, drained out of me. A French speed horse, Obash, shot by me, and he and Alsab ran head to head for the wire. Alsab won, Obash was second, I was third.

I went on to finish that 1942 season—and, as it turned out, pretty much my racing career—by winning four of my final five races. I had won about $200,000 [$211,250]. I had started in twenty-two races, won twelve. I came in second eight times. In the other two races, I was third. In two years of running against the very best, I had never finished out of the money, so you can see why the railbirds loved me for reasons other than my flowing tail. For the second year in a row—and this was something no horse had ever done before—I was selected the Horse of the Year.

Most important—what's more important than your health?—I had finished three seasons of racing as healthy as I had started them. Newspapers called me the "Iron Horse." In three years I had finished fifty-eight races and never had anything worse than a sneeze. Ben Jones said I was strong. Like iron, he said. I said, "Nonsense." I told the other horses I was proof that if you took it easy in the first half of a race, when most horses get hurt in wild stampedes to the first turn, you will last a lot longer than those fool speed horses. A race, I have always said when the thinking got deep around the stable—and maybe something else was getting deep too—is a lot like life. It's what you got at the end that counts.

But you can't go on forever. I found that out the next spring, 1943. I had a bunch of bad colds and then high temperatures that made me feel draggy. I ran in two races at Arlington Park in

Chicago, finishing third, then fifth.

Usually, a day or two after a race, I could breeze a mile and come in for a big meal. But after that second race, my legs ached and I had no appetite. Ben Jones looked at me and I could see the worry in his eyes. I heard him tell a vet that I would be carrying more weight and running longer distances as a five-year-old. He was afraid, he said, I might break down.

Two days later, on June 28, 1943, he announced my racing days were over.

I was glad. I didn't want to ache like that after a race—it took all the joy out of the running of it. I reminded myself how, during that last race against Alsab, I had nothing left—for the first time ever—at the head of a stretch. I asked myself: Is your body telling you something—that those wild charges down the stretch are gone with your youth?

All the newspapers and the radio announcers listed my lifetime record. I had reported to the post for sixty races and won thirty-two. I had come in second fifteen times, third in nine races.

I had finished out of the money four times, twice in my last two races. I had won more than a half-million dollars [$561,161], and that beat Seabiscuit's record by more than $100,000.

I rode back to Keeneland in my private railroad car. When the train stopped and the door swung open, I saw a huge crowd waiting at the station. A band blared "My Old Kentucky Home." The people were cheering. Lots of horses come back to Keeneland and the Calumet Farm to retire. But I was one of the few that got a Welcome Home Day. I saw soldiers and sailors salute as I was led down a ramp. I marched down the middle of the street and the people cheered. I know my eyes were wet.

When I got to the farm, Attention stood in a stall and welcomed me to retirement. He laughed and said, "You know, you got here just in time. We are having a meeting tomorrow of the I Beat Whirlaway Club."

"That's fine," I said, "and where are you holding it—in a telephone booth?"

COUNT FLEET

 A lot of Thoroughbred horses spend all their time bragging about their bloodlines, how great their sires and dams were. That's okay, and maybe it's all they have to boast of, because their own records were the kind to hide under a soft spot in the turf. I guess I'm different in that respect. Sure, I can blow off about my parents, and I will for a while, because they were very good runners.

Take my father, for instance. His name was Reigh Count. He won the Kentucky Derby in 1928, and the next year he took a trip to England, where he won the Coronation Cup. He won a few other races, too. When I was born in 1940, I could point to him proudly as my pop.

My dam was a very fast horse named Quickly. She raced mostly at the six-furlong distance, and she won only once at the mile. Mom lived up to her name. She ran for six seasons, and it didn't matter to her what the races were. She was entered in allowance events, handicaps, and claiming, and she did all right. She ran during the time of the big Depression, when purses were as small as an oat in a dinner bucket, but she earned $21,530. She had eighty-five starts. She won

Victory at Belmont and the Triple Crown! Mrs. John D. Hertz leads the Count to the winner's circle.

thirty-two, placed in fourteen, and came in to show thirteen times.

I had everything going for me right from the start, stamina to go the distance inherited from my sire, and sprinting speed that was the gift from my dam. A student majoring in Thoroughbred horses has got to like my chances. But how do you figure human beings who do not have great bloodlines, and yet come on as great champions? You've got to love them, admire them, bust a gut working for them. Maybe that's why I spend my time thinking about two men: Mr. John D. Hertz, the man who started Stoner Creek Stud, and Mr. John Eric Longden, the only jockey ever to ride me in a race. Whenever anybody mentions their names I suck in air and throw out my chest. That's how proud I am of them. Let me tell you about those two gentlemen.

Mr. Hertz was born in 1879 in a small village which was then part of Austria. He came to America when he was five years old and his family planted roots in the Chicago area. When he was ten years old he ran away from home. I never did find out why.

There he was, a kid of ten in the streets of Chicago, earning his keep as an assistant driver for a newspaper delivery wagon. I suppose he got to know about horses by holding the reins, sitting up there in the wagon seat. He was an ambitious kid, always hustling a buck. He worked as an office boy for the old *Chicago Herald*, then he wrote boxing news—he even did a little boxing

43

himself—then he began nosing around racetracks. He worked as a valet. He even worked for a bookie.

As a rule, automobiles and horses do not mix. I never did trust anything with wheels. But in the case of Mr. Hertz it was a fine combination. He became a car salesman, and that was when the money began to pour in. I suppose it was a fluke beginning, because Mr. Hertz made his fortune as the result of a mistake.

He took a bunch of cars in trade—they were big seven-passenger jobs—and he couldn't get rid of them. So he began to rent them out as buses. One thing led to another, and that's how the Yellow Cab Company was formed. Yellow, by the way, became the color of his racing silks.

Maybe now the name John Hertz begins to ring a bell. Now, when somebody wants to rent a car, chances are Hertz gets the business. He became number one in the field, just as he became number one in racing. Talk about a self-made man, that immigrant kid became a big wheel with an outfit named Paramount Pictures. You can add to that a partnership in the Wall Street investment banking house known as Lehman Brothers.

The whole world of racing owes a big debt to Mr. Hertz. A while back Arlington Park was having money problems, and it looked like a hard-nosed gent named Al Capone was going to buy it, which would have been a kick in the teeth for racing in the Midwest. Mr. Hertz rounded up a few other Chicago businessmen and they bought the track to keep it out of Capone's hands.

As for Johnny Longden, all you really have to know about him is the plain fact that he was the absolute best. Okay, so I'm prejudiced, but there was a man who fought his way to the top. Jockeys are small, and so was Johnny, but he had the heart of a giant.

Johnny had great hands and shoulders. He developed strength when he was still a youngster in Canada, working in the mines, leading donkeys drawing cars full of coal. He had terrific balance, and he learned that too while he was still a kid. After he left the coal mines he took to "Roman riding," usually seen in a circus. The rider stands up on two horses with one foot on each horse. In Johnny's day that was a popular type of racing in Canada. He won a lot, too; I think fifteen in a row at one time.

Best of all, Johnny had fantastic timing. He could clock a race in his head even while it was being run. Maybe that's why he got the nickname the "Pumper."

Johnny always wanted to be a jockey, but most of the opportunity was in the United States. He didn't have enough money to get down here, so he hopped a freight train and got off at Salt Lake City. He hung around the racetracks, hoping to get a mount, but they weren't easy to come by. He was just another kid with very little experience, only a burning desire to become a winning jockey. He didn't ride his first winner until he got aboard a nine-year-old gelding named Hugo K. Asher in a $300 claiming race. It was the horse's only win in thirty-three starts that year.

Oh, how Johnny loved to ride! That was what he wanted to do more than anything else. In fact Johnny and a horse named Rushaway pulled a stunt that was talked about for a long time.

Jockey Johnny Longden sits astride his favorite Thoroughbred, Count Fleet.

On a day late in May 1936, Johnny rode Rushaway to a win in the Illinois Derby at Aurora Downs. Then Johnny, Rushaway, and the trainer left town in a hurry. They turned up the next day at a track in northern Kentucky, a few hundred miles away. With Johnny Longden up, Rushaway won the Latonia Derby. Can you imagine that? A horse and his jockey winning two races in two days. Incredible!

See what I mean? Two scrappers, Mr. Hertz and Johnny Longden, both starting out with nothing—no bloodlines, no money, just ambition and pride—and when anybody mentions Thoroughbred racing, their names have to be right on top. That's why I always loved them.

When Mr. Hertz began to buy horses, he didn't have too much luck at first. Then one day he saw a horse named Reigh Count, who didn't amount to anything at that time. Reigh had started six times and still hadn't won, but his seventh outing was something else.

It was a nail-biter of a race, and no doubt Reigh Count was tired of other horses finishing ahead of him. He let fly with a finishing kick, caught the leader at the sixteenth pole, and then he reached over and bit the other horse on the neck. That was enough for Mr. Hertz. He shelled out $12,000, and Reigh Count became the start of something big. Mr. Hertz said, "I always loved a fighter, man or horse."'

When I started to run as a two-year-old, Mr. Hertz must have thought for sure I was my father's son, because I finished second in a race at Belmont Park and then another second place at Aqueduct. But I wasn't about to drop six in a row the way my father did. I won my third race at Aqueduct by four lengths, and I won again at Empire City. I was feeling pretty chipper, like every race was going to be a breeze. I didn't understand that when arrogance and overconfidence take over, the horse gets lazy. In the East View Stakes I just dogged it, and a horse named Gold Shower beat me. Nobody had to stick a finger up my nose, I knew it was my fault and so did Johnny. It was *how* I lost that stuck in my gullet: I hadn't put out a hundred percent.

I had my chance to get back at Gold Shower the next time out, in the Wakefield Stakes at Empire City. Sure, I won. Gold Shower didn't come close, he finished third.

It wasn't a cocky attitude that brought my fourth loss, it was a very good horse named Occupation. He had won four races by an average margin of five lengths, including the Arlington Futurity and the Washington Park Juvenile, and if he wasn't the class of the two-year-olds at that time, he was pretty close to it.

It was the Washington Park Futurity and Occupation was the favorite. He got away slower than usual, but he ran down the other horses and went ahead. I got stuck in traffic and it wasn't until the stretch that I broke free. Occupation led by three lengths when I began to make up ground, but he held on and won by a neck.

I laid off for a month, but I figured to meet up with Occupation again when I came back. My workouts were good, but it was then that I learned another fact of life, that there's a big difference between a training run and a real race.

Before I raced Occupation again I won a couple of allowance races. Allowance races can be peculiar events. The weight a horse carries might be determined by the amount of money he has won, or it can be the number of races a horse has won, in any specific time period. It can lead to confusion. Sometimes a horse has won some races but the competition was nothing special, yet he has to carry the most weight. On the other hand, a horse with real promise who has lost a couple of heartbreakers doesn't carry much weight. Both horses can surprise the track handicappers and the fans. The horse with the winning record fades out, while the horse who's a comer turns in a clear-cut win. Of course the next time out the weights of both horses will be changed.

Four days before Occupation and I had it out, I ran a six-furlong workout in 1:08$^1/_5$. That same day, in a prep race, Occupation ran the six-furlong event in 1:09$^3/_5$, and he won going away. Simple arithmetic said I was one and two-fifths seconds faster at the distance.

Only it didn't work out that way. Occupation broke on top and stayed that way. I mean, he almost burned the dirt off the track, and he won by five lengths. To rub it in even deeper, I came in third. A little lady named Askmenow, the best of the two-year-old fillies, beat me for place money by a head.

It was right then that I grew up. Never mind how many races I'd won, I had already lost five, and the season still had a long way to go. I felt miserable, like I'd let Mr. Hertz and Johnny down. The hell with losing, I wanted to win and I damn well was going to win. Not by a nose or a neck or length, either, that was kid stuff. I aimed to show Mr. Hertz, and Johnny, and the crowds at the tracks—yes, and Occupation, too—that there wasn't a two-year-old alive who could run with me.

I was entered in the one-mile Champagne Stakes, and I got my first look at another pair of pretty good two-year-olds named Blue Swords and Slide Rule. I won by six lengths. My time was 1:34⁴/₅, the fastest mile of the year.

Then it was Occupation time again, the mile-and-a-sixteenth Pimlico Futurity. Occupation was installed as the clear favorite. Well, why not? He'd given away weight to me and beat me in our last two meetings, so he figured to make it three in a row.

We both broke well. Occupation jumped into the lead by a head and held it for five furlongs, but then I took the bit and after that it was strictly howdy-do and see-you-later. I beat Occupation by five lengths. My time of 1:43³/₅ equaled the track record.

I ran once more as a two-year-old, in the Walden Stakes. It wasn't a race. I still don't know what it was. Nobody could believe my margin of victory and there was really no way to measure it. Some old-timers guessed that I had won by thirty lengths. That's right, thirty lengths, and if it was only twenty-nine lengths, would that make a difference?

It's hard to explain this new surge of strength I felt. Maybe it was partly more confidence, because I felt in my bones I was the best. But it was also straight power in my legs, in my body. I was fast—you can bet the rent money I was faster than ever, except that I wasn't sure I could con-

trol my new speed. Longden wasn't sure, either, and for a while he wasn't anxious to find out. Just once he let curiosity get the best of him. It was during a workout. Usually Johnny kept a tight rein in practice, but now he loosened up, clicked his tongue, and tapped me lightly on the flank with his hand. I turned loose and bolted up the track like a cannon shot. I must have scared years off Johnny's life because he pulled me in right away.

My first start as a three-year-old was an allowance race over the strange distance of one mile and seventy yards. I doubt if anybody knows how that amount of track was figured out. It wasn't a mile, but it wasn't a mile and a sixteenth either, just somewhere in between. Track conditions weren't very good, and often it's hard to describe a track exactly. I know jockeys talk about track conditions, and sometimes the odds on a horse go up or down depending on what the track is like. Track conditions can be determined this way, more or less:

A *fast track* is the best. It's hard, dry, and even.

A *sloppy track* is the condition during or right after a downpour. There may be some puddles here and there, but the base of the track is a little firm and a horse can run provided the jockey is careful.

A *muddy track* is just what you'd expect. The ground is soft and wet, and sometimes a horse is up to his fetlocks in the goo.

Then there are a lot of "in-between" track conditions:

A *heavy track* is one that's drying out. Call it between muddy and good.

A *slow track* is still wet, but drier than heavy. It's between heavy and good.

A *good track* is acceptable. It's between slow and fast.

Of course you can generalize, too, by calling it an "off track," which means anything but fast.

So, on this "off track" over the funny distance I beat a horse named Bosseur by three and a third lengths.

That was just a prep. The important races were coming up, and I'd be facing my two favorite patsies, Blue Swords and Slide Rule. Don't misunderstand, they were good horses. Nobody enters a Thoroughbred in the Wood Memorial, or the Kentucky Derby, or the Preakness unless that horse has a chance to win. The mile-and-a-sixteenth Wood Memorial always had a field of excellent entries.

It wasn't the best of track conditions, but neither was it the worst. Nobody really challenged me once I got up a full head of steam. I beat Blue Swords by three and a half lengths and Slide Rule by thirteen.

Just to show it was no freak, I took on the same pair in the Derby. I got away fast and it was a romp, three lengths ahead of Blue Swords, nine ahead of Slide Rule. After that it was the Preakness and it was the same story, me ahead of Blue Swords by eight lengths.

It became monotonous. The Belmont was still four weeks away and I had to keep in shape, so I took on the field in the Withers. The track was muddy—I mean if there had been any more water on it, folks would have left the stands to go fishing. However, the outcome didn't change. I beat Slide Rule by five lengths.

Finally the Belmont was at hand, but now neither Blue Swords nor Slide Rule came to run. There were a few other horses eligible to enter, but none of them wanted any part of me. Still, the Belmont can't be a walkover, it's too big an event; it would be like only one runner showing up for an Olympic race. The only horses who showed up were a pair of nobody-cares named Fairy Manhurst and Deseronto. That was just plain insulting. All they ever won was a few overnighters.

I had my dander up and so did Longden. He had always wanted to find out how fast I could run in a race from start to finish, and now he was about to find out. He turned me loose.

Only it wasn't really a race. Actually, I don't know what in hell to call it. How can anybody tell what's going on when the winner—that was me, of course—comes in twenty-five lengths ahead? I should have set a track record, but I didn't. The mark for Belmont was held by Bolingbroke, who made it in 2:27³/₅, but when he won, it was as a five-year-old and he was also carrying eleven pounds less weight than I was. My time was 2:28¹/₅, which was actually two-fifths of a second faster than the record that Bolingbroke shattered.

Beside, I have another excuse, although it was my own damned fault. Somewhere during the run I kicked myself smack in the right front foreleg. At first it didn't seem to be a serious injury, but it turned out to be worse than anyone thought. My career ended after the Belmont win.

So I was undefeated as a three-year-old. I started six and I won six. Counting the last three races I won as a two-year-old, I ended my racing days with nine straight wins. The overall total was twenty-one races entered, sixteen victories, four place finishes, and just a single show. That's my big boast—I never ran out of the money. And the cherry on top of the frosting on the cake was my Triple Crown, the first horse to turn the trick since the very first Triple winner, Sir Barton. My total purses added up to $250,300.

It never fails, when a horse runs up a big record the cry goes up, "Who did he ever beat? What kind of horses was he running against?" It has happened before, it happened to me, and I

Count Fleet takes the Wood Memorial with plenty to spare. That's Blue Swords in second place.

Roaring into the first turn in the Kentucky Derby. The Count won by three lengths.

suppose it will happen as long as losing bettors have to taste sour grapes. Let's examine some of the very good horses who lost to me.

It's true I lost to Occupation twice, but I also beat him once. Was Occupation any good? Give a listen: he won the Arlington, Washington Park, Belmont, and Breeder's futurities, and also the Washington Park Juvenile Stakes, all as a two-year-old. He had nine wins and three seconds in thirteen starts. Let the losers chew on that for a while.

I made Blue Swords look bad, but he was really a very good horse indeed. As a two-year-old he won the Eastern Shore, Remsen, and Ardsley handicaps. He came in second to me in the Wood Memorial, the Kentucky Derby, and the Preakness. Who knows what he might have done if an injury hadn't shortened his racing time?

Let's consider Slide Rule. As a three-year-old, when I beat him so badly, his record when I wasn't running against him was pretty outstanding. He won the Swift Stakes, the Arlington Classic, the Experimental, the Peter Pan, the Jerome, the Interborough, and Westchester handicaps, and if that kind of record isn't good enough for the sore losers, they should learn

A runaway victory in the Preakness. Count Fleet beat Blue Swords by eight lengths.

something about horse racing.

I could name other good horses I beat, but you get the picture. Okay, so I lost a few when I was still learning what racing was all about, but that happens to just about every horse.

All that time I was trying to make Mr. John Hertz happy, because he was the boss. It wasn't until much later that I learned he didn't own me, his wife did. In fact there wasn't much his wife, Fanny, didn't own. He made a speech when he was honored by the Thoroughbred Club of America, and he said, "She owns the farm called Stoner Creek Stud, she owns all the horses and the stock, and she also owns me."

I bowed out with a lot of praises ringing in my ears. The sweetest words came from my rider, John Eric Longden, who was a terrific champ in his own right. He said, "Count Fleet was the best horse I ever saw."

Notice, he didn't say the best horse he ever rode, just the *número uno* he'd ever clapped eyes on.

But then, Johnny always knew the right things to say. Somebody once remarked to him that the first part on an athlete to go bad was his legs. They asked how his legs were holding up.

He said, "Just fine, because I always get four new ones every time I go to the post." A class act, that gentleman.

One more thing. My sire, Reigh Count, won the Kentucky Derby. I also won the Kentucky Derby. My son, Count Turf, won the Kentucky Derby too. Three consecutive generations of Kentucky Derby winners.

How sweet it is!

The retired champion at stud. Count Fleet's sire, Reigh Count, won the Kentucky Derby. So did Count Fleet's son, Count Turf.

CITATION

It always helps to come from a good home. My home was the best, Calumet Farm, and you don't have to take my word for it, just ask around. The name Calumet is familiar even to folks who don't follow horse racing, because they've heard about Calumet Baking Powder, although that company was sold a long time ago for about $40 million. All the horses at Calumet get along great. We're like one big happy family.

If anybody wants to find out about a man with a sharp eye for horses, a little research into the wheeling and dealing of a man named Warren Wright would be an eye-opener. Mr. Wright didn't make a mistake very often, even when a big bundle of cash was on the line. For instance, he chipped in with another shrewd gentleman, named A. B. Hancock, to buy an English Derby winner named Blenheim II for a whopping $225,000, and all the Limey did was sire a champion horse named Whirlaway, which more than paid for his cost.

Mr. Wright spent a lot less for my sire, Bull Lea. He cost $14,000, but that was in the Depression when a buck was a buck. That price

A clear victory in the Futurity at Belmont Park. Whirling Fox came in second, and Citation's stablemate, the filly Bewitch, finished third.

tag was the fourth highest paid for a yearling in 1936. The three higher-priced horses were bought by a lady named Mrs. Ethel V. Mars, and her bankbook had a row of numbers longer than the straightaway at Belmont. My dam, if you want to know, was a good lady named Hydroplane II. The trainers were Ben and Jimmy Jones.

By the time I was ready to run as a two-year-old—that was in 1947—Calumet was loaded down with some of the best horses in the country. A few of them were my personal relatives, meaning we had the same sire, Bull Lea. They included Armed, once Horse of the Year and a champion handicap, and in my age group there were the likes of Coaltown and a filly named Bewitch. I'll tell you how good the Calumet stable was in 1947: we had thirty-six horses who won a hundred races, and no other stable came close.

Sometimes the Calumet entries played games when they were all in the same race. For instance, in the Washington Park Futurity, Calumet entered me, Bewitch, and a good runner named Free America. Jimmy Jones knew we would finish one-two-three, and he didn't want the horses to even feel a whip, so he instructed the jockeys how to run the event. Whoever was in front after a while would be allowed to win, and the riders would split the fees three ways.

Bewitch went ahead—she was like a whippet—and I just sort of went with her and so did Free America. At the stretch Bewitch eased in and I picked up five lengths on her, but she won.

You should have heard the jockey talk later.

Doug Dodson was up on Bewitch and he said, "I could have opened up the lead any time I wanted to."

Steve Brooks rode me and he said, "Citation was just loafing. He could have gone right past the filly."

Jackie Westrope rode Free America, and he laughed, "You guys are just kidding yourselves. I could have taken both of you and I wouldn't need the whip, either."

The funny part of the story is this: none of us were going flat out, but Bewitch won in 1:10²/₅, which was the fastest clocking for the event up to that time.

Before that little charade I was unbeaten. I started off by taking three straight overnighters in Maryland. There's nothing special about an "overnighter" except for the way it's handled. It's a race for which entries close seventy-two hours or less before post time for the first race on the day the race is to be run (that's not counting Sundays). An overnight can also be a printed sheet of paper listing entries for the following day. Only horsemen pay attention to those things. The betting public shrugs if off and the horses care even less.

After those three wins I set a record at Arlington Park at :58 for five furlongs, and then I won the Elementary Stakes.

With a record of five wins and one loss (that setback to Bewitch is one I never considered a loss, but go argue with the record books), I was shipped to New York for the Futurity Trial.

A lot of races are called "futurity," and in a way it does have something to do with the future. A futurity—*any* futurity— is a race for two-year-olds for which they were entered as foals. A futurity trial is just what it appears to be, a test to see if the two-year-old has potential or runs like a farm mule. You might say a futurity is the exact opposite of an overnighter.

For this Futurity Trial the favorite was a nice horse named My Request. I beat him. In the Futurity itself there were fourteen horses entered, some of the best two-year-olds running.

It was a good race. We were just a furlong from the starting gate and there were six of us bunched

together, maybe a length apart. I didn't like the crowd and began pulling away easily. I won by three lengths. Whirling Fox just managed to beat Bewitch by a neck for second place. I'll say this for the little filly, she could run. Even with a hobble around two legs she could beat a lot of colts. As a matter of fact she could have broken the money record for all two-year-olds, except for something that wasn't her fault. She had finished first in the Matron Stakes, but she was disqualified for interference with a horse named Ghost Run. In an interference call the fault is almost never with the horse. It's the jockey who does the dirt. Bewitch was placed last and her rider, Doug Dodson, was suspended.

The Pimlico Futurity was the last race I ran as a two-year-old. It wasn't a big field for the mile-and-a-sixteenth race. Some pretty fair horses showed up, including Better Self, Ace, and Royal Blood. It was a muddy track, but that wasn't a big deal. My winning time was 1:48⁴/₅. That made my record eight wins and one place in nine starts. My winnings totaled $155,680. I could have had a bigger paycheck and an unbeaten season if the Calumet big wheels hadn't decided to play games. Oh well, what's a race more or less between friends?

Since I was a three-year-old with potential, Calumet wanted to start me off easy. They picked a race they thought might be an easy break-in, a $5,000 overnighter at six furlongs at Hialeah. That showed what might go wrong with an overnighter. A lot of trainers figured it was a good spot, and when the bugler blew his horn for the horses to get to the track, I was practically surrounded by older horses. These were no stiffs, either. I couldn't blame Calumet for entering Armed, a terrific gelding who happened to be Horse of the Year last season, but the others didn't figure to be pushovers. I saw five-year-old Kitchen Police, a six-year-old mare named Rampart, four-year-old Say Blue, four-year-old Travistock. I must say it's a hell of a way to start off a three-year-old.

Kitchen Police broke out in front, but he was no problem. I caught him after one furlong and ran him ragged. At the end of the half-mile it was no contest. I won by plenty, just a mere second off the track record for six furlongs.

A few days later I found myself in the company of older horses again, this time with a slightly different cast of characters. Armed was still there—Calumet liked to hedge its bets by frequently entering more than one horse in an event—but the rest included such veterans as Delegate, Faultless, Gestapo, Round View, and Buzfuz. I won that one, too, the seven-furlong Seminole Handicap.

By then Calumet realized the kind of horse I was, and if they weren't quite sure, a trainer named Sunny Jim Fitzsimmons told them. Sunny Jim was a legend, a wise man who had trained a couple of Triple Crown winners in Gallant Fox and the Fox's son, Omaha. Someone asked Sunny Jim what he thought of me, and that smart old geezer said, "Up to this point Citation has done more than any horse I ever saw." He smiled, paused, and then added, "And don't forget, I saw Man o' War."

I don't know about anyone else, but I'd take Sunny Jim's word anytime.

I'd made my point by beating older horses, and now it was time to send me out against horses my own age. By the way, I wasn't *really* a three-year-old yet. I was born April 11, 1945, so, since I had won those races in February, technically I was still a two-year-old, but why quibble over a couple of months?

The Everglades Handicap was a breeze, and the Flamingo was even easier. I beat Big Dial by six lengths and a horse named Saggy by ten.

A funny thing happened to me in my next outing, the six-furlong Chesapeake Trial Stakes at Havre de Grace. I lost in the mud. I went off at odds of 3 to 10, and no doubt I should have won, bad track and all, but there are always the intangibles, such as other horses doing their own thing, that nobody can ever figure on.

I had a new jockey. In the other races, Doug Dodson was riding Armed and Al Snider was riding me. When the handicap races were over, Al Snider—who rode me both times—was my jockey. Perhaps Dodson's nose was out of joint, because he soon quit the Calumet stable. I had

a pretty damn good jockey named Eddie Arcaro in the stirrups, and it was the first time he had ever ridden me. That's not an excuse, just an explanation.

The horse out of the gate first was Saggy—remember Saggy, I beat him by ten lengths in the Flamingo—he broke on top, and a horse named Hefty followed him out. At the top of the stretch I made my move on the outside, but Hefty started to go outside with me. In the middle of the stretch Arcaro got me clear, but it was too late. I was two lengths behind Saggy then, and all I could do was make up one length. That was Saggy's margin of victory. I will say this about Arcaro, he never went to the whip. He was willing to concede. He said later, "I might have caught Saggy. I think I could have. But I wasn't about to burn up this horse for an $8,300 pot with all those $100,000 races ahead. This was the first time I had him and believe me, I wanted to ride him back."

Saggy was an okay horse, but not that good so as to beat me. I cleared up any doubts in the mile-and-a-sixteenth Chesapeake Stakes. In the backstretch Saggy went by me, but Arcaro and I decided the foolishness had gone far enough. On the final turn I went by Saggy like he wasn't even there. Actually, Saggy didn't run well at all. I beat a horse named Bovard by four and a half lengths, and Saggy was another eleven lengths behind Bovard. Poor Saggy, he hurt himself in that race and didn't start again for over a month. When he did go to the post again he pulled up lame and it was on to the stud farm afterward.

I made one big mistake in the Derby Trial race. I went off at odds of 1 to 10, and I won so easily that not many other owners wanted to start their horses. Can you imagine throwing in the towel even before that big race is run? That's every owner's dream, a Derby win. If any horse except a gelding wins, the stud or mare's fees can be large enough to keep the farm in oats for years.

It was even more disheartening for everybody else when my half-brother, Coaltown, was also entered. Coaltown had won four straight so far, and it sure looked like Calumet was going to finish one-two in the Derby. The only question seemed to be which one of us would win. So the Churchill Downs people did the only thing that could possibly be done, they eliminated all place and show bets. It was like they were saying any horse could lose to Citation and/or Coaltown, so those hunch players who thought their horse could beat us would get a payoff. The betting public was, of course, free to bet Coaltown or me.

Only four other horses showed up to try the "Run for the Roses": My Request, Billings, Grandpere, and Escadru. The Calumet entries went off at 2 to 5. My Request, who had also won four straight races before the Derby, was 4 to 1.

Coaltown got off winging. That horse could really go when the mood was in him to run. At the half his time was a tad over :46 and he had a six-length lead. Well, it runs in the family. However, in a race like the Derby there is no

friendship or brotherly love. Besides, Arcaro had already won four Derby runs and he was hungry for another. Steady Eddie pushed me a little and I cut the margin to three lengths, and at the turn Coaltown and I were about even. Over the last quarter-mile I pulled away, and the sloppy track didn't make much difference, because I took it by three and a half lengths. Coaltown was second, three lengths ahead of My Request.

Calumet wasn't a very popular stable then. A lot of owners were shaking their heads and muttering to themselves about a monopoly, or some such thing. It got worse when I won the Preakness. Only three other horses showed up: Vulcan's Forge, Bovard, and Better Self. I beat Forge by five and a half lengths. Meanwhile, at the Gallant Fox Handicap in New York, two other Calumet horses, Faultless and Fervent, finished one-two.

It was like we weren't leaving any purse money

Winning the Kentucky Derby, with stablemate Coaltown three-and-a-half lengths behind.

A handy win in the Preakness, with Vulcan's Forge five-and-a-half lengths away.

for the others. One trainer at Keeneland said wearily, "The only way now is to stay home or ship a horse for a race in Winnipeg."

A few sourpusses tried to put me down. One of them asked, "Who did Citation beat that My Request did not beat?" The answer was simple enough—I beat My Request.

There was a month between the Preakness and the Belmont, and Jimmy Jones didn't want me to get fat, so he entered me in the mile-and-a-quarter Jersey Stakes. It was just another workout. I won by eleven lengths, and my time, 2:03, knocked $1^3/5$ seconds off the track record for that distance.

However, Calumet's stranglehold on every winner's circle was broken. In the Withers, Vulcan's Forge took revenge by beating Coaltown by almost two lengths. Sorry about that, brother. Nobody wins 'em all.

The horse owners were a lot braver for the Belmont. Seven horses came to test me at the mile-and-a-half distance, and some owners thought I was a sure loser. It had to do with my sire, Bull Lea. Among his sons and daughters were a ton of champions, but none was a good distance horse. I had won at a mile and a quarter a few times, but the Belmont was a quarter-mile longer. If I was the class of the field I'd have to win big, otherwise I'd always be suspect.

Maybe there was something to all that heavy thinking. I was three lengths ahead at the half-mile pole, but Escadru hung in behind me, and with three furlongs to go he cut a length off my lead, and that big Belmont homestretch still lay ahead. But I had plenty left. Arcaro dropped his hands, I dropped my head and went home free. My time was 2:28⅕, not too bad.

It was the second time Calumet had taken the Triple Crown. They'd won it before with Whirlaway.

"See America" is a good motto. I'd run in Kentucky, Maryland, and New York; now I was shipped out to check the action in Chicago. I was entered in a field of mostly older horses; in fact, the only other three-year-old besides myself was a horse named Loujac. This race was the Stars and Stripes Handicap, a nine-furlong event.

It turned out to be a very tough one. Knockdown and Loujac set the pace and I laid off. There was something wrong with me back in the

A tremendous victory in the Belmont Stakes for the Triple Crown. Better Self was second, Escadru came in third.

After the Belmont Stakes, with Eddie Arcaro in the saddle.

right hip area, and I didn't lead the pack until we were in the stretch. There was no finishing kick in me, and maybe it was Arcaro batting me a couple of times that helped me across by two lengths, with Eternal Reward and Pellicle finishing for place and show. Even with that pain my time was 1:49^1/$_5$, which tied Armed's track record.

The pain was real. I had pulled a muscle in my hip, which sidelined me for a few weeks.

When I returned to action, I also returned to winning. There was an overnighter, a prep race for the American Derby, at Washington Park. This run had some very good horses, like Papa Redbird, who had won the Arlington Classic, and Volcanic, and my stablemate, Free America. I won by eight lengths. Calumet finished one-two again, because Free America came in second.

Back in New York, I met up with brother Coaltown again in the Sysonby Mile. Coaltown had redeemed himself for his Withers loss with a

very nice win in the Jerome Handicap. I think I surprised everybody, including Arcaro, because I turned the race into a laugher with just one real burst of speed. There were some good horses in the field, including a sprinter named Spy Song, Natchez, and First Flight. I was six lengths back, then Arcaro made a little clucking sound and I took off. In the next eighth-mile I picked up all six lengths and won by three. First Flight was second, Coaltown was third.

Now I had the chance to make monkeys of everyone who thought I couldn't go for distance. The Jockey Club Gold Cup is a two-mile run, and before the Belmont there were plenty of smart people who'd have bet you I couldn't walk that far, let alone run. I guess the other entries were out to gang up on me, because it looked like a planned race. When I opened up a five-length lead, a couple of sprinters came flying at me, but I beat 'em back. Next, a lady horse named Conniver began to challenge and she was no slouch, being the leading handicap mare of the year, but I got rid of her, too. Finally, the previous year's three-year-old champion, Phalanx, took a crack at me, but it did no good. I beat Phalanx by seven lengths.

There was nothing left to prove with a distance race and it all boiled down to how much of a paycheck I could donate to Calumet. The big money was in the runs against older horses, and the logical choice was the mile-and-five-six-teenths Empire City Gold Cup, which was a $100,000 race. For this one, some of the horses were from out of town—I mean *really* out of town, like another country. There was Miss Grillo, an Argentine horse I'd beaten in the Jockey Club, and Nathoo, winner of the Irish St. Leger, and Bayeux, a champion from Belgium. Add to the field some other dandy runners, like Carolyn A., Phalanx, Better Self, and Ace Admiral. None of them had a chance.

The Pimlico Special was a weird race. As a matter of fact it wasn't a race at all. In those days, like now, the champion horse was decided by a poll, but some people got the bright idea that the championship should be settled by the horses, not the touts and tipsters. It was like a shoot-out at the O.K. Corral: we all meet on the track and whoever wins gets the decision.

Invitations were sent out. Nobody showed up, only me. I went out on the track waiting for the opposition, but I was all alone. In racing language that's called a *walkover*. If the race had been run on grass I could have grazed my way around the oval in a couple of hours and still be top dog. I guess no one else bothered because it was a winner-take-all race, and even a rich owner won't toss away money for nothing.

But my pride was hurt. Arcaro had all he could handle holding me down, because I covered the ground in 1:59⁴/₅. That proved the no-shows had the right idea.

It was on to San Francisco. I won a small prep race and entered the Tanforan Handicap. The two horses to beat in that one were Shannon II and On Trust, but when the assigned weights were announced, both horses were scratched. The rest of the field wasn't much. Just for the hell

of it I set a track record for the mile and a quarter.

That was the end of the season for me. In fact, I laid off completely as a four-year-old, because I developed an osselet, which is a kind of hard nodule on the leg. Still, I hadn't done badly. I won $709,470 as a three-year-old, and add to that my $155,680 the year before, so that my total winnings were $865,150. In all I had won twenty-seven out of twenty-nine starts, with two place finishes. You can throw out both losses. One was a family gift to Bewitch, the other was in the Chesapeake Trial Stakes, when Hefty took me so wide I almost became a grandstand spectator.

I suppose the Tanforan was my last hurrah. I raced a few times as a five-year-old, nine times to be exact, and I won only two, with seven second-place finishes. A horse never really comes back from an osselet, at least not as good as he once was. However, I was never beaten by a lot, maybe a nose in one race, a neck in another. When I won, my time was always good.

Now it became a matter of playing out the string. I ran only seven times as a six-year-old, and the object was to get me over the million-dollar mark in earnings. It was a chore. In one race I was out of the money, the only time that ever happened to me. Other than that I always gave a good account of myself.

I'd lost my first four races in a row when I was entered in the Argonaut Handicap, a one-mile event. I won it. Next came the American Handicap. I won that too, beating Bewitch by half a length. Finally, I ran in the Hollywood Gold Cup, a ten-furlong race. First money was $100,000, and that put me over the million-dollar mark.

Jimmy Jones wanted me to run at least one more time, but Mrs. Wright said no, it was over, I was going to stud. That was okay with me. At least I went out a winner.

All in all I racked up a record to be proud of. A total of forty-five starts, thirty-two wins, ten places, two shows, and, just once, no payoff. Along the way I picked up a Triple Crown. No complaints from me. No complaints from Calumet, either.

Master of all he surveys, the retired Citation at stud. He had won more than a million dollars in purses.

NATIVE DANCER

I am a joke horse. I like jokes. All kinds of jokes. Yes, even practical jokes. Like the one I pulled on Eddie Arcaro. He still doesn't know how I pulled that fast one on him in Chicago. Or should I say, how I pulled that slow one?

Let me give you an idea of the kind of jokes I like. A trainer once asked how he would like the track to be for a race I was running in. The trainer said, "Well, I'd really like a track that doesn't have Native Dancer on it."

That's the kind of humor I like—subtle, you know? You remember how Eric Guerin rode me so wide on the turns at the Kentucky Derby? After the race I heard a Churchill Downs steward say to someone, "Eric took Native Dancer everywhere on the track except to the ladies' room."

Nothing like a good laugh, even after you've lost a Derby. In fact, the only way to be after a race, win or lose—is laughing. Racing's too short a career to take it too seriously.

I can be serious too, of course. What can get me real serious is when I hear a jockey say, "Well, we made our move at the eighth pole and won by a length."

Native Dancer and Eric Guerin look muddy but satisfied after winning the 1954 Oneonta Handicap at Saratoga. Native Dancer never raced again. He died in 1967.

We? What's this *we* stuff? If a jock had to run a race all by himself, he'd still be running when the horses are back in the paddock thinking What's for supper?

Now, I must admit, there are jocks who don't put themselves in front of the horse. Eric always knew who was the important one in a horse race. Once I heard him say, "Sometimes I think Native Dancer has more real sense on how to run a race than I do."

I always had that good sense—when to make my move, when not to, when to sprint, when to lay back, when to look for the hole. I let Eric steer me during most of a race, but if my race sense told me to do something else, I nearly always trusted that sense—and did what it told me.

I was always good at changing leads. You know what that means, of course. When you go around turns, your left foreleg is supposed to hit the ground first—that's your left lead. On straightaways you're supposed to lead with your right foreleg—your right lead. "It's like walking with a suitcase," I heard Eric say once, "you've got to change hands or your one arm gets tired." Some horses don't like to change leads—it confuses them—but it always came natural to me.

Since I knew the way horses think, I knew how to make them shaky. I'd run stride for stride with a horse for a furlong, running at three-quarter speed. The other horse would be snorting and panting, busting a gut to get ahead. Then I'd suddenly shift into full speed and I'd blast right by him, leaving him bug-eyed in my dust.

That will take something out of a horse the next time you run against him. He says to himself before the next race: What's the good of killing myself to stay even with this guy? He can run away from me whenever he wants. When they think like that, you have an easy race for yourself. And being a fun horse, I loved easy races.

Maybe I liked easy races so much that it cost me the Derby that Dark Star won. A lot of people said I took it too easy in the first half of a race and then made up ground in the last half. That was true of me, I'll admit it, and maybe in the Derby I took it easy for just a couple of inches too many.

But I hadn't counted on hitting into that wall—"the wall of noise" is what the other horses call it. Churchill Downs is built in such a way that all the noise from the crowd is funneled into the stretch. It's like one of those tidal waves you hear about swamping some island in the ocean. Imagine a tidal wave that could be streamed into a channel the width of the Downs. The wave would build into a huge wall, right? It's that wall—not of water, but noise—that you hit as you enter the stretch at Churchill. It's so loud, so overpowering, it can stop you in your tracks if you are not ready for it.

Dark Star was ready for it. He had run in the Derby Trial. He knew what was coming and he braced himself, he told me later, to go through it. I had heard about the wall, but I never expected what I hit. I knew it cost me a couple of seconds fighting through it.

I know that sounds like an alibi. Maybe it is. But don't go away thinking I've spent my life alibiing for that Derby. Actually, until someone like you or another horse brings it up, I seldom think about it. Really. One, Eric made a mistake. Two, I didn't trust my instincts. Three, there was the wall, which I hadn't expected to hit so hard. Add it all up and what does it mean? I didn't win the Triple Crown. Look, to me a bad day is a day when I don't get a good belly laugh, and you don't get a lot of belly laughs thinking back to how you won or lost a Triple Crown.

I think back to Eddie and me at Arlington,

okay. Then I get a belly laugh. And whether we won or lost, I know I would have gone away from that race laughing. Let me tell you how I got that way.

I was born on March 27, 1950. I grew up on the Glyndon Farm in Maryland, which is owned by Mr. Vanderbilt [Alfred Gwynn Vanderbilt]. Only one in a hundred Thoroughbreds, they say, is gray. I was the one in a hundred. Actually, you look at me close, you can see I am a gunpowder gray speckled with white and black. To grooms and trainers and other horses, I was always "The Gray" or "The Big Gray." When some racing writers got fanciful, they called me "The Gray Ghost of Glyndon." Now *that's* a name.

Even as a two-year-old I was playful. One day at the farm I watched two steeplechasers learning how to leap over the hurdles. I wanted to do that, but of course my trainer [Bill Winfrey] wouldn't let me near a bar. He was afraid, for one thing, I'd hurt my knees, which were always knobby and would finally mean the end of racing for me. And I miss the racetrack. Who wouldn't, when you nearly always won?

Anyway, the day after I saw the steeplechasers, I was working out on a track. The sun had just peeped over the barn and the light cast long shadows as it hit the furlong poles. As I ran down the track, I saw the striped shadows and thought how much they looked like hurdles. I came up to each shadow and leaped across it like I was sailing over a barrier. It was great fun, pretending to fly. But when we got back to the stable, Bill Winfrey bawled out the exercise boy, thinking the boy had put me up to it. Horse people, they'll give you no credit for having a little imagination.

In the winter of 1952 I went to California, where I worked out as a two-year-old at Santa Anita. One day I heard Bill talking to a reporter and he said, "The gray is the fastest horse I've ever trained. He shows good times in workouts, but that's not what's impressive. It's the fact that the big gray does it without any effort. He actually seems to be holding himself back."

He was right. I never believed in killing myself to win a race. That's probably the big reason why I didn't set a lot of records. Someone's going to

Polynesian, Native Dancer's sire, as he looked about a year before he sired Native Dancer.

break the record, right? No laughs when you hear your record's just been broken by some horse you never heard of, right? So who needs records? Give me laughs anytime.

I never did race in California. I went east to New York and ran my first race—at Jamaica. Word had jumped across the country about my fast clockings at Santa Anita. I went off as the 7-to-5 favorite and won by four lengths.

That was the way I won all my races as a two-year-old—easy does it. I won almost a quarter of a million dollars [$230,495]. In one race they loaded 130 pounds on me, which was the heaviest cargo any two-year-old had ever carried [except Man o' War and Count Fleet, who also were assigned 130]. I was the first two-year-old to be picked as the Horse of the Year.

It was about then, that summer of '53, you may recall, that TV began to go to the tracks to telecast the big races. In those days there were only black-and-white pictures. I looked good on screens with that shimmering pepper-and-salt look. I was the first horse to be a TV star, and I got lots of letters, mostly from young girls. In fact, one magazine that summer [*TV Guide*] picked me, Arthur Godfrey, and Ed Sullivan as the number-one attractions of the TV season—although not, I guess I should say, necessarily in that order.

I won the Gotham Mile and the Wood Memorial in New York, so naturally I was the heavy favorite to win the 1953 Kentucky Derby. When I got to Churchill Downs, I heard talk about a big, husky bay, Dark Star, who had won the Derby Trial. But I was still the favorite, and in fact I went off as one of the shortest-priced horses ever for a Derby, 7 to 10.

Later we learned the strategy of the Dark Star

The two-year-old Dancer (above), as New Yorkers called him, shows his heels and long legs to the also-rans as he wins a 1952 race at Jamaica. Later in 1952, Native Dancer and Eric Guerin face the cameras (below), *after winning the Grand Union Hotel Stakes at Saratoga.*

people. Hank Moreno, the rider, was told to go out in front right away and set the pace as the front-runner. You look up the charts of Kentucky Derbys and you will see that the front-runner wins a heavy share of the time. In those big stampedes to the first turn, nervous three-year-olds bump each other or block someone else. And it isn't easy trying to come from behind when you first have to run through that wall of

noise at the top of the stretch. You read about those thrillers—a horse charging from way back to win the Derby—but they don't happen all that often.

Dark Star got a great start—and he needed it to be a front-runner because he came out of the next-to-outside gate. That quick start gave Moreno space enough in front of the field. He crossed over to take the rail and lead the field into the first turn. I tried to tuck into a place along the rail, but around me horses banged into one another, riders swore and screamed, clouds of dust billowed into our eyes. I kept my head down, eyes fixed on the hooves around me so I didn't trip or run up someone else's back. As we came to the turn, Money Broker swerved in from the outside and bumped me. Eric pulled me back behind Money Broker so we wouldn't be hit again. We went around the turn, me in eighth or ninth place, or so I was told later. Me, I knew how a blind man must feel in a dark room with a dozen other blind men and all of them groping and bumping into each other to find the door.

Up front, meanwhile, Dark Star was running clear along the rail. Moreno tugged the reins to hold him back and save him for the stretch while holding on to the lead. "He had me bent over almost double," Dark Star told me the next day. "I wanted him to know that he had a lot of horse under him and he should just let me run."

Dark Star piped the tune and Moreno heard the melody. He let out the reins and Dark Star sprinted away from the pack as we curved into the backstretch.

I wanted to run, too. I could see that the leader, whoever he was, was getting too far away. My instinct told me that this was the time to burst free of the pack and move up closer to the leader so we could jump on him at the top of the stretch.

Instead, Eric moved me wide to the outside so I could get clear. I thought we should have kept straight near the inside rail because now the field had strung out and there was room to run. The move to the outside cost us time and distance.

We did pass four horses along the backstretch and, later, when I watched a newsreel of the race on television with the grooms, I heard the track announcer shouting, "And here comes Native Dancer!" I had swung into fourth place, still on the outside. I saw I was running maybe six lengths behind Dark Star, who led Correspondent by maybe a length and a half.

We curved around the turn, the four of us, with me still on the outside. Going into the stretch, Correspondent and the third horse swung to the outside.

Eric and I saw the opening at the same instant. We shot to the inside and I popped by Correspondent into second place.

Dark Star streaked ahead of me by a length and a half. I could see the enemy now, knew it was Dark Star, and I was sure he was ours.

I went forward—and I thought someone had cracked a baseball bat that hit me right between the eyes. I had hit the wall of noise.

It stunned me for maybe a split second. I know I stumbled. Eric said later that I just wouldn't run. For the first time ever, he hit me with the whip.

I never felt the sting. That sound drowned out everything else, including what you always hear in the stretch—that *tumpa-tum, tumpa-tum, tumpa-tum* sound of hooves pounding the track. I felt like I was standing still smack in the middle of the noisiest parade I had ever heard.

Eric whacked again and my brain got the message. I felt like I was running again. And now, my head clear despite the noise, I saw I was gaining on Dark Star. I came abreast of his flying tail. I could hear his bellowing—I guess the two of us sounded like a pair of exhausted elephants ready to keel over.

I came even with his saddle. I knew he was done. His ears flapped down. He didn't even have the energy to pin them back. "My horse had nothing left," Moreno told Eric the next day.

But I was running short of track. I got about even with Dark Star's neck, then shot by him. But I knew we had gone under the wire. There was no doubt about it—Dark Star had won by a head.

Maybe, the more I think about it, maybe I didn't take the Derby seriously enough. I never took any race very seriously. Eric, I know, was nervous before a race. I could feel his legs quivering after he mounted me in the paddock. He steadied by the time we got to the track. Me, I was always as calm before a race as I am talking to you right now.

Once, just before the Travers Stakes at Saratoga in 1955, I think it was, a bunch of my fans from TV got so excited when they saw me in person that they swarmed right by the guards in the paddock. They crowded around me. They patted me on the flanks; some of them even jumped up to rub their hands between my ears. One girl tried to pull hairs out of my tail. She shouted that she wanted a souvenir. A lot of skittish horses I know might have reared up and clobbered them all with a pair of steel hooves. I liked it. I stood very calmly. Later, I heard a trainer say it was the first time that a horse was almost trampled to death by humans.

After the Derby, of course, everyone in racing looked ahead to the Preakness at Pimlico and another stretch duel between myself and Dark Star. Some people argued that Dark Star, a 25-to-1 long shot, won the Derby on a fluke—the fluke being that Eric took me everywhere on the track except to the ladies' room. I don't buy that. Many people quickly forgot, but Dark Star's time in beating me was the fifth fastest Derby time ever. Dark Star had won the Derby Trial, so he didn't come out of nowhere. Dark Star, and I should be the first one to say it, ranks high in my mind among the most underrated horses of all time.

So we get off in the Preakness. For the first mile of the mile and a quarter, Dark Star and me gave the people what they paid for. It was a nose-to-nose duel, neither of us giving an inch. But as we turned for home, Dark Star pulled away from me to lead by half a length. Then, suddenly, Dark Star slowed. He faded right through the pack to finish way back—I think eleventh. Later it was discovered he had bowed a tendon. He never raced again, going right to stud. I was sorry to see him go and I told him so. He held on to finish that Derby when all he had left was heart. We could have given people a lot more thrills. If you see him—he's in stud over in Kentucky—tell him I said he was the greatest horse I ever stood with in a starting gate.

I won the Preakness after Dark Star faded, although Jamie K. gave me a scare by making a run at me and coming to within a neck of winning.

Now I heard talk that I was a short horse. My mom was Geisha, my pop Polynesian—and out of that someone came up with that goofy name of Native Dancer. Mom and Pop were sprinters. The New York railbirds said that I'd surely trip on

my pedigree in what the Big Apple likes to call the "True Test of Champions"—the mile-and-a-half Belmont Stakes, and the third leg of the Triple Crown. Short horses don't win the Belmont Stakes.

I always liked New York. I could understand why the great radio comics—Durante, Berle, Hope—always wanted to play the Palace on Broadway. When you go to New York and you step out of your railroad car, greeted by the photographers' flashing lights and the white lights of the TV crews, the shouted questions from the reporters, you feel you are in the center of a gigantic spotlight. At least I did. And who doesn't love a lot of attention?

When we lined up in the starting gate, I told myself: Keep your mind on what you're doing. Don't be too calm and easy-going like you usually are. If you lose, remember, no more attention.

I led nearly all the way but as we came into the stretch, Jamie K. drove once more at me. We went down the stretch head to head. I bet lots of people were thinking that the son of Polynesian would fade after nearly a mile and a half of hard running. Instead, I pulled away to win by a neck and that was the last time I heard anything about my being a short horse.

That was my fourteenth victory in fifteen starts. I'd won over half a million dollars in a year and a half of racing [$522,745]. That was more money than any other horse had ever earned in that short a time.

Naturally, all that money made me *número uno*, as the Latin jocks say, around the stable. I got most anything I wanted. When Bill Winfrey suspected that I yearned for what most racehorses want, a stable pet, he got me a cute little black cat. When the cat dozed off, I nuzzled her with my nose. I liked doing it, and it also brought the newspaper photographers around to take pictures of me nuzzling the cat. When you're in show biz, and racing's show biz after all, you want the newspaper guys to like you. They can make you look bad, especially the photographers.

I have a funny story to tell you about that cat.

The Derby disappointment behind him, Native Dancer (above) holds off a late surge by Jamie K. to win the 1953 Preakness. Eric Guerin, looking exultant, and Native Dancer, looking noble, parade to the winner's circle after a 1954 race at Belmont Park (below).

My handler, Les Murray, is always saying to me, "You big bum; get over here, you big bum." He's only kidding, he thinks I can do anything. One time we took a trip by train in our special car to Chicago. The cat came along. She was always the "Black Cat" to Les and everyone else, just like I was the "Big Gray." Anyway, I see that the cat is pregnant by the way she's dragging herself around. Back in New York, she gives birth to five kittens. They're all gray.

Lester never stopped carrying on about those gray kittens. He'd tell people who came to visit me, "That cat always had nothing but black kittens. When we came back from Chicago, she had five kittens and they was all gray. Gray like him! He's a powerful horse, he is, a *powerful* horse."

Les always got laughs when he told people how much I ate. I always was "a big doer," as they say of horses with a huge appetite. Usually I had two quarts of hay at eleven in the morning, another four quarts at four in the afternoon, and then I'd get a snack of another four quarts at one in the morning. The hay was mixed with clover on the days I wasn't racing. I ate too much of it to race with that much in my tummy. I loved the sweet buds in the clover. I ate the clover and hay, Bill Winfrey once said, like kids eat chocolate bars. On the days before I raced, so I wouldn't gorge myself, they mixed the hay with timothy. The timothy is not as sweet as the clover, so I ate it only sparingly. Who doesn't have a sweet tooth?

By this time, that summer of 1953, I had decided that those two by-a-neck victories over Jamie K. in the Preakness and Belmont Stakes were shaving things a little too close. In my next four races—the Dwyer Stakes, the Arlington Classic, the Travers, and the American Derby—I won by at least a length and I won the Arlington by nine.

The Arlington brings me to that practical joke I played on Eddie Arcaro. For months Eddie had been telling people I was a good horse but not a great horse like Citation. That riled millions of people. I was their TV matinee idol; that's what one magazine [*Newsweek*] said about me. They wrote angry letters to Eddie. They booed him at the track. How could he say those things about their wonderful Native Dancer?

Well, just imagine how furious those fans were when Mr. Vanderbilt hired Eddie to ride me in the Arlington. For the only time in my career, Eric didn't mount me—he'd been suspended for a week or so for some kind of riding error, what the stewards call an infraction. Mr. Vanderbilt and Eddie got thousands of letters from my fans demanding that someone else, instead of what they called "the non-believer," ride me.

When Eddie got to Chicago, he rode in a race at Arlington a day or so before the Classic. The fans booed and shook their fists at him. The uproar shook Eddie. The night before the race, I heard him say to someone, "If I get beat, I'm the biggest bum alive."

That's when I got the idea. I'd make him think until the very last moment that he was the biggest bum alive.

Eddie knew how I liked to romp along during the first half of the race, then blaze through the second half. But I had him worried halfway down the backstretch at Arlington. We were dead last. Eddie hollered at me and shook the reins—he knew he wasn't supposed to go to the whip unless he had to in the stretch.

I picked up my speed and passed three horses. As we went by, I turned to gaze leisurely at each one—another old trick of mine. That really got to where Eddie breathed. He began to shout, "Go! Go!" I kept on running at a steady pace, keeping the leaders in view while not letting them get any farther ahead.

We turned into the stretch. I am fourth or fifth. Eddie is screaming bloody murder. No doubt he is wondering if he can exit this track without getting killed for losing on an odds-on favorite. I know he is thinking whip.

I beat him to the punch. I flatten my ears, lower my body, and I streamline down that stretch to make what I still believe was my strongest stretch run. I flew by the pack to win by those nine lengths. My time [1:48²/₅] was only one-fifth of a second off the track record, which had been set by a horse carrying 118 pounds. I was weighted down with 128.

Eddie looked ashen when he got off me at the winner's circle. But he is a tough son of a gun. He stood by what he had said. When a reporter asked if he had changed his mind about me and Citation, he said, "The best horse I ever rode was Citation."

That didn't bother me, of course. When I heard people or other horses arguing about one horse being better than another, I always said, "Let the track decide." And since there was no way I could run against Citation, who was retired, there was no way anyone could see who was better.

I would have liked the track to decide who was the better 1953 horse—Tom Fool or me. Tom Fool got the nod as the Horse of the Year. I was picked as the three-year-old of the year. Who else could they have picked? Tom Fool had a fine record, but not any better than my eight firsts and and a second. What hurt me a little, I'll admit, was being picked the next year, 1954, as the Horse of the Year. If I'd won it by 1953, I would have been the first horse to win that award three years in a row.

I had to quit racing in August of 1953. I had bruised the heel of my left forefoot while winning the American Derby and got out of bed the next day limping. I seemed to be all right the next spring, 1954, and won my first two races. Then I went after another Triple Crown, the Triple Handicap Crown, which is the Metropolitan, Suburban, and the Brooklyn, all at New York tracks. I went off in the Metropolitan as the 1-to-4 favorite and ran my usual race. Carrying the top weight of 130 pounds, I came into the homestretch fifth, about seven lengths behind Straight Face. I streaked by three horses and caught Straight Face thirty yards from the finish to win by a neck. My time was just a fraction off the track record, but I told myself I was getting too old for these hair-thin finishes.

We went up to Saratoga. No one wanted to race against me, Tom Fool having been retired to stud. That was too bad, since there had been talk about a match race between the two of us. Mr. Vanderbilt wanted to match me against Tom Fool. If he had, I think I would have been the 1953 Horse of the Year. But then I got the stone bruise and Tom Fool retired, so there wasn't a race.

At Saratoga I entered the Oneonta Handicap. The handicapper threw 137 pounds at me. Even so, no owner wanted to put up an entry fee he knew was money lost. Only Gigantic, who had won the Louisiana Derby the previous year, and one of my stablemates, First Glance, a cheerful fellow who snored a lot, were entered. Naturally, with only three horses entered, there could be no betting, which didn't make the track happy. I won by nine lengths.

It was then, I think, that Mr. Vanderbilt decided to ship me to Europe. I heard him say, "Well, at least he can find horses and owners who'll race him." He planned to enter me in two of England's biggest races, the King George VI and the Queen Elizabeth Stakes.

Everyone was excited. The grooms said we would go by boat and that the trip would take five or six days. I began to work out by running around the track the wrong way—what my exercise boy called clockwise. That's the way the horses run in England, I heard Bill Winfrey say. They do everything the wrong way there, he said, like driving on the wrong side of the road. I was looking forward to seeing what the wrong side of a road looked like.

Then, one morning, I got up and my left front foot ached like someone had been hitting it all night with a hammer. Bill called a vet and he said I had more of those stone bruises. Whenever I ran, he said, the bruises were going to keep on coming back. A day later, Mr. Vanderbilt called off the trip to Europe. He told a huge mob of reporters, who gathered around my stall at Saratoga, that he was retiring me to stud.

That made sense to me. No sense in trying to run on sore feet. And I thought I had done all I could do in racing. I had topped Man o' War's record of 20 wins in 21 starts by winning 21 of 22. I had won almost three-quarters of a million dollars [$785,240] and that made me the fourth of the all-time money winners, behind Citation, Stymie, and Armed.

What I liked best was what one writer put in the paper. He wrote that in those 22 races, I had lined up against about 150 of the best American horses and beaten all of them except Dark Star, who I did beat two weeks later.

The Gray Ghost of Glyndon is back here at Sagamore and I am a very active stud. I heard yesterday that there are applications coming in for me to service mares as far ahead as four years. In fact, do you know when the first application was entered in my stud book? When I was two years old. When I was two, I didn't know what a stud was.

SILKY SULLIVAN

The interviews with this horse, if indeed they actually took place, seem to have been done at Churchill Downs during the week before the 1958 Kentucky Derby. A careful check of the material left by Slips has found no other material on Silky Sullivan, who was one of the favorites to win the 1958 Derby.

 You know what the other horses call me? Especially the Kentucky horses, like that snooty Tim Tam. They call me "Hollywood." They're jealous of all the attention I've been getting here. You should have seen jaws drop in one stall after another when the TV cameramen came by yesterday. They wanted to get all kinds of views of me. They're doing a special show just on me before the race starts this Saturday. When the TV people set up the lights, I heard one horse say, "I guess Hollywood is the only horse in the Derby this year."

The horses don't understand. I'm a star. I sell tickets, as they say in the studios back home. I drew the biggest crowd ever to go to the Golden Gate track on a weekday afternoon. That crowd at Santa Anita this March, it was the biggest crowd [61,151] ever to watch the Santa Anita Derby. They came because they knew I'd be doing my thing—and, boy, you know that I gave them what they came for. I guess you want to know about that Derby and how I came from—what was it?—almost thirty lengths back.

First, take a look at that scrapbook in the corner. One of the grooms has been putting it together for the owners. Look through it. You'll find one clipping that I heard the groom read. It says that I am "the most dramatized horse since Man o' War." Big Red looked like me, you know, a big horse with a flaming red coat. One writer called me "a flaming chestnut." I know that if one of the studios wants to make *The Silky Sullivan Story,* it is going to have to use only flaming-red Technicolor.

The press is going right after the Hollywood angle. One writer in Los Angeles put in the paper that I should get an Oscar nomination as the best actor of the year. He said, "Silky milks every scene for all it's worth." One of my owners, Tom Ross, told a reporter, "Silky is a hambone actor who hates to leave the track. I swear that the reason why he walks onto the track so slowly is because he wants to count the house."

It's true. I like to see big crowds. I like to *hear* big crowds. That big crowd at the Derby at Santa Anita—when they yelled "Here he comes!"—of course it gave me a lift during that drive down the stretch. Every star gets a lift from applause.

I look like a star. Everybody says so. In that book there's a clipping that says I look more like an artist's idea of a war charger than a racehorse. That's because I'm a hunk. I'm almost twelve hundred pounds, about two hundred pounds heavier than most of the horses here. I stand sixteen hands, which means I look down on Tim Tam—and don't you think that makes him even more peevish.

Silky has come from behind to catch Tyhawk in the 1959 Roy Campanella Purse at Hollywood Park. Jockey Don Pierce is letting the long-necked Silky do his thing—his whip is not being used.

I dress like a star. I wear those red leg bandages, the red shadow roll, the red saddle cloths. They make my flaming red coat even more striking, don't you think? And when you're a star, you flaunt it, right? I don't see that Marilyn Monroe babe hiding anything she's got, check?

I think the people who run Churchill Downs and the Kentucky Derby are awfully happy I'm here. They needed something to jazz up this show. It's been running with the same tired cast of three-year-olds for some eighty years now. Look in that book and you'll see what Paul Lowrey wrote about me in the L.A. *Times*. He wrote that he's been coming to Churchill Downs for a quarter of a century and he's never seen anything compared—let's see, how did he put it?—"to the adulation and hero worship bestowed upon Silky Sullivan." Something like that.

And he's right. You heard what CBS is doing, of course. They are going to have two cameras covering the race at all times. One camera will be aimed at the leaders. The other camera will be aimed only at me. *Me.* All by myself. People at home will see what the CBS people call a split screen. On one half of the screen you will see the leaders. On the other half of the screen you'll see me way back in last place, waiting to make my move and come from behind.

Come from behind. That's me. Maybe that's a better title for the movie than *The Silky Sullivan Story. The Come from Behind Horse,* starring Silky Sullivan and Ann-Margret. It could be another *National Velvet.*

I've been thinking about that fellow Walt Disney and those cartoons he makes about animals. Maybe he would want to make me his new hero. Don't you think people are getting tired of watching that mouse and the duck that Disney's been drawing for so long? How fast can a duck run?

But you want to know how I came from so far behind to win the Santa Anita Derby last month. I was about thirty lengths behind in the backstretch. For me, that was being laid up close. I've come from more than forty lengths back. But I knew that Tom and Phil [Tom Ross and Phil

Klipstein, his owners] would be at the race. Their doctors gave them strict orders not to watch me run. Both Tom and Phil have heart trouble, and so far I haven't been so good for their tickers. So I tried not to give them too bad a scare.

You know, of course, that I run my own race. Not like Tim Tam and those Kentucky horses who have to be banged with a whip to get them moving. The Shoe [Willie Shoemaker, his jockey] knows better than to hit me with a whip. Fat Reggie [rotund Reggie Cornell, his trainer] has told reporters, "This horse is like no other horse I've ever seen. He wants to run his own race and we let him run his own race." The Shoe, he lets out a little chirp and rattles my bit. That's when I know it's time for us to come from behind.

Before I tell you how we came from behind at Santa Anita, I'd better give you a backgrounder bio on myself. "Backgrounder bio," that's the way the Hollywood flacks—the press agents—talk when they are telling reporters about their clients. I met one press agent, heard him say he was betting fifty dollars on me against the field in the Kentucky Derby. That's confidence.

Anyway, I was foaled in California in 1955. My sire was a big stallion imported from Ireland. His name was Sullivan. They named him after some boxer who went around saying he could lick any man in the house. My dam was Lady N Silk. The old man was big, with a chestnut coat, so you can see I took after him. He had a big appetite and so do I. None of that tea and crumpets stuff like those Kentucky horses eat. They're nibblers. I'll stow away fifteen buckets of oats in a day. I bet Tim Tam can't put away that much in a week.

When I was a yearling, I left the Merryman Farm—it's near Moreno—for a sale where I was bought by Tom and Phil, who are L.A. businessmen. They paid $10,000. Right from the start, when I began to train with Reggie, I raced the way I wanted to race. Reggie called me an upside-down horse. Most two-year-olds sprint through the first half of the race. They gallop home with what they have left. I galloped the first half, sprinted the second half.

I broke my maiden at Hollywood Park in May [of 1957]. I won two other races in six starts as a

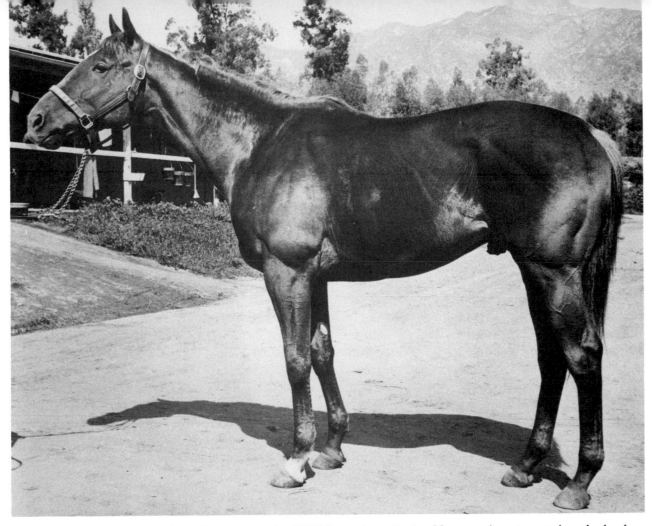

Silky stands proud a few days after winning the 1958 Santa Anita Derby. He came from twenty lengths back.

two-year-old. My first stakes victory came in December, my last race as a two-year-old, and it was then that people began to train their binoculars on what someone called "that flying red horse."

The race was the Golden Gate Futurity at Golden Gate. I hung some twenty-seven lengths behind the leader halfway through the one-mile race. The Shoe rattled the bit and chirped. Off we went to win going away.

Earlier that year I was running some forty lengths behind Old Pueblo, who was rated among the best two-year-olds in the country. As Old Pueblo turned into the homestretch, Eddie Arcaro, who was his jockey, turned to look behind him. He didn't see me because I was still on the far turn some forty lengths behind. When Eddie and Old Pueblo were an eighth of a mile from the finish, he heard something, turned and saw me coming. "It was like Silky came out of nowhere," Eddie said later. I missed catching Old Pueblo by a neck.

I made up for that miss—and got people talking again—in one of my first races as a three-year-old. I fell forty-one lengths back in a six-and-a-half-furlong run. Going into the far turn, I couldn't see the leader. I saw him down the stretch, caught him, and won going away.

So by March, as the Santa Anita Derby came closer, Californians knew all about me and my wild finishes. That's why all those people showed up at Anita for the race. Word spread across the country, even to New York, where they think there's nothing in California except grapes and movie stars. Ask your average New Yorker—I met a few of them here at Churchill Downs—where the Derby is, he'll tell you it's held in Kentucky early in May. He's never heard of the biggest Derby of them all, the Santa Anita Derby, which pays its winners almost twice as much as I'll win here on Saturday.

Anyway, from New York, *Life* magazine sent photographers to show me coming from far behind. I didn't want to disappoint anyone, figuring this was my chance to upstage horses like Tim Tam and Gone Fishin', who'd been grabbing headlines by winning stakes races in Florida. Right from the start, I told myself, You do your thing, Silky.

I bounced out of the gate as leisurely as I could and still look respectable. The loud *yahoo* shouts of the jockeys and the pounding of the hooves faded quickly away behind a wall of dust and a line of bushy-tailed rear ends. I followed at a gentleman's gallop.

I tried to keep my distance for the first half of the mile-and-an-eighth race. At the halfway point I was twenty-eight lengths behind. As we came down the backstretch in a long line with me at the tail, Alawar and Old Pueblo struggled for the lead. Later, I learned that in the middle of the backstretch I was ten lengths behind—not ten lengths behind the leader, ten lengths behind the next-to-last horse.

Then the Shoe chirped and jiggled. I agreed—it was time to go. In fact, maybe it had been time to go a furlong earlier.

I zipped past horses, but as I bent into the far turn I was about twenty lengths behind Alawar, who led Old Pueblo by about a neck.

We had to go outside to pass the posse of horses that trailed the two leaders. Going around the turn, we put in our hip pockets half the horses in the field. As I straightened out for the run down the stretch, there were five horses in front of me. The nearest was Harcall, the farthest was Alawar, who was a healthy nine lengths away.

The Shoe told reporters after the race that he expected I would want to stay outside as I came down the stretch. Other jockeys said they had expected me to do the same.

But I had seen a hole on the inside, just to the inside of Harcall. I burst through the hole. Later, I heard Eddie Boland, who was riding Harcall, say to the Shoe: "Silky went by me so fast he darn near sucked me under."

Harcall was a stablemate of mine, a fine fellow when he was awake, a snorer when he slept, but I liked him anyway. He saw me go by and decided to let me draft him home. In fact, Boland told the Shoe that "all I saw to the finish was Silky's tail."

The crowd was roaring, "Here he *comes!*" I loved it. I felt I could bound to the moon just to hear one more "Here he *comes!*" Within seconds I caught the fourth horse, the third horse, then Old Pueblo and Alawar. Harcall followed me through to finish second by three and a half lengths.

From twenty-eight lengths behind to win!

I bet *every* story out of Santa Anita that day and for the next week had that line in its lead—*Silky Sullivan comes from 28 lengths behind to win the richest race.* There was newspaper talk that Wilbur Clark, a big Las Vegas casino operator, wanted to buy me from Tom and Phil for about $300,000. That would have made Tom and Phil a profit of $290,000, right? I wouldn't have blamed Tom and Phil if they had sold me. How much more could their hearts take?

The Florida tracks wanted me to run against Tim Tam, Jewel's Reward, and the other Kentucky horses who had been making a big splash at Hialeah and Gulfstream that winter. But Tom, Phil, Reggie, and the Shoe decided that we should come here direct to get ready for the next big enchilada, the Kentucky Derby.

When I got here last week, I heard mixed reviews, as we say in show biz. Everyone wanted to see me, of course, and Eddie Arcaro said that Silky Sullivan had created more interest in the Derby than any other horse in his career, and he goes back to before World War II, for Pete's sake. Another jockey, Ted Atkinson, picked me to win. In the early line, I understand, I'm right up there with the favorites, Tim Tam and Jewel's Reward.

One of the stablehands said this morning that he had been talking to a man from Western Union. The Western Union man said that reporters here are sending out thousands of words more than they did before any other Derby ever—and most of those words are about me. A *New York Times* reporter came by the other day and told Reggie that a lot of their readers, who didn't ever go to racetracks, wanted to know all about me and what my chances were of winning.

The thumbs-down reviews are coming—what would you expect?—from those trainers of Kentucky horses. They're saying, "Look at the record. Tim Tam has been first in eight of ten starts against the best horses in the country. What's Silky Sullivan's record and what kind of horses has he beat? Nothing but California speed horses."

Okay, let's look at the record. I've won seven races in twelve starts. Two were stakes races. Tim Tam has won five stakes races. But I've beaten some good horses. Old Pueblo and Alawar can run with Tim Tam or any of those eastern horses.

The Shoe spoke up for me. "When you ask this horse," he told reporters after yesterday's workout, "he's there."

Willie was kind of embarrassed when he got here a few days ago. He didn't say much, but I saw the sheepish look on his face when he talked about last year's Derby. He was riding Gallant Man. He mistook the finish line and stood up too soon. Gallant Man lost a race he should have won. Yesterday Willie rode four winners here at Churchill Downs. The joke around the stable is that Willie finally has found where the finish line is.

Reggie has been comparing me to that fighter Rocky Marciano, who talks funny when I see him on the television. I think he comes from Boston, which is somewhere in the East, you know. Reggie says I'm just like Rocky because I'm big and tough like Rocky. He said to a reporter yesterday, "Rocky can beat anything he can hit. Silky can beat anything he can catch."

When the other trainers pan me, though, I think they hit below the belt. I heard one say the other day as I was being walked by his stable: "If Silky Sullivan wins the Derby, I am going to hold a dispersal sale and get out of racing for good." Those types think that if you weren't born and raised in the Kentucky bluegrass, you can't run. I call 'em blue bloods. I'm a red-blood Westerner and proud of it.

Some of those Kentucky trainers have been whispering to reporters—I hear this from my grooms—that I got a bad breathing problem. It's true that I had a bad cold last winter. When I got over it, I had what the vets call "a wind condition." I let out a whistling sound when I run. People say that's why I can only gallop during the first half of a race—until my wind is okay and I'm not whistling anymore.

But I *always* galloped during the first half of a race, even as a two-year-old, *before* I had the cold. I have always liked to come from behind.

Reggie told reporters that my wind condition had nothing to do with my sprinting at the end of a race.

"This horse," I heard him say, "is the greatest climax runner since Red Grange." Who was Red Grange? Anyway, when they asked Reggie if the whistling bothers me, he said, "I wish I had a stableful of horses who whistled—and then ran the way Silky runs."

I was taken over to Tim Tam's stable this morning so photographers could take a picture of us. He began to talk to me about his sire, Tom Fool, and what a great horse Tom Fool had been. He went on blabbering about how Calumet Farm, *his* farm, has won more Kentucky Derbys than anyone else. I waited until he had finished and then I said, "How many Santa Anita Derbys have they won? That's the biggest jackpot of them all, you know."

He turned away like he hadn't heard. I whinnied all the way back to my stable.

But I think maybe all this talk about eastern horses being better trained and better endowed than western horses is getting to the Shoe. The other day I heard him say to another jock: "This is a lot tougher than the field we beat in the Derby at Santa Anita."

Apparently it was. Silky finished twelfth of fourteen. The next morning's *New York Times* bannered a headline across the front page of its sports section: "Tim Tam Wins the $160,500 Derby; Silky Sullivan 12th." Silky may have become the first horse to finish twelfth and still be part of a banner headline anywhere. But the prominence of Silky's name in that headline was another sign of the attention given to the most famous come-from-

behind horse of them all; Whirlaway is an arguable other choice.

That Derby was run on a muddy track. Silky made a brief spurt near the far turn—the crowd roaring, "Here he *comes*!" But then he fell back into the ruck. After the race Shoemaker said, "The horse just didn't like the track."

Two weeks later at the Preakness, however, the track was fast and Silky ran eighth behind the winning Tim Tam. Again he made only a brief and ineffectual spurt. "California," said Reggie Cornell, "here we come."

Never again was Silky the exciting horse that had come from twenty-eight lengths back to win the Santa Anita Derby. He won twice, then retired with twelve victories in twenty-seven starts. His only stakes victories were the 1957 Golden Gate Futurity and the 1958 Santa Anita Derby.

The colorful actor in him, however, must have bubbled with pleasure when he paraded each Saint Patrick's Day at Golden Gate, the site of his first important win. The son of Sullivan wore bright green ribbons as he pranced around the track while a band played Irish jigs. He was always a special favorite at Golden Gate. The crowd he drew for a weekday, 18,532, was still a record twenty-five years later. After his death, in 1977, Silky was buried at the track. A bronze plaque, posted above the grave, bears this tribute:

Out of the gate like a bullet of red,
Dropping behind as the rest
sped ahead,
Loping along as the clubhouse
fans cheer,
Leisurely stalking the field in
first gear.

Silky stands in the winner's circle after winning the 1959 Ralph Neves purse at Hollywood Park. Jockey Neves, out of racing at the time with an eye injury, is set to present Silky with a winning bouquet. On Ralph's right is co-owner Tom Ross. Don Pierce is aboard Silky.

KELSO

A clipping from *Time* magazine, dated November 22, 1963, was attached to Slips's notes on Kelso. The *Time* article begins: "A psychiatrist who knew the lingo could make a living at the track. Some horses love mud, others sulk if they get their hooves wet. All horses are brought up on grass, but that does not mean they can run on it. Nobody knows why, or ever will—unless he can talk to horses."

Of course I don't like to race on grass. Only T.V. Lark or an idiot—they're the same thing—would like to race on grass. There you are, flying high, all four hooves off the ground. Then you come down to hit a slick stretch of grass while traveling at forty miles an hour. How would you like to race on ice? No thanks, right? You know you would break a tailbone. Horses were never meant to race on grass. Grass is for nibbling, grass is for romping. Dirt is for racing.

I had a mental thing about grass, I'll admit it. But when I had to, I could win on grass. Just ask old Gun Bow, right? He found out I could win on grass. And so did those idiot writers. I guess you want to know all about that race and how I fooled a lot of people.

I thought you [Slips] might come by after I heard about that article in the magazine you got there. Other horses told me about you—how you put down what we say on little scraps of paper. One of the grooms read that magazine. He told an exercise boy that he thought one day humans could talk to horses. If he's right, you seem to be the first who can do it.

I'm glad to talk to you so that you can put down what I am really like and not what some writers and horses say I am like. For example, the grooms say I'm gruff and mean. Okay, I like to have fun with the stablehands. I bite them. I nip their arms, their hands, their fingers whenever they get too close. But there's a reason—I don't like to be petted. I am not a cat or a dog, damn it. One of the grooms got me right when I heard him tell a reporter: "Old Kelly, he doesn't like to be petted, but you've got to notice him. He insists on that." Don't fawn over me, I say, but give me a little respect.

The horses say I'm dirty. In a workout, even during a race, I'll swing my head and take a bite out of a horse's flank. I admit it. But that's not dirty tactics. Hell, I know I can beat nearly everything that wears a saddle whether I bite them or I don't. My bites are a message—keep your distance.

In fact, that's what I'm all about—I like to be noticed, but from afar. I think you get more respect—and attention—when you keep everyone at a distance.

The only one who gets close to me is Charlie Potatoes. That's my pet dog. He's over there in the corner of my stall. When he gets up in the morning, we nuzzle each other nose to nose. That's my way of saying good morning to Charlie Potatoes, because dogs don't talk our language. But we never get any closer than that. That's what I like about dogs—they know their place.

In a familiar position, Kelso pounds to the wire ahead of the pack and wins the 1961 Suburban Handicap at Aqueduct. Head low, the jockey needs no whip.

Even my fan club members, I don't let them get too close. You know about my fan club, don't you? I'm just like that Elvis Presley fellow I hear on the radio—I got a fan club. A little girl [twelve-year-old Heather Noble of Falls Church, Virginia] saw me on the TV one day as I paraded to the post. She thought I winked at her. She got so excited she and her friends started a fan club. They call themselves Kelsolanders. There are more than a thousand of them. I get about three thousand fan letters a year. The secretary of Mrs. du Pont [Alleare du Pont, the owner of Kelso] comes by and reads them to me. You can't imagine how gushy they get. Like, "You are our great and noble King Kelly of Kelsoland." They send me gifts. One girl sent me a camera. She wrote, "Now you can take pictures of all the horses behind you!"

They come to the track and wave banners, like "Kelso, we love you!" I heard snickers from the other horses as we paraded to the post. I bit the nearest snickerer and told the others they were jealous. Everybody shut up.

Not that I crave attention, mind you. I have always said I am glad I never won the Triple Crown as a three-year-old. You win the Triple Crown and those snoopy reporters come by, notebooks in hand, to ask the groom what you ate for breakfast.

Now that I have been named the Horse of the Year for the past four straight years [1960, 1961, 1962, and 1963], of course, I have to stand still while those pesky, shouting photographers shoot lights into my eyes. And the reporters pull the stablehands aside and smirk while they ask all kinds of stupid questions about the sex life of a gelding.

Well, you have to take the bad with the good. The good is that I have won thirty-one of forty-four races so far. I could be the Horse of the Year for the fifth straight year, especially after the Gun Bow thing. Nobody else has ever won it more than twice. I saw a headline the other day that said, "Move Over, Man o' War!" The writer said I had to be put right up there at the top with Man o' War, who was my grandpop, you know. I've won more money, about a million and a half

dollars, than any horse ever except Round Table, and you watch—I'll catch him before they put me out to pasture.

Speaking of being put out to pasture, do you hear the talk about what the du Ponts plan to do with me when I stop racing? One of the stallions here [at the du Pont farm in Chesapeake City, Maryland] put a buzz in my ear the other day and it's got me worried. He said to me, "Oh, Kelly," which is what they call me around the stables even though I hate the name, "have you seen that gelding"—and he mentioned the name of a horse I've since forgotten—"around here lately?"

I said I hadn't.

He grinned and said, "They don't seem to keep geldings around for very long after they stop racing, do they?"

I asked him what he meant.

"If you're too old to race and you can't do stud duty," he said, "what good are you?"

I said nothing. But it made me worry. And lately I've been thinking that it would be strange if they gave me the Big Needle because I can't do stud duty, when it was stud duty that saved my pop's life. And saving his life brought me into the world to make all this money for Mrs. du Pont.

My pop was Your Host. He won about twelve races and was rated the best three-year-old in California. But he fell at Santa Anita, broke a shoulder and messed up a leg, so that one was shorter than the others. His owner said, "Destroy him." Then he'd get money from an insurance company.

Your Host had made a lot of fans. They wrote to the owner and begged him not to kill Your Host. The owner said nuts to that, he wanted his insurance money.

Someone at the insurance company had a heart. They decided to keep Pop alive, even though he could only hobble around and sometimes seemed to be in pain.

Pop was a tough one. Pain or no pain, he turned out to be a valuable stud. The insurance company got back the money they paid the owner. Pop did so well he was sold to some people here in the East, including Mrs. du Pont,

A handler shows off Your Host, Kelso's sire, whose fans saved him from an early death, sending him to stud duty, which produced Kelso and many more fans.

for a lot of money [$140,000]. Pop mated with Maid of Flight, whose mother was a daughter of Man o' War. The result was me, born April 4, 1957.

Mrs. du Pont had a lady friend named Kelso and I was named for her. I hope the lady wasn't too shocked when she first saw me. I've heard the grooms say I was a scrawny runt with a stumpy neck. A trainer named me Skin and Bones, said you could hang a hat on my hipbone, and told Mrs. du Pont I was too weak ever to be a racehorse.

I wonder where he is today.

It's a wonder Mrs. du Pont didn't send me to a farm to pull a plow, which happens to horses who were like me—not good for racing, not good to people. I had a nasty way with people. I began to bite them, maybe because I knew they thought I was ugly. I kicked the walls of my stall. Even to this day, I think the gangster in me hates the idea of being locked up.

A trainer told Mrs. du Pont that I should be gelded. Trainers think that gelding will calm down and fatten up horses like me. I once heard a fellow from another country—he spoke funny—tell an American that the trouble with our trainers is that they use gelding as a first resort instead of as a last resort.

Gelding me was a blunder—a costly blunder. Mrs. du Pont hears talk almost every day about how much money she has lost because I can never be a stud. She gets quite angry, I know, when the subject comes up, so if you talk to her, don't use the word "gelding."

I did get heavier. But I also got meaner. I had lost all faith in the human animal. If they take away your sex life just as easily as they slip you an aspirin, how can you trust them?

I did forgive Mrs. du Pont. I know she likes me for what I am and not as a money machine. I heard her say one day that if I ever got hurt in a race, she could never forgive herself for letting me run so long when most horses my age are retired. I hope she likes me just as much when I'm

81

retired, and now that I'm almost nine years old, that should be pretty soon.

While I did get heavier as a two-year-old, I will never be one of those heavyweights like Man o' War was. I go on the scale at about a thousand pounds, while most racehorses are 50 to 150 pounds heavier, and most are a hand or two taller. Once a runt, I guess, always a runt.

Mrs. du Pont and her trainer [Carl Hanford] didn't think I was strong enough to do much running in 1959 as a two-year-old. I started three times, won one and finished second the other two times. That was not bad for a horse I heard one groom call "the weakling." But at the start of the 1960 racing year, when I became three years old, Hanford didn't think I had the strength or stamina for a shot at the Triple Crown. In fact, I didn't even start a race until June of 1960, when the last of the Triple Crown races had already been run.

I won my first two races as a three-year-old; the second was a mile race that I won by twelve lengths. About then, I think, Mrs. du Pont and Carl began to think that their ugly duckling might make them a pretty penny or two.

We went to Chicago for the Arlington Classic, which is run on grass. I finished eight lengths behind T.V. Lark. After the race I told T.V. Lark I worried about slipping on grass. He said—can you believe this?—there is no way a horse can slip on grass. I said that was like a jet pilot saying there was no way a plane can crash. Right then I knew he had the brains of a dodo bird.

That was the only race I lost in 1960 in nine starts. I tied Man o' War's Belmont record for the mile and five-eighths when I won the Lawrence Realization. Grandpop's record had stood, I heard, for forty years. I won the Jockey Club Gold Cup and set a new American record for two miles—on a sloppy track, mind you. I remember seeing Mrs. du Pont wading through the slop to the winner's circle, her shoes and stockings all muddy, but she could buy a lot of shoes with the money I won for her that year [$296,690]. I was the first three-year-old who hadn't won the Derby, Preakness, or Belmont to be picked as Horse of the Year.

When I hear horses brag about some stablemate who won the three-year-old Triple Crown, I snort and say I won a Triple Crown that was a lot tougher to win than the Derby, Preakness, and Belmont Stakes. Everyone runs under the same weight, in those three races. As a four-year-old, in 1961, I won a Triple Crown when I had to carry as much as 136 pounds while the others carried as little as 118. The three races I'm talking about are run on New York tracks—the one-mile Metropolitan Handicap, the mile-and-a-quarter Suburban Handicap, and the mile-and-a-quarter Brooklyn Handicap. I won all three. In the Brooklyn, with 136 pounds on top of me, I came within a split second of tying the track record set by Sword Dancer some ten years earlier when he was lugging only 126 pounds.

I lost only two races as a four-year-old, one of them in Chicago when I carried twenty pounds more than any of the three horses that finished in front of me. The second loss was at Laurel in Maryland, the International, which is across grass, and that's when the talk really got loud that I couldn't win on grass. I think some of those writers who said those things were using grass themselves, but that's only going to get me into more trouble, so maybe you should leave that out.

In the race is T.V. Lark, that empty-head who was the only one to beat me as a three-year-old the previous year. His name tells you something about his brains, doesn't it? Anyway, I try to forget my nervous thoughts about slipping on this spinach. I ran at maybe nine-tenths of my normal speed on dirt. That allowed T.V. Lark to stay about even with me and we ran one-two, me in front, through the first mile and a quarter of this mile-and-a-half race.

As we go by the eighth pole, I decide it is time to kick and leave T.V. Lark in my wake. That was a good thought. My second thought was a bad thought. It was this: To kick, I have got to take off on my rear legs for one long bound. Suppose I slip? I see myself sliding across the finish line on my rump. I can see my jockey hanging on, staring upward at the blue sky, as I skid on my tailbone over the green stuff.

The bad thought made me pause. Just then

Winning the 1960 Jockey Club Gold Cup at Aqueduct, Kelso leaves second place Don Poggio and the rest of the field far behind on a sloppy track (above). Kelso won this race four times from 1960 to 1963. Eddie Arcaro sits aboard Kelso on the way to the starting line for a 1961 race at Aqueduct in New York (below). Kelso's ears are perked, his eyes—unlike Eddie's—wide open.

Trainer Carl Hanford and Eddie Arcaro walk Kelso out of the paddock for the start of the 1961 Whitney at Belmont (above). Spectators crane their necks to see a New York favorite. Kelso, No. 9 (below), nips All Hands at the wire to win the 1961 Metropolitan at Aqueduct. Sweet William is a distant third as fans once more roared, "Here comes Kelso!"

T.V. Lark made his move. He thrusts his head in front. I am still picking my way tippy-toe and thinking about sliding. T.V. Lark pulls ahead to win by half a length. The rest of the field is twelve lengths back. Both T.V. Lark and myself break the old track record by about a second and a half.

So what do those writers put in their papers after I've broken a track record and lost on a track I don't like by *half a length*? They write— you guessed it—that Kelso proved he can't win on grass. If I had won by half a length, they would have written that Kelso proved he *can* win on grass. Half a length proves one thing—another half a length proves the exact opposite. You figure it out. Racing would be a lot more fun, I tell you, if there was as much horse sense in the press box as there is in the stable.

No matter I lost. For the second straight year I was the Horse of the Year. No more than a couple of other horses, Whirlaway was one, had ever won the Horse of the Year twice.

The next year, the spring of 1962, I came down with a bad virus and I felt weak. When I could run, I had a new jock, Willie Shoemaker. The vibes didn't quiver just right between the Shoe and me—I never knew why. We had four races and lost three of them. By September of 1962 the Horse of the Year of 1960 and 1961 had yet to win a stakes race.

By then the headlines raved about two younger horses: Carry Back and Beau Purple. One figured to be the 1962 Horse of the Year.

Then I went on a tear to make it a three-horse race. I had a new jockey by this time, Milo Valenzuela, and Milo and I had the good vibes. He once said to someone within my earshot, "This horse is a runner. You ask him to go and from there on it's whoop-de-do all the way."

Well, it was whoop-de-do for the rest of 1962. At Saratoga I won my first stakes race that year, the Stymie Handicap. I ran away from Beau Purple in the Woodward Stakes. I won my third straight Jockey Club Gold Cup, the two-mile grind, winning by ten lengths in a time of 3:19⅘, which broke the old record set by Nashua.

Beau Purple beat me by two lengths in the Man o' War Stakes, maybe because I was still a little bushed after that record two-miler, but Beau won fair and square. Now the Horse of the Year picture looked less clear, what with my beating Beau in the Woodward and Carry Back finishing fifth in the Man o' War.

We went—the three of us—to my nemesis, the International, that green monster at Laurel. Reporters wrote that this would be the last "battle royal," as they put it, among Kelso, Carry Back, and Beau Purple—the winner likely to be the 1962 Horse of the Year.

Most writers favored Beau or Carry Back to win. "Kelso can't win on grass." They repeated that refrain so often I thought they should have put a melody to it and let Patti Page sing it. Never, or hardly ever, did they write that I had never finished worse than second on grass, which was better, I thought, than some of those writers could say about themselves.

Before the race Carl Hanford and Milo had a strategy talk and, like all smart jockeys and trainers, they let me listen in. We knew Beau Purple liked to take the track and try to sprint everyone into exhaustion so no one could challenge him in the stretch. Beau doesn't like challenges. I once heard his trainer say that challenges gave Beau a headache.

Carry Back liked to tag along in the middle of the pack, then come on in the stretch to catch the leaders. So we had a sprinter and a lingerer— what to do? Carl told Milo: "Don't let Beau Purple steal the thing by getting so far out in front that no one can catch him. But no one will want to come into the stretch exhausted, because they're afraid of Carry Back coming from behind. No one will want to sprint with Beau Purple. We will have to do it, then hope we have enough left to hold off Carry Back."

Sure enough, as expected, Beau and I go out together and sprint madly through the first quarter, the rest of the field strung out behind us, Carry Back maybe fourth or fifth. As we go into the far turn, Beau and I still running about even, I tell myself to think of what I am running on as green dirt. I lunge forward and I can hear Beau Purple wheeze. He doesn't like what's happening. There is a half-mile of exhaustion left, and Beau decides to step out for lunch. He quits.

I go into the stretch, still running smoothly. I think to myself that maybe I've got this green bugaboo licked at last. Then I hear action on my right. It's Carry Back making his run. He comes alongside of me and we run like one horse for maybe an eighth of a mile.

Then he fades. Trouble is, so do I. That mile sprint with Beau and then that duel in the stretch with Carry Back has sucked everything out of me. On the outside comes a big French horse, Match II, who races nearly always on grass. He zips by me in the final quarter to win by a length and a half. I'm second, Carry Back third, Beau a distant eleventh.

I'd lost my second straight International, finishing second for a second time in a row. But I had beaten Beau at his own game and Carry Back at his. That had to impress people. For the third straight year I was the Horse of the Year— a first.

As 1963 began, I had won more than a million dollars, second only to Round Table. Mrs. du Pont, as you know, needs another million dollars about as badly as Nelson Rockefeller, so it wasn't

all that money that made her like me. I think what she likes is the gangster in me. She sees how I always fix the good horses with a glare just before we step into the starting gate. I have heard that a boxer named Sonny Liston does the same thing just before a fight. The grooms claim that Liston's glare turns the knees of other fighters to jelly. I try to drill the same scare into horses. I give them my look that says, No way you can beat me today.

I know that Mrs. du Pont smiles when she sees me give that look. I have heard her say to reporters that she could name any number of horses that Kelso has retired to the farm. And I have heard her name them—tough lady that she is, horses like Ridan and Tompion. The other day I overheard her telling a friend that "Jaipur wasn't worth a nickel after Kelso beat him in the Woodward."

The gangster, the beat-'em-up guy, whose weapons are his legs, his teeth, and a glare— that's the way I think of myself. I often wonder what those little girls—the ones who write, "with all my love, dear Kelso"—would think if they ever saw Kelso the Gangster. They'd run away, squealing.

Kelso lets Eddie Arcaro show the jockey's banana nose to the photographers while Kelso looks at Mrs. du Pont (wearing white gloves), the lady who pays the feed bill.

In 1963 I put together a streak of eight consecutive stakes victories. I won the Woodward for the third straight time and the two-mile Jockey Club Gold Cup for the third time in a row. Then I went down to Laurel for my annual two minutes of agony, the International. As usual, I had to hear that Kelso could not win on grass. I heard it before the race, I heard it after the race. Another big foreigner, Mongo, beat me by half a length. His time was the fastest International since T.V. Lark beat me two years earlier. Now I had finished second three years in a row at the International, beaten twice by the two fastest times in the history of the race. But I was still the horse that couldn't win on grass.

All those stakes victories earned me the Horse of the Year award for a fourth straight year. I heard a guy say on radio that maybe there should be two awards for Horse of the Year—one to Kelso, the second to someone else. "There may never be another Horse of the Year except Kelso," he said, but I knew different.

As 1964 began I was seven years old and that's old, even for a gelding. I had started 44 races and won 31, finishing second in 9. When you finish in the money in 40 of 44 races, the railbirds like you. In New York, where I had done most of my racing, the crowd would let out a loud, expectant kind of roar as I came into the stretch during a race. And they really whooped when the track announcer let out that cry that meant money in pockets—"Here comes Kelso!"

I had earned about a million and a half dollars for Mrs. du Pont. [His earnings at the end of 1963 totaled $1,711,132, which was only about $38,000 shy of the retired Round Table's then-record earnings of $1,749,869.] Mrs. du Pont paid me back with more than fond glances. I got royal treatment. She had a special brand of bottled spring water flown in from Hot Springs, Arkansas, so my gizzard should be flushed with only the best. I insisted on being fed my favorite fruit, apples, *before* dinner. I slept on the softest possible bed, the sleeping sack filled with sugar-cane shavings. And Mrs. du Pont's secretary personally answered each letter from my fans, sending them an autographed picture of myself.

Those fans. They wrote dozens of letters to me each week. They came by the hundreds each year to visit me at the du Pont farm at Chesapeake City in Maryland. They published a newsletter, sent to all club members, that gave the latest news about me. Take one of those newsletters with you—I've got dozens of them here in the stall.

Attached to one of Slips's scraps was a December 1963 issue of "The Kelsolander," from which we have taken this excerpt.

Kelly really put on a show in the post parade, looking at everything. He loved every minute of it. It was an unforgettable race. People just went wild when Mr. Caposella, the Aqueduct track announcer, said, "HERE COMES KELSO!" WOW! Pandemonium broke loose. Kelly knew he had to get his nose in front, and he did. People all around us were crying and pounding on one another. When he came to the winner's circle, KEL KNEW EXACTLY WHERE HE WAS AND WHAT HE HAD DONE. His gift to us that day is one of eternal joy.

When this year's racing season [1964] began, all I heard was: Can Kelso be the Horse of the Year for a fifth straight year? Only two horses, Challedon and Whirlaway, had won it more than once—and each had won it only twice. But I know that Mrs. du Pont worried more about my getting hurt than about my being Horse of the Year for the fifth time. Often I heard Carl say that he didn't know how much longer she could bear to see me race, fearful I'd get hurt. I suppose that means I'll be one gelding who won't get the Long Goodbye when his racing days are over, since she likes me so much, but I still worry.

Near the end of 1964 I had won only two stakes races, while Gun Bow, a four-year-old, had won eight. Head to head, I had beaten him twice and he had beaten me twice.

Gun Bow's trainer said that the voters for the 1964 Horse of the Year shouldn't be swayed toward me by sentiment, everyone wanting me to take five in a row. Carl and Mrs. du Pont decided they wouldn't depend on sentiment. They decided to take on Gun Bow, head to head, in the 1964 International at Laurel. It's the race on grass in which I had finished second three years in a row. Almost everyone agreed: If Kelso, the horse who can't win on grass, beats Gun Bow on grass, he has got to be the Horse of the Year.

We went to Laurel and I ran on grass for a week. I heard Carl tell someone, "The only time he's had his feet on grass this year has been when he was grazing or lazing up for the winter." But I thought Carl was looking for an alibi if I lost. I told myself: It's about time you grew up and realized that lots of horses run on grass without skidding across the finish line on their cans.

As we trotted to the start, I gave Gun Bow as mean a look as I could scare up. Gun Bow stared right back, telling me I would have to win this with my feet and not with my glare. I knew how bad he wanted this. He was prancing off to stud duty after this race. His owners might get $5,000 for each mare he, uh, serviced—is that the word?—if he won. If he lost, he might get only about a thousand. For me, of course, both the money and the mares were things I'd never get close to.

Walter Blum sat on Gun Bow. He and Milo eyed each other. Both sensed, I later heard, that this was a two-horse race and neither wanted to let the other get too far away.

We took off together. I tucked into second behind Gun Bow as we rounded the first turn.

The rest of the field hung way back and fought for third. Right away I knew what Blum and Gun Bow wanted to do—sprint the first mile and an eighth of this mile-and-a-half race. The horse who had the mostest left staggered home the winner.

We had no choice—we had to run their race. We couldn't let Gun Bow get too far in front.

I fixed my eyes on Gun Bow's brown rump. I told myself—don't even think green.

We shot by the mile mark in a little over a minute and a half, which is fast for a mile race when we still had half a mile to go.

As we came around the turn, I sensed Milo telling me it was time to whoop-de-doo. I passed Gun Bow on the outside and thought he sounded awfully strong. I told myself—one of us, or both, will crawl home.

I came out of the turn ahead by a neck. We went by the mile-and-a-quarter pole in two minutes flat. That was the fastest any horse had ever run a mile and a quarter in a mile-and-a-half race.

I came down the stretch still ahead by that outstretched neck. Now Gun Bow sounded awful—bellowing loudly. I thought my lungs were afire, scorched forever.

Gun Bow suddenly shuddered. For a moment I thought he'd fall down. Blum felt his horse sag. He hit Gun Bow a wallop with the stick. The blow drove poor old Gun Bow at least a couple of feet toward the rail. He banged into me and for a moment I was staring down at that green spinach. But I was too exhausted to even think about skidding. All I could think about was how happy I would be to stand still in a stall and lap up buckets of cold water.

For about a hundred yards Gun Bow and I slammed against each other like two grooms careening home to the stables after a night closing up a tavern.

Gun Bow cracked. He wobbled home second while I came across eased up—and glad of it—about six lengths ahead.

When we got to the winner's circle, I saw Mrs. du Pont running toward me, tears streaming down her face. She burst out bawling as the band struck up "The Star-Spangled Banner," which meant our country had won the International. After three straight seconds, I had finally put this one in my bag. I felt like rearing up and pumping my hooves toward the press box while I whinnied, "Who says I can't win on grass?"

Slips's notes on Kelso stop here. Kelso was named Horse of the Year for the fifth straight year, a record no other horse has come close to equaling. In 1966 Mrs. du Pont gave in to her fears that Kelso might be injured. She retired the nine-year-old King Kelly. He had gone to the starting post 63 times and won 39 races, finishing second in 12, those 51 in-the-money finishes in 63 races making him among the all-time favorites of horseplayers. He won $1,977,896, to go by Round Table as the biggest money winner up to then in racing history. Some twenty-five years later, despite the inflation that skyrocketed purses, Kelso still ranked fifth on the all-time list of money winners.

His rewards included an eight-acre playground on the du Pont Woodstock Farm at Chesapeake City. His loving owner frequently rode him on leisurely jaunts across the Maryland hills. Kelso appeared often at tracks and horse shows, the fees for his personal appearances donated to a foundation for equine research.

In October of 1983 Kelso went to New York's Belmont track to be saluted before the running of the Jockey Club Gold Cup, the two-mile race he had won five straight times from 1960 to 1964. Now twenty-six years old, wearing the canary yellow and gray colors of Mrs. du Pont's Bohemia Stable, a yellow ribbon around his neck, Kelso pranced like a yearling that October day as he led the horses to the starting post. The huge crowd let out an emotional roar of welcome as the track announcer called out one last time, "Here comes Kelso!"

The next day Kelso was stricken by an attack of colic and died. His longtime groom, Gene Moore, spoke the words that belong on Kelso's tombstone: "He had to show everyone he was the boss."

BUCKPASSER

In my opinion a Thoroughbred racehorse has a little bit of every ancestor inside the bloodstream. That means good and bad traits. Sometimes the good part shows up right away, and the bad parts don't surface until a couple of years later. That's the story of my life. When my family tree is examined, everything becomes clear.

First, I looked terrific, every bit a champion. It was like somebody drew a diagram of the perfect horse and there I was, big as life. Don't take my word for it, ask around. For instance:

Dr. Manuel Gilman was an important horse inspector at New York racetracks. He had seen them all come and go for twenty years, and there wasn't much he didn't know about Thoroughbreds. He said, "Generally, every horse has about a hundred faults of conformation. I would defy anybody to pick a flaw in Buckpasser."

A very fine animal artist named Richard Stone Reeves painted my portrait not once but twice. He said, "Buckpasser was the most perfectly proportioned Thoroughbred I have ever seen."

So much for my personal good looks. But both my parents were good-looking, too. Let me explain about my dam first.

Her name was Busanda, and like they say, she was all-around royalty, to the manor born. Her father was Triple Crown winner War Admiral,

Buckpasser winning as a four-year-old.

and her grandfather was the horse whose name is spoken in whispers, Man o' War. Not only was my mom beautiful to look at, she could also run like hell. She ran a nice race to win the Alabama. When she won the Suburban, she beat a couple of colts. And when she took first place in the mile-and-three-quarters Saratoga Cup, she wasn't content with winning it once, she had to do it twice. That's my bloodline on Mama's side.

My sire was Tom Fool, a handsome Thoroughbred if ever there was one. To him distance didn't mean a thing. He could win at five and a half furlongs and he could win at a mile and a quarter. He won honors as a two-year-old, and in time was named Horse of the Year and champion sprinter as well. My father was a running demon at ages two and three, but as a four-year-old nobody could beat him. That means *nobody*. He went 10 for 10, which is about all any horse can do in ten races. In his last four outings the tracks wouldn't take bets and he ran just for the purse and the joy of the fans.

Yet there was one funny thing about my father. Some colts keep sniffing after the fillies so much they have to be gelded. When Tom Fool went to stud, for a while he wasn't interested in the ladies. Can you imagine, all those passionate mares running after him and he had to be coaxed to return the favor. Maybe he was too much of a gentleman. When he did lose his inhibitions, the result was sometimes spectacular. For instance, one of his kids, named Tim Tam, won the Kentucky Derby and the Preakness.

Buckpasser—often said to be the horse without a flaw in his conformation.

So far, my bloodlines are all to the good, right? I've got champion ancestors all over the place, I've got good looks, I must have inherited speed from horses like Tom Fool, Busanda, Man o' War, and War Admiral. But there's another champion in my background, on my father's side. He won twenty-nine out of fifty-one races, with ten seconds, four thirds, and the rest just heart-break. He could cover the distances and he could carry weight, which boggles the mind when you consider *he was not a sound horse.*

He was my great-grandfather. His name was Equipoise.

Almost all his life he ran in pain. He had bad feet, including a chronic quarter crack in one hoof. You talk about guts, you talk about not giving in to *any* horse, and you are talking about Equipoise. Nobody will ever know how good he might have been if his feet were normal. Of all my ancestors, including Busanda, Tom Fool, War Admiral, and Man o' War, I guess I admire Equipoise most of all. And if I put them all together, sometimes I feel kind of humble. I had so much to live up to. Maybe that's why I tried never to throw my weight around.

You know who noticed that about me right off? That artist, Richard Stone Reeves. He liked my looks, but he also admired the way I handled myself. He said, "Buckpasser is the kindest and most beautifully mannered horse I ever painted.

I'm serious. Sometimes I almost expected him to invite me into his stall, to have a chair and perhaps a drink."

There was one flaw in my personality, and I don't know where it came from. Sometimes I was lazy. That character trait almost drove my owner, Mr. Ogden Phipps, up the wall, and gave my first trainer, Bill Winfrey, a few more gray hairs. Mr. Winfrey was a fine trainer, and he did well with a lot of Thoroughbreds, including Native Dancer. He thought I had great possibilities. I was entered at Aqueduct on May 13, 1965, in a race against nine other maidens.

I finished fourth. Probably none of the entries felt like running that day. The winner was a downright plater named Lonely Gambler, who was a Thoroughbred in name only. In fact, Lonely Gambler didn't win another race for a year, and when he did take first-place money it wasn't because he won the race. The event was a $3,500 claiming race, and the horse who went across first was disqualified. Lonely Gambler was second and sort of backed into the victory.

Bad-mouthing the winner didn't change anything. In my first race I was an also-ran, and that hurt. I knew what was in Bill Winfrey's mind—he knew I *could* run, but he wasn't sure I *would* run. With all those speed genes built into my body, I should have given everybody on the track a diet of my dust, but I loafed, I practically idled in neutral. Even I wasn't sure I would ever shake off my laziness.

My immediate goal was to start winning a few races. Two weeks later I won a five-eighths-of-a-mile sprint in one minute, and then I took an overnighter in nice time. Both races were tune-ups for the National Stallion Stakes.

I almost gave Winfrey and Mr. Phipps heart failure by the way I ran that race. I was practically out of it, nine lengths behind, when I finally made my move. A horse named Hospitality had been setting the pace and he was still leading when I took out after him. I caught Hospitality, but I couldn't pass him. We finished in a dead heat. Would you call that "half-a-first?" Maybe that's what a tie really is. I wasn't second, but on the other hand, neither was Hospitality.

I knew I was better than Hospitality, and I proved it in the Tremont Stakes, but once again it was the same old story. I hung back and was in last place when I turned up the heat. I won by a neck. Second place went to a horse named Spring Double. Hospitality was third, two and a half lengths back.

I won again at Monmouth Park, and that time my margin of victory was a surprising seven lengths. I guess Bill Winfrey was also puzzled, because I wasn't in the habit of running away from the opposition with so much of a lead. He couldn't figure me out, although he knew I was fast enough and had the stamina. Bill fussed and fumed when I loafed through a workout. My attitude was, why bother when nothing is on the line? Looking back at my career, my average margin of victory was only about half a length. In twelve of my wins the margin was less than one length. And it didn't matter who the opposition was. I beat the good horses by the same margin that I beat the so-so horses.

In the Sapling Stakes I convinced everybody that I was the class of the two-year-old colts. When the gates sprang open I was left at the post. I spotted the field a good five lengths before I got under way. A very fast horse named Our Michael, the favorite, had set the pace, but I had a lot of other horses to pass before I could challenge him. Near the wire I caught Our Michael, and I beat him by a half-length.

One win followed another, but they weren't all easy. I took the Hopeful Stakes at Saratoga by

Winning the Hopeful Stakes at Saratoga. One of his many wins as a two-year-old.

In the winner's circle after the Hopeful.

two and a half lengths. In that one I beat out my stablemate, a good prospect named Impressive. In the rich Arlington-Washington Futurity I had a lead of four lengths at the sixth pole, and I eased up because I thought the field had quit. That was a mistake. Father's Image bore down on me and I just managed to sneak under the wire by half a length. It was close, but a win was a win, and that extended my streak to eight straight. I hadn't lost since my first time out.

It was a different story in the Aqueduct Futurity. Everybody was thinking I was unbeatable, but there was this filly named Priceless Gem, a half-sister to another speedy filly named Affectionately, who had won some nice races. The Gem went into the lead and I was right on her heels because the girl was a real sprinter and I didn't want her to get too far ahead. Into the backstretch I pulled to within a neck of the young lady, but that was as far as I could get. She beat me by half a length.

Listen, it's not such a big deal for a colt to lose

to a filly. My own mother, Busanda, had taken the measure of a few colts in her day, and Priceless Gem won fair and square. As a matter of fact there was still another filly, named Moccasin, and she was also a two-year-old, but she could beat almost any four-legged critter under a saddle. Moccasin was so quick that sometimes the track would not allow a bet on her. Two of those races were the Alcibiades Stakes at Keeneland, which she won by an amazing fifteen lengths, and the Selima Stakes at Laurel Race Course in Maryland, which Moccasin won by five lengths. With two great fillies like Priceless Gem and Moccasin on the scene at the same time, there was talk about entering them both in an upcoming event, but the showdown never happened. Priceless Gem developed sore shins.

The fact remained that I had lost for the second time and I had to make up for it. The next race was the Champagne Stakes and I won it by four lengths. Poor Priceless Gem was seventh.

The year 1965 had been a great one for the

crop of two-year-olds. Among the colts were the likes of Kauai King and Graustark, and let's not forget yours truly. In the female ranks one could find Priceless Gem and Moccasin.

The voting for best two-year-old was interesting. Graustark was undefeated that year, but he didn't win the honors for best colt. I did, even though I had lost two of eleven. Maybe it was because of my earnings: $568,096, which was a record for two-year-olds at that time. The best horse, male or female, was Moccasin, who was also undefeated. I always thought she deserved the championship.

A few changes were made before I began campaigning as a three-year-old. Bill Winfrey resigned as my trainer. My jockey, Braulio Baeza, decided he wanted to ride Graustark. Winfrey was replaced by Mr. Eddie Neloy, and my new jockey was that sterling rider named William "Willie the Shoe" Shoemaker. I think the Shoe could give a good ride on anything from a hobby horse to a rodeo bronc.

However, when an experienced jockey teams up with an experienced horse, some adjustments have to be made. The horse has to get used to the rider's way of using the whip, the strength of his hands. A jockey has to find out how much the horse has in reserve for a finishing kick, the rate of acceleration. Just as jockeys are not the same, neither are horses.

My first race with Shoe up was a learning experience for both of us. I started as a three-year-old the same way I started as a two-year-old: I didn't win. But I didn't finish fourth, either. My stablemate, Impressive, took first place, I was second, and another stablemate, Stupendous, was third. Maybe Mr. Phipps wanted me to win, but as far as he was concerned, the race wasn't a total loss by any means.

It took only that one race for Willie and I to get to know each other. I won the Everglades by a head, with Stupendous second. That showing warmed the cockles of every racing fan's heart. I was back in form, and now the early line on the Kentucky Derby had me as a projected winner, with a nice chance for the Triple Crown. It was conceded that Kauai King and Graustark would

have something to say about the winner.

Actually, there was so much Buckpasser sentiment that the betting windows for the Flamingo Stakes were shut. No money could change hands for the nine-horse race, unless an unwary bookie could be found who liked to live dangerously. Not everybody was exactly thrilled with the no-bet status. A great New York sportswriter named Red Smith—some said he was the best in the business when it came to writing about Thoroughbreds—thought it was a dirty shame. He called the race "The Chicken Flamingo."

When the starting gate opened I got away fast and had the lead at the three-sixteenths pole. I began to think maybe the odds-makers were right, this was strictly no contest, and I got bored. Shoemaker was riding his usual race but I got sloppy, and just then a horse named Abe's Hope shot ahead of me. He was in front by two lengths before I woke up.

I think at that moment all the track officials went into cardiac arrest because this was one hell of an upset in the making. How could they explain a no-bet race if the favorite lost? For that matter, how could I face Eddie Neloy, Mr. Phipps, or Willie the Shoe if I didn't win?

I let go with three giant strides—count 'em, three—and I had Abe's Hope on the ropes. If he tried to get the lead back, I didn't notice. I won. I heard later that Miss Cynthia Phipps, the daughter of my owner, was bubbling with glee. She said, "I have never seen a horse demolish that much ground with only three strides. It had to be seen to be believed."

Victory was sweet, but all talk about a Derby victory suddenly ended. I had the genes of Tom Fool, Busanda, War Admiral, and Man o' War in my blood, but there was still one more ancestor to be heard from. A superstitious individual might call it "the mark of Equipoise," because that was the ghost who came to haunt me. Like Equipoise I developed a crack in my right front hoof. Eddie Neloy was not about to have me tough it out like Equipoise often did. I was out of action for three months until the crack healed. I never did enter any of the Triple Crown races.

There was no need for my fans to start dripping crocodile tears because I missed the Classics. Sure, the Kentucky Derby is a tradition all by itself, and it's great to win it, but some pretty terrific Thoroughbreds never ran in the Churchill Downs epic. My own sire, Tom Fool, was scratched because of a fever and a cough. Seabiscuit, the horse that beat War Admiral, didn't run in the Derby, and neither did Man o' War.

But suppose I had entered the Kentucky Derby and lost. That wouldn't have been such a terrible disgrace. You want a list of some big ones who came in second? Try Discovery, Coaltown, and Native Dancer. You want a hunk of trivia? In one Derby, Iron Liege edged out Gallant Man. You remember that race? It was the one in which Willie Shoemaker aboard Gallant Man was in the lead, and he stood up in the stirrups when he thought he'd crossed the finish line, but it wasn't the finish line, and Liege won by a whisker. However, that's not the point. The big chuckle is, both those horses beat Round Table and Bold Ruler in that Derby. Round Table and Bold Ruler are in racing's Hall of Fame, Iron Liege and Gallant Man are not.

There were three of us who were touted for the Derby-Preakness-Belmont when the season opened: Kauai King, Graustark, and me. I was out of it, and it appeared that Graustark was the horse to beat. He had won the Bahamas, another race at Hialeah, and then came down with a bruised hoof, but he recovered and won a couple of races at Keeneland. Then, wouldn't you know it, he broke down in the Blue Grass Stakes and had to be scratched from the Derby.

That left Kauai King alone of the original trio. He won the Derby all right, and the Preakness, too, but failed on a bad track at Belmont. A horse named Amberoid beat him.

Meanwhile, the crack and infection in my hoof healed. The hoof knitted with the use of a fiberglass patch invented by a man who trained trotters. I came back in time to run at Belmont on the same day the big race was run. It was a six-furlong job, and I never was too choked up about six-furlong races. A lot of experts, folks who know about such things, agree with me.

A six-furlong race is really nothing more than a long workout, an extended sprint. The speed horses that jump into an early lead can keep up the pace in short races, but then they tend to fade. The odds are against a come-from-behind horse. That type has to stay close to the leader to keep from falling behind with no chance to make up the gap.

The longer Classic races, like the mile-and-a-quarter Kentucky Derby, have their own drawbacks. It depends so much on how the other horses run. A good finisher might be caught in traffic, and even when he has a lot of finishing kick left, there's just no room to let it out. Sometimes it seems a horse has nothing left at the mile pole, but somehow a last chunk of guts rises up and the horse hangs on. That's what brings the crowd to its feet.

So, by compromise, the best all-purpose test of a Thoroughbred racehorse is at one mile. If the colt or filly can win the mile run again and again and again, that's your champion.

However, like it or not, my distance in my Belmont comeback was a six-furlong race and I won with no trouble. Once more Baeza was in the saddle because Graustark wasn't running. Baeza watched the main event and later said to his employer, "Boss, I think we started the wrong horse today."

Two weeks passed and I ran in the Leonard Richards Stakes at Delaware, which I won by three-quarters of a length over a horse named Buffle. It was a tough race. Buffle was nobody's patsy, a point he proved later when he won the Suburban.

Now it was time for the Arlington Classic, which was billed as "The Race of the Century" because this was one terrific field. I had to face the likes of Kauai King, who had won the Derby and the Preakness, plus the very good Crème dela Crème, winner of seven of his last eight races, and my stablemate, Impressive.

Kauai King should have been scratched. Anybody could see he was in no condition to run even in a workout. For an hour before the race his left foreleg was hosed down. Kauai's trainer, Henry Forrest, wanted to send the horse back to the paddock, but Kauai's owner, Mike Ford, in-

In a playful mood, Buckpasser seems to be giving his handler fits, and a horse laugh to the camera.

sisted the colt have his chance. Kauai ran.

It was a fast track. Out of the gate it was Impressive and he really turned it on. He ran the first quarter in :22^1/$_5$; at the half-mile his time was :43^3/$_5$; at the three-quarter mark he was clocked at 1:06^4/$_5$. Then he was challenged and lost the lead to Crème dela Crème.

Baeza was in no hurry. He knew I had plenty of power left and he picked his time for the charge. I was next to last going into the final turn, and in the stretch he turned me loose. I moved up, went through openings, went around other horses. I caught Crème, left him behind, and won by one and three-quarter lengths. My time for the mile was 1:32^3/$_5$. I'm not sure if it was a track record or a world record, but I know for damn sure it was a fast run.

Kauai King wasn't in it. He broke down during the race. His owner should have allowed him to walk away from the track without racing, which would have left Kauai with a lot more dignity and a lot less pain.

The rest of my three-year-old season was a delightful time for Mr. Eddie Neloy and Mr. Ogden Phipps. I just couldn't lose—not that I had losing on my mind—and the events went by in a blur. I was first in the mile-and-an-eighth Chicago Stakes; first in the mile-and-a-quarter Brooklyn Derby against older horses. I set another track record in the American Derby, covering the mile-and-an-eighth course in 1:47. In that one I beat some very fine competition in Jolly Jet and Stupendous.

By then it seemed everyone had forgotten about Derby and Preakness winner Kauai King and Belmont winner Amberoid. They weren't winning the important stakes races consistently, I was.

The victories piled up: the Everglades Stakes, the Woodward, the Lawrence Realization Stakes, the Travers at Saratoga, the two-mile Jockey Club Gold Cup. In almost all those events my margin of victory wasn't very much, but a win is a win—that was my style—and if it worked for me, why change it? On December 31, 1966, I ran my last three-year-old race, the seven-furlong Malibu at Santa Anita. I won.

It had been an interesting year, to say the least. I had won thirteen out of fourteen with one second place. I tacked on $669,078 to my previous winnings, going over the million mark in purses. There was only one choice for Horse of the Year and that was Buckpasser, going away.

In the past I had begun each racing season with a loss. Now I reversed the order of things. As a four-year-old I began by winning the San Fernando Stakes at Santa Anita, and it was assumed that would be merely a warm-up for the Charles H. Strub Stakes, but I never made it. Once more, "the mark of Equipoise" visited me and I was sidelined for more than four months with a quarter crack in my right front hoof. When I returned it was with a victory in the Metropolitan Mile at Aqueduct. It was my fifteenth consecutive win.

For a while there was some talk about entering me in the Grand Prix de Saint-Cloud in France. That race was run on grass and I was tested on that surface just to see how well I'd do. It was the mile-and-five-eighths Bowling Green Handicap, and just to make the test harder, I had to carry 135 pounds. That was too much. I finished third, four and a half lengths out, behind my stablemate Porker, who carried 112 pounds, and Assagai, who toted 127 pounds. That ended the talk about a trip across the Atlantic.

My next start was in the Suburban, carrying 133 pounds, which was top weight in the race. I was up against the winner of the Widener, Ring Twice, who was toting 22 pounds less. He was leading by two lengths with about eighty yards to go, but I ran like hell and beat him by half a length. The fans who watched the race said it was my most spectacular finish, and maybe it was. As things turned out, it was also my last win.

In the Brooklyn event they saddled me with 136 pounds, which made me think the handicapper was trying to turn me into a swaybacked stallion. I just didn't feel like running under such conditions and I finished second by eight lengths to Handsome Boy, who was carrying 120 pounds. In the Woodward I had to face Damascus, who was a true champion if ever I saw one. I was second by ten lengths, but had the satis-

98

Buckpasser wins at Aqueduct

faction of edging out another outstanding horse, Dr. Fager.

And my boss thought it was time I called it a career. I had raced thirty-one times with twenty-five wins, my total purses amounted to $1,462,014. I was syndicated for $4,800,000.

Now that's my idea of a whole bunch of cash.

What I liked best was Mr. Eddie Neloy's observation when I left for Claiborne to stand at stud. He said, "Buckpasser overcame all my mistakes. That's a great horse."

SECRETARIAT

 I came into the world exactly ten minutes after midnight on March 30, 1970. I mention that in case you might want to send me a birthday card. It's always nice to be remembered.

First, let me tell you about Meadow Farm, where I was born. In a way it's like a part of American history. It was built in 1810 by a gentleman named Charles Dabney Morris, at Doswell, Virginia, not far from Richmond. In those days it must have been like something out of *Gone With the Wind*, with horses, and ladies in hoop skirts, and all that good stuff. Then the family lost it after the Civil War, just like Tara. A lot of years passed, and in 1936, it was bought by a man who loved horses. His name was Christopher Chenery. He used to go fox hunting and play polo—you know, a real Virginia gentleman. Mr. Chenery was actually some kind of relative of old Mr. Morris, and he just decided to buy back the old homestead. He was going to raise Thoroughbreds.

Some of Mr. Chenery's friends told him not to buy the place. It wasn't in a good location, a lot of the twenty-six hundred acres were just bogs of swampland, and the grass wasn't very good. Mr.

As a three-year-old, victory in the Gotham Mile at Aqueduct. Secretariat broke on top and never lost the lead.

Chenery went ahead anyway. He was quite a man, that Mr. Chenery, a self-made millionaire, an engineer, owner and manager of a few utility companies. He always looked ahead. In fact he financed the first offshore oil drilling in the Gulf of Mexico. He did some thinking, some exploring on his new farm, and what he did was a joy to behold. Mr. Chenery found what was left of an old levee built before the Civil War. It was meant to hold back the water of the North Anna River. He had it rebuilt, drained off the swamp water, planted pasture grass, then took care of the buildings. You should see the place now.

In time Mr. Chenery became old and he got sick. He couldn't run the farm and the business was turned over to his daughter, Helen Chenery Tweedy. "Miss Penny"—that's what everybody called her—knew a little bit about horse breeding, but she had a lot to learn. She had help from an old friend of the family, Arthur Boyd "Bull" Hancock, Jr. What Bull forgot about Thoroughbreds a lot of big-wheel experts still don't know.

Old Mr. Chenery had made a deal to breed a couple of his mares to a great sire named Bold Ruler. Hell, you've heard of him; anybody older than forty who walked over to the $2 window knows about the Ruler. But Miss Penny had her doubts. Bold Ruler had all the right bloodlines, but somehow, a lot of his kids went lame early on. Miss Penny decided to stop using Bold Ruler after her two mares had made the scene with the big stud. One of the mares was a beautiful lady named Somethingroyal. That was my mom.

You'd think with my background I'd have a name with "Bold" in it, or maybe "Ruler." I'll tell you how I got my name. It was in honor of Miss Elizabeth Ham, the farm's general secretary, the woman who kept the place glued together when Mr. Chenery got sick. With us it was love at first sight. Read her entry in the farm log:

> July 28, 1970—Three white stockings— well made colt—might be a little tight under the knees—stands well on pasterns—good straight hind leg—good shoulders—good quarters. You just have to like him.

Foals don't get to see their sires, and in my case that was a blessing. I'm told my pop was a grump, like his father before him, Nasrullah. Mama was completely different. She loved all her kids. Usually, a mare licks her newborn foal clean and that's more or less the end of it, but Somethingroyal was different. Even after I began running around the pasture like a young idiot, she'd kiss me and lick me. Every kid likes to have an affectionate mom.

My first summer was full of sunshine. I'd hear folks talking about me, calling me "precocious"—whatever that's supposed to mean. I had no bad habits. Sure, I liked to roughhouse with the other foals, kick out at times, maybe even take a soft bite now and then, but that's normal. I never really hurt another kid and they never hurt me.

With all that running and playing I developed an appetite. I sure did enjoy the groceries, like four or five quarts of grain a day, plus, of course, a little mare's milk to wash it down. But the milk was coming less and less. I guess it was part of the weaning process. Like all creatures, sooner or later you get off mother's milk and into the stuff you'll eat for the rest of your life. Sure enough, one day I had to leave my beautiful mother and go off with a few other youngsters.

Weaning is hard to describe. Some foals stand around quietly and just tremble, others try to climb the walls of their stalls. I was somewhere in between. I pawed the ground, let go with a few

whinnies, and felt lost. I ran around like a crazy kid looking for my mama in the morning, but even then something told me the baby part of my life was over. I quieted down eventually. We all did. It was time to go into the family business— horse racing.

I met my first trainer, Bob Bailes. He was a very nice, very patient man. You know, Bob and me seemed to communicate somehow. Not many people can—he could. So did Bob's son, Meredith.

We went through the preliminaries: putting a saddle on my back, getting fitted with the right bit. I always did have a sensitive mouth, and they thought that was good, because I'd be able to respond to any slight pull on the reins. Then I was introduced to the weight of a man. That's tricky for a lot of horses. It's called "backing a yearling." A man lies on his belly over the saddle, and if the yearling gets too nervous, the man's ribs can be sore for a long time. Meredith did that with me. Hell, I wouldn't hurt Meredith. The next day he got into the saddle astride. That was the real beginning. My new groom, Chuck Ross, took me outside and for a couple of weeks he led me in circles, or figure eights, while Meredith pulled the reins this way or that way, just to get me used to the signals. Finally I went out on the track with Meredith on my back. I walked some, jogged a little, getting the feel of moving with somebody on my back.

You know what they called me at first? "Ol' Hopalong," that's what my name was. I was just a gorgeous, fat kid. Man, how I could put away the grains! I was getting bigger, fatter, and clumsier by the day, a walking tub of lard. And it wasn't so funny. Fat means slow, and I practically invented slow.

Meadow Farm was great, but it wasn't the place for serious horse training. And I also needed a full-time trainer, somebody who had— you should excuse the expression—a track record as a winner. Roger Laurin should have been the man, but he got this big offer from a horse owner named Ogden Phipps, one of the big wheels in the game. Roger talked his father, Lucien, into taking the job. Poor Lucien, he wanted to retire; he was sixty years old and all he wanted to do was take naps in the sunshine, but he shrugged and agreed. I was shipped down to Lucien's stable at Florida's Hialeah racetrack. It was there that I first met my new groom, Eddie Sweat.

I have never, not in my whole life, met anybody who loved horses more than Eddie Sweat. It was almost like people didn't matter to him. Once, when the help went on a wildcat strike, Eddie didn't join in, even though he was a member of the union. All by himself he took care of seventeen horses. Now that's my kind of a guy.

But it wasn't love at first sight where Eddie was concerned. I didn't impress him much. He took one look at me and started shaking his head. Right to my face he said, "You're too pretty. You're too big. An' you're too fat." How could I get mad at that? Eddie was right. But my feelings were hurt when he refused to give me a rub. He said he'd rather spend more time giving rubs to my stablemate, Riva Ridge.

I'd heard about Riva before, and at first I thought he was too good to be true. Lucien trained him. Right away, as a two-year-old, Riva showed more class than any colt was entitled to. Like he won the Saratoga Flash, the Belmont Futurity, the Champagne Stakes, the Laurel Futurity, the Garden State Stakes. Hey, that was a record to shoot at. Now I was a two-year-old; Riva was three, ready for his shot at the big time.

But I've got to admit, right then I was more trouble than I was worth. I don't remember if I couldn't or wouldn't run fast, but it's a fact that I *didn't*. For instance:

I'd practice running around the track with a horse named Gold Bag. Yeah, he was a horse. He had four legs, a tail, he ate grain. But he wasn't much of a runner. Yet he would open up in what was laughingly called a sprint and I'd be grunting and galloping like I was six months' pregnant. It took time before they stopped calling me Ol' Hopalong.

And I thought it was a big laugh to dump my rider. I didn't mean any harm, I was a clown, nobody held it against me. But they shoved a special bit into my mouth and that cured me.

In March I was shipped north to Belmont Park, Long Island. I was still the slowest horse you ever saw, until one morning in June. And then I woke up. Maybe it was because of Riva Ridge. I mean, that colt was beating everybody in sight. He won the Kentucky Derby. He lost the Preakness because the track was like a muddy slime pit, but Riva came back to win the Belmont. So I decided to get Lucien's attention.

I'll never forget the look on his face after that big workout. I tore off five furlongs in exactly $57^3/_5$ seconds. He shook his stopwatch to see if it was still working, and he kept muttering, "Why didn't you do that before?" He made arrangements to enter me in a five-and-a-half-furlong maiden special weights race at Aqueduct on July Fourth.

Right after the starting bell I was introduced to the real world of horse racing. I was on the rail with Paul Feliciano up, and when I left the post I thought the whole world was ganging up on me. Some horse named Quebec—I don't know if it was the colt's fault or his jockey's—ducked in toward the rail and there was a traffic jam in front of me. I almost got slammed into the rail. I guess if I hadn't been that big and strong I'd have taken a spill right then. I stumbled and jittered for maybe a hundred yards before I could get back in stride. I guess Lucien and Miss Penny almost had heart attacks.

No, I didn't win, or even finish in the money. Hey, I was lucky to be running at all. But I showed the rest of the field what they could expect in the future. At the top of the stretch I was in tenth place, but I made up eight lengths and finished fourth, only a quarter-length behind the winner.

Eleven days later I was back at Aqueduct. The odds-makers had me pegged, all right. I went off a 6-to-5 favorite, and nobody was disappointed after the six-furlong race was done. I breezed in by six lengths. All Paul Feliciano had to do was hang on and not fall off.

Saratoga was next. Ron Turcotte was supposed to be my jockey but he got hurt in a spill. He was healthy by opening day. Again I was the favorite, this time 2 to 5, which scared away

Secretariat's first victory as a two-year-old. He was a 6-to-5 favorite as he won the Aqueduct event with jockey Paul Feliciano aboard.

some bettors, I suppose. After all, why risk five bucks to win only two? But it was a sure thing. Nobody pushed me, there was no point rubbing it in. I crossed the finish line with a one-and-a-half-length lead. Just a piece of cake.

I like what Ron said about me after that race. It was his first ride with me, and he said, "He just floats. You don't feel like you're goin' that fast, but then you look up and you're passin' horses like they were standin' still."

The six-furlong Sanford Stakes was next. That race has a big history. It's the only one Man o' War didn't win. You remember that race. Sure you do. The winner was a horse named Upset. Maybe some folks who wager cash money thought I'd eat dust in this one, because a lot of smart money was on a little guy named Linda's Chief. More than a few people thought he was the best two-year-old running. He'd won five races in a row, and that's something to think about. Linda's Chief was the favorite. Why not? He'd earned it.

I got off slow, which was the way I always ran. Like I was spotting the other horses a few yards, just to make it interesting. For a quarter of a mile I was dead last, then I passed one horse, and kept running easy until we turned into the homestretch. Oh, wow, I was looking at a roadblock of horses' rumps in front of me. Trust Ron to find an opening. I squeezed through, and ran the last quarter in :23⁴/₅ seconds. I won by five lengths in 1:10, the fastest six furlongs run at Saratoga that year.

The most surprised guy at the track was Al Scotti, the trainer of Linda's Chief. Surprised? Hell, he was walking around like he'd just seen the ghost of Christmas past. He said, "I don't think any horse alive could have beaten my horse that day. He had a good lead at the stretch . . . it was unbelievable. Secretariat ran away from me like I wasn't even there."

Remember how I moped along in a workout? No more. Tuning up for the $86,550 Hopeful Stakes, I turned in a half-mile in :46²/₅. In his workout, Linda's Chief covered the same ground in :49¹/₅. Scotti checked his stopwatch and scratched his horse from the race.

It was just as well. I took the Hopeful by five lengths, my time for the six and a half furlongs was 1:16¹/₅, only three-fifths of a second off the track record for that distance.

Eddie Sweat sponged me down later, and he whispered to me, "I think you might be as good as Riva Ridge." Praise from Caesar!

Now everybody who followed the ponies was talking about me. They said I was not only fast, I was also beautiful. They were right. Should I lie? I stood sixteen hands three-quarter inches high (in case you forgot, a "hand" is four inches, and the measurement is from the point of the withers to the ground, so I was five feet four and three-quarters inches tall), and I had the most soulful, intelligent eyes (ask Ron Turcotte), and a good, broad head. Everywhere I went the photographers came like somebody started a new gold rush. For me it was a big hoot. I made sure nobody wasted film, because I had a few poses ready that made me look like a movie star. They all got profile or full face, or maybe they wanted my special "flaring nostrils" bit, or it could be I'd prick up my ears—that always got 'em.

Next came the Belmont Futurity. After one of my workouts, the competition dropped from ten horses to six. But a couple of days before the race, there was a big tragedy. I mean you could almost feel the sadness, like a blanket of sorrow. Bull Hancock, the great guy who helped Miss Penny so much, had died at the age of sixty-two.

I couldn't let Bull Hancock down. And I didn't. I went under the wire one and three-quarter lengths in front.

All the talk now was about Barn 5, where Riva and I had adjoining stalls. Naturally, the gentry who make a living writing about horses wanted to compare us. Ron and Eddie told them all to forget it.

"They're completely different types," Ron said. "Secretariat hits the ground a little harder. Riva seems to skip over the track."

Eddie Sweat's opinion of us was different. He said that when he bandaged Riva's legs, Riva just stood there nice and peaceable. But I liked to play. I might try to nip at Eddie, or aim a soft kick in his direction. He knew I didn't mean any harm. He wasn't mad, just careful.

I don't know why anybody wanted to compare me with Riva. If you wanted to say we were alike you could. We both stood sixteen hands three-quarter inches high. If you wanted to say we were different, you could do that too. Riva was a year older, but I measured three inches more around the girth than he did.

I was primed for the October Champagne Stakes, and there was some worry at first about the distance, one mile. That's eight furlongs, and I hadn't run that far in a race. Not to worry. I had a couple of workouts and I actually saw Lucien smile. But he was also afraid that my come-from-behind way of running might backfire. He was right, but he was also wrong.

I went off a 7-to-10 favorite and I trailed so far back some fans thought I might be an early entry in the next race. This time I didn't fool around trying to shove through a lot of horses. Ron took me to the outside and I let it all hang out. You never heard so much noise. I practically exploded. But, as I pulled up, the tote board blinked. There was an "inquiry."

The place horse was a pretty good colt named Stop the Music. His jockey claimed I had "brushed" his mount when I went for the finish line. But I didn't slow Music. Geez, I almost shoved him ahead! But the stewards ruled against me. I lost—if you want to call that losing. Even Jock Whitney, who owned Stop the Music, said he didn't want to win that way. I was the best horse on the track, the whole crowd saw that.

It was the second time I'd lost a race through no fault of my own. I'm not blaming Stop the Music, he didn't complain, his jockey did, but the loss went on my record just the same. I had my chance for revenge in the $133,800 Laurel Futurity.

Six horses were entered. I might just as well have run around the track alone. It was a muddy track, but it didn't matter to me then. When we turned for home I ran away from the field like the other horses were out for exercise, and I was still pouring it on with a lead of eight lengths when I went across the finish line. I was so happy I pulled a silly stunt on Miss Penny. I rested my muddy head on her shoulder, slopping up her arm and her dress. She loved me anyway.

But it wasn't a perfect day. Rain also fell at Aqueduct, where Riva was running in the Jockey Club Gold Cup. He came in third. A horse named Autobiography won it by fifteen lengths. Riva just can't run in mud. Hell, no horse ever born is fifteen lengths better than Riva on a normal track.

I ran one more race as a two-year-old, the Garden State Stakes in Cherry Hills, New Jersey. I ran as an entry with my stablemate, Angle Light. Ron rode me; his brother, Rudy, rode the other horse. We finished one-two, with me ahead by three and a half lengths.

All in all it wasn't a bad year for Meadow Stable. I had earned $456,000, Riva made over $395,000, and our track records weren't too shabby, either. I had seven wins in nine starts, and those two losses were just flukes. Riva won five out of twelve, with one second and one third. Just to frost the cake, the good people in racing land voted me Horse of the Year, the first time the honor went to a two-year-old.

Wait a minute, I know what all the purists who study up on racing are going to say. Native Dancer won it as a two-year-old in 1952, and so did a great two-year-old filly named Moccasin in 1965. But there's a big difference. This is how I heard it:

The award is given by three organizations: the Thoroughbred Racing Association, the *Daily Racing Form*, and the Turf Writers of America. They used to give out the awards *separately*. In fact, the Thoroughbred Racing Association gave the award to Dancer and Moccasin. By the time I won it, the three groups voted together. One award, not three, see?

But you can't have the good things without some bad thrown in. On January 3, 1973, Mr. Christopher T. Chenery, the big boss himself, passed away at the age of eighty-six. He'd been sick for a long time, so sick that I'm not sure he knew how well Riva and I were running.

When the owner of a horse farm dies, that's when the big headaches begin. Bull Hancock's sons found that out when they had to pay a lot of taxes to settle the estate, and the ready cash wasn't there. They sold off about twenty of their Claiborne Farm horses. One of them was a big, good-looking dark horse named Sham. I found out plenty about Sham later on.

Now, only a few months later, it was Miss Penny's turn to learn the facts of life. Naturally she turned to the sons of Bull Hancock. In horses or people, you can always tell good bloodlines. Seth Hancock was only twenty-three years old, but his father had given him an education about horses. Seth did everybody proud. The answer was to syndicate me, with the price $190,000 a share. Syndication is a very complicated deal, but the horse breeders from all over the world jumped on the bandwagon. According to all the totals, I was syndicated for a little over $6 million. When you consider that the stock market wasn't so healthy then, I must have looked like a great investment.

Now I was a three-year-old, bigger and fatter than ever. That's when the real work begins for a racehorse. Back I went to Barn 5 at Belmont to begin serious training. My first big test was the Bay Shore Handicap on a chilly, cloudy day in March.

I think the other horses and jockeys wanted to gang up on me. When I tried to make my move from behind, it was the same scene all over again: a wall of horses' rumps strung across the track, blocking my way. There was only one way to pass the mob and that was to force a lane through them. That's just what Ron and I did. We won by four and a half lengths.

My next outing was the Gotham Mile at Aqueduct, and this time Ron took no chances. I broke ahead and led all the way. Maybe it was smart to work that way, because a strong colt named Champagne Charlie kept on coming, but I held him off and won by three lengths.

I suppose I began getting too cocky. When the head gets big, trouble is bound to show up. In this case trouble was named Sham, the colt Bull Hancock's kids sold when they needed money.

Secretariat had a point to prove as he was led to the track by groom Eddie Sweat. He had just lost the Woodward Stakes and now he was out to redeem himself in the Man o' War. The champion colt set a world record for the mile-and-five-fur- longs distance.

Sham made a big rep for himself with wins on the West Coast in races like the Santa Catalina and the Santa Anita Derby. Only good horses can beat the competition in those runs. Sham was good.

I'll give it to you in a nutshell. The race was the Wood Memorial and I finished third. Angle Light won, Sham was second, and I was four lengths out.

No alibis, I just plain lost. There was the small matter of my bit. When I make my move, I sort of lean into the bit. When I was examined the day after the race, they found a small boil in my mouth, right where the bit hit that exact spot. I'm not saying that's why I lost, but the boil in my mouth sure didn't help.

Once I got beaten the rumors began to fly. According to one piece of garbage, I had a bad knee. Or I wasn't being worked right. Or I was too fat, too temperamental, a clown. How can you figure it? So far I'd gone to the post twelve times and won nine. Not many horses did better than that. But I didn't let it get to me. I was out to show everybody I wasn't just another pretty face.

Relaxed? I'll tell you how relaxed I was on Derby day. At about noon I ate two quarts of oats—just a snack—then I lay down and conked out for three hours.

There were thirteen of us walking to the starting gate and I had drawn post position 10. Then there was a commotion. All of a sudden a horse named Twice a Prince reared up, fell over, and threw his jockey. The horse got to his feet but then was all shook-up and an assistant starter had to come over to help quiet him. The colt he left unattended was Sham. When the gate opened Sham stumbled and cracked his head against it.

That hard shot to the face knocked two teeth loose. There was blood in his mouth, but Sham ignored it and ran. Oh, Lordy, how he ran! A horse named Shecky Greene was in front but Sham caught him and took the lead; going into the turn it was still Sham. I had been moving up on the outside, and now there was only Sham ahead of me. Ron tapped me on the flank a few times and I opened up for him. At the eighth pole Sham and I were even, then I was ahead and across the line.

I broke the record. My Derby time was 1:59²/₅, three-fifths of a second better than Northern Dancer's mark. I'm not sure but I think that Sham—bloody mouth and all—also broke the record. He would have breezed in if I hadn't been there.

Another thing, I went faster with each quarter of a mile. There were five quarters and the clock read :25¹/₅; :24 flat; :23⁴/₅; :23²/₅; and :23 flat.

So the Preakness shaped up as mostly a two-horse race between me and Sham. I heard that losing two front teeth wouldn't bother him much (hah!) because horses chew oats and grain mostly with their back teeth, but Sham couldn't pick up grass right away.

There was no fuss at the gate this time. It was a clean start for everybody. I held back and the

pace was slow, but Ron wasn't about to let me get boxed in. He took me to the outside so I could loop around the field and take the long way home. Coming out of the backstretch I had the lead.

Laffit Pincay was up on Sham again, and he went to the whip all the way in. Poor Sham almost bust a gut trying to catch me. Dammit, that's one hell of a horse, he just doesn't quit! He got to within two and a half lengths of me and that's where he stayed. My official time was 1:54²/₅, just two-fifths of a second behind the record set by Canonero II. If I did that well, Sham must have been running a pretty good race, too.

The Belmont, the third leg of the Triple Crown, is a mile and a half, which everybody knows. That's a long way to run. The rap on my sire, Bold Ruler, was that almost none of his kids could run that far and still have enough breath left to walk back to the paddock. To be honest, I wasn't so sure I could, either. Six quarters of a mile; gee, that could take forever.

It was a beautiful day and there was a big crowd. They came out to see if I could become the first horse in twenty-five years to win the Triple. Five of us were entered, but the only colt I counted was Sham. The others were Pvt. Smiles, My Gallant, and Twice a Prince. I was on the outside, Sham was on the inside at the start.

All of us enjoyed a clean getaway. I grabbed the lead on the straightaway, but Sham came right at me and he wasn't fooling around. That big colt wanted the win badly, and he kept coming, and coming, and we were even. Then Sham started inching ahead.

Oh no you don't, buddy! Not today you won't!

The two of us were flying. We did the first quarter in :23³/₅, the next in :22³/₅. The crowd was going crazy; you never heard such screaming. Who could stay the distance at that pace?

Sham didn't have it, I did. I went back into the lead, and I mean it was a *lead*. The third quarter was over in :23³/₅, the fourth quarter in :24³/₅. I was seven lengths ahead and I wanted a lot more. Distance? Who cared about distance? Right then each quarter was like a step in the

Just out for a little gallop at Belmont with an exercise rider aboard.

clover to me. I had the mile and a quarter in 1:59 even, with one more quarter to go, but I wasn't through yet.

Funny, but I didn't hear the crowd anymore. I didn't see anybody. I wasn't even sure if the other horses were still there. It was like I was running in a dream, with no people and no other entries, just Ron and me, with the finish line up ahead. I took the last quarter in :25 even.

I'll never forget that race because so many things happened.

First, I set a new Belmont record, 2:24 flat, which was a big two and three-fifths seconds better than the old mark.

Second, I won by thirty-one lengths. Let that sink in—*thirty-one lengths.* Who wins a big race with that kind of a lead? I did, but I still don't believe it.

Third, I won the Triple Crown.

Sham was finished. He never raced again. Not because I broke his spirit—nobody can do that to a colt as good as Sham—but they found a

fracture in a cannon bone. The hard-luck horse went to stud.

Then the comparisons started. I guess it's because horse*players* don't have horse *sense.* Right away I had a new nickname, "Big Red," the same handle that was stuck on Man o' War a long time ago. Was I as good as the first Big Red? Was I better? What difference did it make? Things have changed since Man o' War ran; tracks aren't the same; the competition is different, so are training conditions. They began calling me "The Horse of the Century." Hey, I've always been a big ham and I liked the fuss, but I'll tell you who wasn't too thrilled—Riva Ridge.

He got depressed; he wouldn't have anything to do with me. Everybody was giving me the big hello, and Riva got lost in the shuffle. I couldn't blame him for sulking, but he had no cause to get sore at me.

Wise old Lucien and Miss Penny had a cure for Riva's blahs. They entered him in the $50,000 Massachusetts Handicap. They hadn't forgotten him after all. Neither had the fans. And Riva showed 'em that he was still a champ. Not only did he win, but he equaled the record of 1:48¹/₅ set by another horse nicknamed Mr. Longtail—Whirlaway. Along the way he beat out Bee Bee Bee, the horse that had beat him in the muddy Preakness and kept him away from the Triple Crown.

Riva wasn't through yet. On July Fourth, he ran in the Brooklyn Handicap at Aqueduct, and all he did was break the record for the mile and three-sixteenths with a time of 1:52²/₅. Furthermore, his purse was $67,200, and that brought his earnings to about $1 million, a total I had not yet reached. Miss Penny and Seth Hancock hatched another syndication plot, and Riva went for something over $5 million.

Meanwhile, I hadn't exactly been asleep, and I earned my keep, too. I ran at Arlington Park, which is a track near Chicago. It was just exercise. I won by nine lengths, and Miss Penny took $125,000 to the bank.

The racing season opened at Saratoga and that's where I went next. Normally it's dog days in August, but in upstate New York nobody tries to predict weather. Wouldn't you know it, we ran into a bunch of dank, rainy days that sloshed up the track. Funny though, I had a good workout, mud and all. Even Lucien thought I'd breeze in the Whitney Stakes.

There was some good opposition. A horse named West Coast Scout had won a few races, so had Rule By Reason, and a gelding named Onion could burn up the track. What with a muddy track, this wasn't just another quick payday.

The mud was softer and deeper on the inside. When Onion took the lead, Ron had two choices: go around him and lose ground, or go to the inside where the goo was heavier. I'd had a good workout in the slime, so Ron reasonably took the shorter route. I don't know if that tired me or not. When the time came for the big finishing kick, I just didn't have it. Onion won by a length.

I had no alibi, I got beat fair and square. It can happen to any horse, especially at Saratoga, which is supposed to be a jinx track. That's where

Man o' War lost for the only time in his life, to Upset, in the Sanford. And Gallant Fox lost to an outsider named Jim Dandy in the Travers. But I'd be meeting up with Onion again. The result would be different.

Right after the Whitney I got sick with some kind of fever. Everybody at the stable started biting their nails because another race—a real biggie—was coming up.

A while back Miss Penny had made a deal with the Philip Morris Corporation—they make cigarettes and a lot of other things—to enter me and Riva in a race, to be called the Marlboro Cup. It would be run in September at Belmont. I got well in time to make it, and there never was competition like that before. For instance:

Me, Secretariat, a Triple Crown winner. Riva, who won the Derby and Belmont. Cougar II, a seven-year-old stakes winner from California. Kennedy Road, Canadian Horse of the Year in 1971, running as an entry with Cougar. Key to the Mint, who beat out Riva in 1972 for Horse of the Year. Annihilate 'em, who had won the Travers. And Onion, set for a rematch with me personally. What a group! Among us we had won more than $6 million, sixty-four stakes races, and only God knows how many awards and honors.

To me only Riva mattered, the other entries didn't worry me. He and I were the best on the track, and anybody who didn't know that didn't know horses. Suppose I beat him, would he go back into his sulk? If he beat me I could handle that, but I didn't want to lose. What the hell, stablemate or not, I couldn't spend my life thinking about hurting a pal's feelings. I'd run my race, Riva would run his, and when it was over, maybe we'd both forget it.

Out of the gate Onion and Kennedy Road went ahead, with Riva right behind them, followed by four horses—Key to the Mint, Annihilate 'em, Cougar II, and me. Kennedy fell away some and Riva took up the chase, and I began making my move. Turning for home it was just me and Riva, stride for stride, the way it was always meant to be, but it was my day and I went over by three and a half lengths. It was a record for the mile and an eighth, 1:45²/₅. The top money, $150,000, made me a million-dollar winner, too.

Onion? He finished fourth, fourteen lengths out. In your face, baby!

I'm not sure why Miss Penny and Lucien decided to do it, but they said I'd start running on turf next. It was a big difference. I'd always run on dirt. Some horses can make the switch, others can't. I suppose they had the Woodward race in mind, followed by the Man o' War, two very important meets.

Sometimes the odds-makers are right, but often they're wrong. They said the horse I'd have to beat was Cougar II, and I'd already beaten him. The others in the race—Amen II, Prove Out, and a mare named Summer Guest—didn't figure. Maybe they were smart, especially because of the weather. It rained. Belmont was muddy.

The experts were right about one thing, that I'd be challenging, but the horse wasn't Cougar at all, it was Prove Out. The track was slow. I didn't like it at all, and I didn't have the come-from-behind drive. Prove Out won, and he won big, by four and a half lengths.

It was different in the Man o' War. That's a very long race, a mile and five furlongs, and the big challenger was Tentam, the grass champion. But I'd never lost two races in a row and this wasn't the time to do it. I almost pulled Ron's arms out of his silks, and he had to hold me back. Nobody could catch me that day. My time was 2:37⁴/₅, the fastest time for that distance ever run by any horse on any track, grass or dirt.

I guess Miss Penny and Lucien thought I'd had just about enough. There was only one more race to run, that was at Woodbine in Toronto, Canada. After that I was finished running. I thought a lot about not riding anymore with Ron after that, but it turned out I was wrong. Ron didn't ride me at all. It was Eddie Maple. Ron got himself suspended for five days because of some foul claim, and suspensions hold good for all tracks. That was okay. I liked Eddie Maple. He rode Riva in the Marlboro.

Only, Eddie's heart wasn't in the Woodbine, and neither was mine. Just the day before, Eddie rode Riva in the Jockey Club Gold Cup, and my stablemate finished last. Can you imagine that? Riva Ridge was last. Unbelievable!

The day of my last race was dark and damp and misty and the grass was like glass underfoot. And another thing I had never had to contend with: Part of the race was run into the wind, and there was a lot of wind that day.

And Kennedy Road tried to make my life miserable. He was a Canadian, running before his own countrymen, but I guess he was sore at me from the Marlboro, because at the half-mile pole he bumped me a shot that almost took me down. I got real mad about that, and I poured it on. I copped the duke by six and a half lengths.

So it was goodbye to racing, but not goodbye to the fans. Tuesday, November 6, was "Farewell to Secretariat Day" at Aqueduct. It was a nice day, a little cool, but sunny. A lot of people made speeches, including Miss Penny, and a lot of gifts were handed out. Then Ron mounted up and we moved out on the track.

It was funny walking out on an oval with no other horses around. Just a lot of people cheering and crying and yelling goodbye to me. I moved up to the quarter pole, then Ron turned me around and we paraded past the stands. Finally we went to the winner's circle and a ring of flowers was thrown over my neck. That was stupid if you ask me. I didn't run, I didn't win. How can a racehorse go on a track, then go into the winner's circle and not run against other horses? Sure beats me.

So we packed it in, Riva and I. We flew to Kentucky, and got side-by-side stalls at Claiborne Farm, the place run by Seth Hancock. I saw my groom, Eddie Sweat, crying a little bit.

If you want to see two champs in adjoining stalls, drop in some time. Riva and I always have time for visitors. And now that racing's behind us, you never saw two closer pals.

FOREGO

Weight. That's the story of my life in one word. In practically every race I ever ran, the handicappers piled weights on my back. They must have thought I had the strength of a Clydesdale pulling a beer wagon. But I survived, no thanks to those people. Still, all the added weight was sort of a left-handed compliment. The system of weights was instituted so that ordinary horses had a chance against the better Thoroughbreds. There's some kind of rule-of-thumb that every pound of weight means one length in a given race. For instance, when I'm carrying 132 pounds and another horse is carrying 120 pounds, the handicappers think I'm twelve lengths better than my rival. That's crazy, if you ask me.

And then there's the matter of gelding. A horse is gelded for any number of reasons. Some like the fillies too much and can't keep their minds on business. Some don't train very well, they're nasty.

In my case it was just that I grew too fast. My shins were always sore; I had splint trouble and that made me mean. My ankles bothered me. I guess there was nothing else to do but make a gelding of me.

The funny thing is, maybe half the horses you

Forego as a five-year-old, beating Wajima in the Woodward at Belmont.

see on a track are geldings. I mean like Kelso, and like Armed and Exterminator. They won a lot of races. Maybe they wouldn't have been winners if they had been allowed to grow into stallions. Gelding changes a lot of things.

I was born in 1970, the same year as Secretariat, who definitely was *not* a gelding. My sire was a South American stud named Forli, my dam was Lady Golconda. I was the property of the Lazy F Ranch, and I became the special pet of the boss lady, Martha Gerry. A canny old geezer named Sherrill Ward took over my training at first, and he had help from my groom, Shotgun Hampton. That should take care of the preliminaries. I like to get those things out of the way first.

For a long time I was one of the best-kept secrets in racing. That's not a complaint, it's just the way things were. Maybe some horses are born with a racing instinct, but I wasn't one of them. After my first few races I began to wonder why Miss Martha even bothered with me, because I didn't seem to be getting anywhere. I began to run as a three-year-old, and my first time out was in the Florida Derby at Gulfstream. I was a 2-to-1 favorite, and I led for a while, but Royal and Regal caught me and I finished second.

Why then should I be entered in the 1973 Kentucky Derby? I asked myself that same question, and the odds-makers must have had their doubts, too, because I went off at 28 to 1. You know who won that race, don't you? It was the Big "S"—Secretariat. Me, I was all over the track.

About the only place I didn't hit was the men's room in the clubhouse. Going into the far turn I was bumped into the rail, then my jockey took me wide on the outside. To be honest, I surprised myself, because I started to come on strong in the stretch and finished fourth, eleven lengths behind the winner.

Next was the Withers Stakes at Belmont. I was third in that mile run. So far, one second, one third, and once out of the money. That's a hell of a way to start a career.

I got another test in the Jerome Handicap at Aqueduct, carrying 124 pounds for the mile race. I think it was about then that my jockey, Heliodoro Gustines, began to find out about me. He handled me a lot better, even though I lost. The winner was Step Nicely, carrying 118 pounds, and the winner set a Jerome record at 1:34. My effort wasn't bad as second-place finishes go. I felt a lot more confident.

It had to happen that I should start winning. I took the Roamer Handicap, which was a mile and three-sixteenths, and then I took the Discovery Handicap toting 127 pounds. Perhaps it's true that winning can become a habit. In 1973 I went to the post eighteen times. I won nine, was second three times, third three times, and unplaced three times. I won a total of $188,909 in purses. At last I had found my station in life. I was a handicap horse.

That was when they started to pile on the weights. It didn't matter if the race was a sprint or over a distance, I always had to carry the heaviest load. That was why I never took an early lead. Hey, I had to have some muscle left for the finish, and I couldn't burn myself out early, could I? Heliodoro knew that too. He always knew how to handle me.

I opened the 1974 racing season with the Donn Handicap at Gulfstream. I carried 125 pounds, and beat out a game little horse named True Knight, a five-year-old carrying 123 pounds. Two weeks later I ran in the ten-furlong Gulfstream Park Handicap, and for that race the geniuses upped my weight to 127 pounds. I worked hard for that win. On the final turn I caught the tiring Strictly Business, and then I held off that

gamester True Knight, who was carrying the same 123 pounds.

Naturally, it figured that the big brains would add a couple of pounds in my saddlebags. For the ten-furlong Widener Handicap at Hialeah, I struggled under 129 pounds. I won it. And can you guess who came in second? True Knight, naturally, behind by a length.

Carrying weight is tolerable at a mile or even a little more. It's the shorter runs and the distances that cause the most wear and tear. The Carter Handicap at Belmont was a seven-furlong event, and sometimes it takes that distance just to hit stride. I carried 129 pounds in the Carter, and I won it.

In the one-mile Metropolitan Handicap they piled me up with 134 pounds. Geez, 134 pounds! I felt like I was carrying a whole extra jockey. I tried, but it was no use. The winner was Arbees Boy, who paid off at 60 to 1. You know how much weight Arbees Boy carried? Exactly 112 pounds. How in hell did they expect me to give away 22 pounds and still win? At the rate of a pound-per-length, did they think I was 22 lengths better than the eventual winner?

Maybe I was still sulking, but I finished second again in the seven-furlong Nassau County Handicap. However, I snapped out of it for the mile-and-three-sixteenths Brooklyn Handicap, which I won by three-quarters of a length in 1:54^4/$_5$. I was saddled with 129 pounds for that one. Second was a horse named Billy Come Lately, carrying 114 pounds. Third was Arbees Boy, with 116 pounds.

In the ten-furlong Suburban I was back up to 131 pounds. I came in third. Those two extra pounds meant two lengths, right? The winner was True Knight, just coming into his own, and second was a speed horse named Plunk. The distance between me and the winner was a length and a quarter. Take away those extra two pounds, which add two lengths for me, and I'd have won by three-quarters of a length. That's only simple arithmetic. It's their system, not mine.

The Marlboro, a nine-furlong race, was just not my bag of oats. For openers, the track was sloppy. I carried 126 pounds; the winner, Boy

Spruce, carried 120; the show horse, Arbees Boy, had 119 pounds. Hell, maybe I wouldn't have won the race anyway. I just didn't have it in the stretch.

The Woodward wasn't exactly a handicap race, it was a "weight-for-age" event. That has always been a puzzle to me. Usually, the added pounds are assigned in an arbitrary way, and the factors include—I'm not kidding—the age of the horses, the distance to be run, the month of the year . . . and for all I know the phase of the moon. For this Woodward, three-year-olds carried 119 pounds; older horses carried 126 pounds; and the champions—whoever they were—were not penalized but were all at equal weights on the scale.

It was a fast track, the kind I enjoy. There were eleven of us in the race and I was next to last after a mile. The field was strung out across the track and Heliodoro had to take me wide, and then even wider because there was no room to get through. I was so far outside I could practically nod to the fans on the rail, and I must have run twice as far as the other entries. I rode them all down and won by a neck over Arbees Boy. A good horse named Group Plan came in a nice third.

I won another seven-furlong Vosburgh Handicap, which was a prep race for the Jockey Club Gold Cup, a grueling two-miler. There were three horses in the field of eight that I had to watch out for: Arbees Boy, Group Plan, and a French horse named Copte. But I liked the odds now because all four of us were carrying the same weight, 124 pounds. It was a hell of a long race. At the quarter pole I caught Group Plan and left him behind. Even Copte caught him; Group Plan was just plain bushed. Arbees Boy was fourth.

By the end of 1974 I had become a celebrity. I raced thirteen times, winning eight, placing twice, third twice, and once out of the money. I added $545,086 to Miss Martha's cashbox. Best of all, I was selected Horse of the Year.

I felt even stronger as a five-year-old, especially in the Florida sunshine. If only the handicappers would have knocked off a couple of pounds in a race here or there, life would have

been complete. But it was business as usual. I carried 129 pounds in the nine-furlong Seminole Handicap and I won it. In the Widener, I carried 131 pounds, which was a record weight for the race. I won. Then I was pointed toward the New York handicap series. That's where the money was.

It was the same old story, the handicappers seemed to be trying to make me sag in the middle. In my opener, the Carter at Aqueduct, I was hit with 134 pounds, but I managed to win. It was a mistake to win, because they slapped me with another couple of pounds for the Metropolitan Mile, so now it was 136 pounds. I did my best, covering the distance in good time, but the weight was just too much. I was third, less than a length behind Gold and Myrrh, with 121 pounds, and Stop the Music, who carried 124.

The track officials for the Brooklyn Handicap had mercy on me. Sure, mercy—if you can call it that. They took off a couple of pounds and I was allowed to run with "only" 132 pounds. The secret of my success in that one was my stretch run. I went flat out like a runaway freight train and beat Monetary Principal by a length and a half. Not too bad, considering I gave away 23 pounds to the place horse.

In the mile-and-a-half Suburban, I had to beat Arbees Boy all over again. I really didn't want to pick on him because it was getting monotonous, but hell, there I was carrying 134 pounds and all he had to tote was 118.

I met up with some new rivals in the nine-furlong Governor's Stakes. To be sure, I carried top weight in the field of ten—what else did anybody expect—and it was 134 pounds again. But we were quite a group of horses, I must say. There was Ancient Title carrying 130, and Foolish Pleasure with 125, and Wajima with 115, and a couple of horses named Media and American History at a mere 111. It wasn't my day. Wajima won by a head, with Foolish Pleasure second, and Ancient Title third. I was fourth, out of the money.

I met up with Wajima again in the Marlboro Cup. It was a rugged run and the winning time for the nine-furlong race was 2:00 flat. Unfortunately, I wasn't the winner. Wajima was, by a head. I could only console myself with the knowledge that I'd given 10 pounds, me at 129, Wajima at 119.

I had to beat that sucker, and my opportunity came in the Woodward Stakes. One of the entries was Avatar, the winner of the Belmont. Heliodoro had a new strategy for me: to go out and challenge right away. Avatar and Wajima got off winging, but so did I, which surprised every fan at the track. Around the turn and into the backstretch I stayed with them, all the way to the far turn. At the three-eighths pole it was just Wajima and me, and I wasn't about to let him beat me three in a row. I began to draw away at the sixteenth pole and beat him by a length and three-quarters. You never heard such cheering. I was a real crowd-pleaser. By the way, Wajima had a seven-pound edge in the weights.

What kind of a year was it? Well sir, in 1975 I ran nine times. I won six, placed once, showed once, and was out once. My earnings were $429,521. And I was Horse of the Year for the second consecutive year.

Probably I could have won more money if I had entered the Jockey Club Gold Cup, but a couple of days before the race I pulled up lame. The vet said something about pulling the suspensory of my left foreleg. The leg filled with fluid and I began to blister. Maybe it was just as well. I was starting to get pooped. In three years I'd been entered in forty races, which is a whole lot of running for any horse.

Then a lot of things began to change. First, my old pal and trainer Sherrill Ward had to retire because of his arthritic hip. The man was in pain, and I knew all about pain. His replacements were Frank Whiteley and his son, David. I understand Sherrill told Whiteley that I would do even better as a six-year-old; I was just coming into my own. A smart man, that Sherrill Ward.

Another change was Whiteley's decision about when and where to race me. I always liked Florida and won quite a few events there. Whiteley wanted to skip Florida and go right to New York. He didn't want me to run as often, only in the big purse events. That made sense to me. Racing is

a business, but there's no point in using up the inventory too fast.

I started in a seven-furlong run at Belmont, and I won it, and then, carrying 130 pounds, I took the Metropolitan Mile. Then came another change. In the nine-furlong Nassau County, my rider was Jacinto Vasquez. It didn't make much difference, Vasquez was a good jockey. I won.

Heliodoro was back on board for the Suburban, and I was assigned 134 pounds by New York racing secretary Tommy Trotter, which might have been correct, except that I had to take on Foolish Pleasure, and he had a 9-pound edge in the weights. Maybe it was because of the way I ran in the Metropolitan. In that one the horse I had to beat was the previous year's Preakness winner, Master Derby, who had improved as a four-year-old. I gave away four pounds and still beat him.

But you can't give away that much to a horse as good as Foolish Pleasure. I gave it my best shot. Foolish Pleasure was ahead most of the way, and my stretch run just fell short. The crowd was rooting me in but I couldn't catch up. I lost by a nose. A pound less for me or a pound more for Foolish Pleasure might have made the difference. Well, like they say, that's what makes horse racing.

Maybe Tommy Trotter got the message, because in the Brooklyn Handicap I was still in at 134, but all I had to give Foolish Pleasure was 8 pounds. As it turned out, Foolish Pleasure wasn't much of a factor. I won, and in second place was a fast horse named Lord Rebeau who had only 114 pounds on his back, which was nothing. Foolish Pleasure was four and a quarter lengths back.

Now Whiteley was faced with another problem. Evidently Heliodoro Gustines thought the grass was greener with Greentree Stable, or maybe they made him an offer he couldn't refuse, because he signed on with them. Jacinto Vasquez rode me in the Amory L. Haskell Handicap at Monmouth Park and I finished third. Vasquez wasn't around for the upcoming Woodward because he hurt his foot. Now Whiteley had to find another jockey for me. He hardly hesi-

Now as a six-year-old after winning the Metropolitan Stakes at Belmont, with Heliodoro Gustines in the saddle.

tated long enough to have a cup of coffee. The call went out to get Willie Shoemaker.

What can anybody say about Willie the Shoe? It was said of him that he weighed two and a half pounds when he was born, and throughout the years he didn't add a whole lot more weight. Nobody I ever saw ride a Thoroughbred had stronger hands, more savvy or courage than that little man. Willie always was all heart.

The Woodward had been changed. It had been a mile-and-a-half weight-for-age event, but now it was a mile-and-a-furlong handicap. I got a whopping 135 pounds. One of the best milers around, Dance Spell, was in at 115, while a crack three-year-old, Honest Pleasure, carried 121.

Whiteley instructed Shoemaker how to ride me, and for the record, Willie obeyed to the letter. He was patient. We were both veterans; he instinctively understood that I knew how to run my race, and I trusted him to make the right move at the right time. We didn't really begin to

rumble until the three-furlong pole, and then I let it all hang out. I got out in front and stayed there, with one and a half lengths between me and Dance Spell. Honest Pleasure was in a dead heat for third. My time was 1:45⁴/₅, only two-fifths of a second off the American record for that distance. The record, by the way, was set by Secretariat.

Everybody said I had a lock on another Horse of the Year championship, but there was still the Marlboro Cup to run, and I dreaded the weight announcement. I had *every* reason to be upset. Those chowderheads assigned me 137 pounds. I thought the whole world of racing had just flipped out. That was the second highest weight assigned to any horse in a major New York race for the past ninety years. Just to make things worse, the Belmont track was like a thin mud pie. Racing secretary Tommy Trotter must have had his bags packed ready to get out of town fast. He said, "If Forego gets hurt out there today with all that weight and the mud, the crowd could very easily string me up from one of those big trees in the paddock—by the thumbs, or worse."

Just how good did Trotter think I was? There were eleven horses in the field, one of them being Honest Pleasure, and I was giving him 18 pounds—in the mud yet! I gave away up to 28 pounds to the others.

I'll tell you who else was worried, Frank Whiteley and Martha Gerry. They went up and back about scratching me from the race. They asked Willie Shoemaker, but he flat refused to tell what he thought. The track was almost like a country road washed out in a rainstorm. In the end they let me run.

The field didn't run out of the gate—I swear we all swam out. Honest Pleasure was having a ball in the mud, because at the clubhouse turn he was up by two lengths. I was back in eighth spot, wondering if I'd get back to a dry stall in one piece.

When we went into the long turn I was twelve lengths out, still looking for a firm footing somewhere. The Shoe was so covered with sprayed mud he could barely see any of the other horses. At the top of the turn I found my sea legs, and then I let 'em have it. I sloshed and I splashed and I sailplaned on the outside, picking up the distance. I don't know how Willie kept me or himself on course, but he did. He had his stick raised but he didn't bring it down on me.

After the race he told his heartfelt thoughts to a racing writer. The Shoe said, "I wanted to go to the whip. I thought he could never make it, but what was there to lose. But then I thought, for God's sake, don't touch him. He's doing the best he can."

Just before the eighth pole I could make out the voice of the track announcer. His voice had risen so high he sounded like an opera singer doing her final aria. I kept passing horses, and then the wire was maybe fifteen or twenty feet away. Honest Pleasure still had it, but I lowered my head and pulled up some juice from somewhere deep inside. It was over. I won by maybe a nose. Miss Martha wasn't sure, Frank Whiteley wasn't sure, maybe even Willie wasn't sure, but I was. When you've got it, you know it.

It matters a lot when you get praise from somebody who has been around the scene for a while. Willie Shoemaker had been up on some of the greatest Thoroughbreds since racing became a sport. I mean horses like Swaps, Round Table, Damascus, Sword Dancer, Cougar II, Dahlia. Willie had brought home thousands of winners. He said, "That is the best horse I have ever ridden."

He wasn't alone. A lot of people with long memories began comparing me with the great Thoroughbreds they watched in the past, and they pointed out that only Exterminator, Native Dancer, and Man o' War won while carrying 137 pounds or more, but never in a big race. I'm not sure they ever had sore legs like I did, especially my right foot.

Somehow, Frank Whiteley put me back together again and there I was a seven-year-old. You should have seen my fans, it was like a love-in—kids walking around wearing T-shirts that read "Forego Forever." My first race was a seven-furlong run, and I doubt there was much action at the window for me because I went off at 1 to 20, which meant if a man plunked down his $2, he won enough money to buy part of a cup of coffee. I beat Dance Spell by half a length.

There's no use reciting a litany of the races I won or lost, or how much weight I had to carry. What is more to the point is that I was long in the tooth, and my legs bothered me, and I lost one race to Great Contractor by eleven lengths. The funny part of that outing was that I came in second. Racing is a crazy business. As a seven-year-old I won four, placed twice, and was out of the money in one race. My earnings that year were $267,740.

Now it became not so much a question of how many more races I would win or lose, but the total of my earnings. Kelso's record was $1,977,896. If I could win just $82,000 more, I'd become the first horse to win $2 million. It was a tough decision. Maybe, my bosses thought, I could just enter a couple of races, take my shot, and if I made it, okay, and if I didn't, that was okay too. I didn't have to prove anything to anybody, not anymore.

So, early in June, I won a seven-furlong event

Forego at Belmont, winning his first race of the year as a seven-year-old by half a length (above). Forego as an eight-year-old, winning by a nose at Belmont (below). But the end was near for the great competitor.

Farewell to the fans. Forego is paraded out onto the track for his final appearance in September of 1978. As if to say, "So I'm retiring and it's about time. What's all the fuss about?"

120

at Belmont, and now I was just $39,000 behind Kelso. I tried again on July Fourth in the Suburban. By the end of the day it was all over for me and I knew it. The track was muddy, I was slow, and my legs were killing me. In a field of six I was fifth.

Miss Martha had a vet examine me, and the X rays showed them what was wrong. They held the dark picture against the light and they almost fainted when they saw that calcium deposits on the joint were forcing a bone out of place. They knew that if my ankle went it would not merely break, it would practically explode.

That was what had happened to Ruffian. Remember Ruffian? Frank Whiteley never forgot her. He had nightmares about that fantastic filly.

God knows what might have happened to him if I had gone out the same way.

In September of 1978 my New York fans said goodbye to me at the Belmont track. Well, let's say I was a very good extra, added attraction, because two other Thoroughbreds—hey, I love that word *Thoroughbred*—were about to meet up. I mean they were Triple Crown winners Affirmed and Seattle Slew. But I made the crowd happy. I tossed 'em a nod and a swish of my tail, and let them dream about a horse named Forego who won twenty-four stakes races.

Mrs. Martha Gerry said it all: "If I had three Triple Crown winners, I doubt that I should ever feel quite the same about any other horse."

RUFFIAN

Everybody in racing knows about Claiborne Farm. It's a big place, about five thousand acres, with trees and pasture and a whole lot of horses. The Hancock family owns Claiborne. The house they live in is over a hundred years old.

I was born at Claiborne in 1972. My sire was Reviewer, a pretty good horse. He'd raced thirteen times and won nine. My mother was Shenanigans, and she wasn't a bad runner, either. But my two grandfathers got most of the attention before I began racing. My father's father was Bold Ruler and mother's father was Native Dancer. That's a pretty good family tree.

The Hancocks didn't own me. I was the property of Mr. and Mrs. Stuart Janney. The Janneys owned Shenanigans, and they were also part owners of Reviewer, so the match between the horses was a natural. Where the Hancocks were concerned it was strictly business. They were breeders in my case, and when the foal was born they took care of it; they got the youngster "people-broken" and used to a saddle, ready to be track-trained. The Janneys figured I'd stay at Claiborne for a year or so, give or take a couple

The second leg up on the Filly Triple Crown. Ruffian sweeps to victory in the Mother Goose. Vasquez is in the saddle.

of months, and then I'd be turned over to Frank Whiteley, the Janneys' trainer.

Come to think of it, a name like Ruffian isn't proper for a filly. A ruffian is a boy, a rowdy, a roughneck. As a matter of fact, the Janneys once did own a colt named Ruffian, but they sold him, and rather than let the name go to waste they hung it on me.

Practically all young horses are frisky, especially Thoroughbreds. I was about normal. When the morning was cool I'd chase a bird, or run every which way and poke my nose where it hadn't been before, and then when the afternoon sun warmed the air I'd go looking for a shade tree, maybe crop a blade or two of grass and just hang out. I got bigger and fatter and sassier all the time. It was one terrific summer.

By the time summer ended I'd gone through all the usual stages, from weanling to yearling. I was introduced to a saddle and a rider, I got a bit for my mouth and a surcingle [or girth]—that's the strap that goes under the belly. Then I was taken to Xalapa Farms, which is the training area of Claiborne Farm.

I had already begun to look like a racehorse, now I had to learn how to act like one, and Claiborne was not the place for that. I was shipped out to the training stable in Camden, South Carolina, and it was there that I began to think that maybe Ruffian was always meant to be my name. I fell in with three tough hombres.

First, take my groom, Dan Williams. Dan was

tough because he had to be. Some years back his wife died and left him with four kids to raise. Somehow, with help from his relatives and friends, he got through the bad time, but he had his heartaches. One of his boys was killed in Vietnam.

I was Dan's horse from the beginning. He didn't take any guff from me. Like I'd take a nip at his rump—don't all young horses do that to a groom?—and he'd shove my head away, not hard, but a real solid push. But he knew how to get around me too. He'd scratch me under the chin and look me in the eye. I guess I became his private girl friend.

Then there was Frank Whiteley, my trainer. All trainers have been around horses most of their lives, and so had Frank. In fact it could be said that Frank Whiteley's job was so important to him that he thought nothing of missing dinner or a night's sleep, because his horses came first and everything else was strictly out of the money. But Frank was different in one respect. He never jumped to conclusions about a horse, he always reserved judgment. In his mind some horses were smart and others dumb, some liked to run and others took the bit only when the jockey went to the whip, some were born winners and others forever also-rans. I had to prove myself before he would agree I had possibilities.

The third tough guy was my jockey, Jacinto Vasquez. That was one feisty little man. He was a street kid from Panama, a fist fighter with a temper like a box of matches looking for a stray spark. He was always getting himself suspended for one reason or another. In fact Jacinto was my jockey in eight of my ten races, and the only reason he missed two outings was because he'd been suspended.

I remember the first time he rode me. It was just a practice session. Jacinto wanted to see how fast I was. I showed him. For about a quarter of a mile I tore up the track, and when he tried to rein me in I almost unhinged his fingers. When I stopped he got off, looked at me, and started to smile. He said to Frank Whiteley, "I never ran a horse like that."

Training was boring and I thought it would never end, but at last Frank found the right spot for me. It was a five-and-a-half-furlong job for fillies at Belmont. The crowd had never heard of me, so they looked at the other entries, fillies like Alpin Less and Garden Quad and Suzest. It turned out that they weren't competition, just opponents.

I broke a little slow—after all, it was my maiden race—but everything changed in a finger-snap. I took the lead and began to lead my own private charge; the rest of the field never had a chance. I was past the half-mile marker in forty-five seconds and the crowd couldn't believe what was happening. I kept pulling away, and crossed the finish line fifteen lengths ahead. No colt and no filly had ever equaled my time, which was sixty-three seconds flat for the five-and-a-half-furlong distance.

After that I began attracting attention. It wasn't hard. When a horse wins that big, people notice. After the next four races the horse players were ready to take me out to dinner and a movie if I'd go.

I made a shambles out of the Fashion Stakes at Belmont. I won that one by six and three-quarter lengths. Next came the Astoria Stakes at Aqueduct, and I guess other filly owners wanted no part of me, because only three other horses were entered. I took that one by nine lengths. I didn't set a record in that race, but I was only four seconds off the mark that had been set eleven years earlier by Raise a Native. After that came the Sorority at Monmouth Park, which I won by only two and a half lengths, followed by the Spinaway Stakes at Saratoga. There were thirteen lengths between me and the runner-up in that outing. I set new stakes records in both races.

I wasn't the only horse that had won five in a row. A colt named Foolish Pleasure had the same record. About then the people who write about racing in the newspapers began to compare us, and they began to toss around the idea of a match race between Foolish Pleasure and me. After all, we were both two-year-olds, both undefeated. Maybe it sounded good on paper, but Frank Whiteley wanted no part of it, not then anyway. He liked my chances against any horse, colt or filly, but he said I was still a frisky kid. Maybe he'd listen to the offer later and advise the Janneys one way or another. He was pointing me toward the $100,000 Frizette Stakes.

The way things turned out I never did make it to the Frizette. All of a sudden I got pretty sick. I ran a temperature, and the lower part of my left rear hoof felt achy and sore. Frank was worried about the fever, and when he saw me stumble and favor my leg he got very nervous. Even after the fever went down he called the vets and scratched me from the Frizette. They X-rayed the hell out of my leg.

The trouble didn't show up right away, but those vets were like eagles looking for anything that wasn't exactly right. They went over those X rays again and again until they finally spotted the trouble. I had a hairline fracture in the lower right pastern. That's a bone just above the hoof.

When a horse has a bum leg it becomes a complicated job to fix it. People who don't know much about horses can't understand all the reasons; they think a broken bone is a broken bone. They couldn't be more wrong. In order to get a handle on why a bone gets broken without the horse's falling down, they should study a Thoroughbred's gait.

When a Thoroughbred is running, for just a fraction of a second its whole body is up off the ground. When it comes down only one hoof at a time touches the ground. For that fraction of a clock-tick all the weight is on that hoof, maybe a thousand or twelve hundred pounds of horse. It's a jolt through every bone in that leg each time it hits the grass or dirt.

When a person breaks a leg it's put in a cast. That happens with a horse, too, but that's the only similarity.

A person can walk around with a crutch. Can a horse walk around with a crutch? End of joke.

How about a horse in a wheelchair while the bone is knitting? That's as funny as the first joke.

Okay then, just lie down in the hay and take it easy. A horse can't do that very long. It's bad for the circulation, it cramps the heart and lungs, muscles lose tone, and above all, waste builds up

in the body, which can be very dangerous. It's possible for a horse to get real sick just from being down on its side too long.

So, if the break isn't too serious, the best cure is a cast and as little movement as possible. The vets have become pretty good with casts and slings, although a lot depends on the horse. Some horses don't like any kind of cast at all; they try to kick it off and the leg gets hurt all over again. Slings are okay, but the horse can't be left hanging all the time. Remember how much a horse weighs. It has to get off the sling for a while at least.

I was lucky. The vets put what's called a "jelly cast" on the leg. That kind isn't stiff; it's almost like a support bandage, and can be changed every day or so without fuss. It didn't bother me. But for a few months I couldn't race. Foolish Pleasure did. He won twice more before his owners called it a year.

It wasn't much of a winter. I couldn't run because of my leg, and I didn't eat much because Frank was afraid I'd get hog-fat through lack of exercise. He cut down on oats and I filled up with hay, which is okay but doesn't have much taste.

Although I hadn't run for a few months it was nice to know the racing world didn't forget me. I won the Eclipse Award as the best two-year-old filly of the year. The same prize for two-year-old colt went to Foolish Pleasure. That started the talk about a match race all over again.

At last I was healed and shipped to Camden again for new training. Frank set up the "Portapaddock" again and I began to have a little fun after being so quiet for a few months. A Portapaddock is just what it sounds like, a portable paddock. Frank figures out how much room I'll need to run around, then he encloses it with a high fence. The fence comes in sections, so it isn't hard to put up or take down, to make the area it encloses larger or smaller.

I drove Frank and the stablehands crazy. For instance, I'd dig a hole somewhere; they would find it and fill it in. I'd dig the hole again. They filled it in again.

Or, I'd be standing around like an innocent baby, and all of a sudden I'd make a dash right for the fence. Just when it looked like I'd bash my fool head against the fence and break my neck, I'd veer off and swish my tail. Maybe it wasn't so funny to Frank, but there's not a lot of games a horse can play in a small area.

Once I began running, everything else was forgotten. It was like I'd never been away, except that with another year tacked on I was bigger and stronger and faster than ever.

I started my comeback at Aqueduct and all the results were the same. There just wasn't a filly in my class. I won that by nearly five lengths, and a couple of weeks later it was the Comeley Stakes. It's hard to run when nobody is challenging, but I did my duty and won that race by eight lengths.

Now I was pointed toward three of the big races.

There are all kinds of Triple Crowns in horse racing. The big one in the United States, of course, is the Kentucky Derby-Preakness-Belmont. In England, it's the Two Thousand Guineas, the Epsom Derby, and the St. Leger. A few other countries probably have their own version, and there are a few states in America that have some kind of Triple. In New York they have their own version for fillies: the Acorn Stakes, the Mother Goose, and the Coaching Club American Oaks.

Meanwhile, Foolish Pleasure was running too. All he did was win the Kentucky Derby, and nobody can argue with that. He was the kind of

Ruffian going to the post and victory in the Comely Stakes. That's Vasquez in the saddle.

126

The start of something big. Ruffian near the starting gate for the start of the Acorn Stakes (above), the first leg of the filly's New York State Triple Crown. Ruffian won big with Vasquez up. And there's the third win in the Filly's Triple (right), a big victory in the Coaching Club American Oaks. Vasquez is her rider.

driving horse that just wouldn't quit; he'd run as long as there was still a piece of track ahead. The fans liked his style and I couldn't blame them. It looked like a match race had to happen, a race between horses who were considered the best two-year-old colt and the best two-year-old filly less than a year ago.

Personally, I always thought match races were silly. One race doesn't mean much, doesn't prove anything. A horse can feel out of sorts on any given day and not feel like running. Still, racing fans seem to like match races. Years ago an American horse named Zev, who won the Kentucky Derby, was matched against an English horse named Papyrus, who won the Epsom Derby. So Papyrus took a trip to the United States and got beat in the mud by five lengths. The last big American match race was maybe twenty years ago, That was between two very good colts named Nashua and Swaps, which was won by Nashua because he got away with early foot and held on.

But this match between Foolish Pleasure and me was different. First, it was a boy horse against a girl horse, and that alone was enough to spark a lot of conversation between horseplayers and their women. Even more important was the money put up by Belmont. The winner would get $225,000, the loser would take home $125,000; but if a horse didn't finish the race for any reason, that entry wouldn't get paid. The date was set for July 6.

As race time got closer the deep thinkers whose bible is the daily scratch sheet began calling the race a toss-up. Those who liked my chances pointed out that I was bigger and heavier than Pleasure and therefore possibly stronger. In another comparison, Pleasure and I had run on the same tracks, and distance for distance covered I had run a little faster. When anybody said that a colt could beat a filly, my backers said that wasn't so. For instance, a filly named Regret won the Derby in 1915. A filly named Priceless Gem beat Buckpasser when they were both two-year-olds. And that's not to mention a filly named Moccasin, who was so fast that some tracks

wouldn't accept any bets on her, regardless of the opposition.

But Foolish Pleasure had his fans. They said he ran against better competition, and that was true. They said nobody ever challenged me, and that was true too. They liked his chances when he began to boom down the stretch, because that colt loved to run as much as I did, and when two horses go head to head in that situation, it can be a joy to behold.

But I had never been beaten. Foolish Pleasure had lost his last two races. A colt named Master Derby beat Pleasure by about a length in the Preakness, and Avatar beat him by a neck in the Belmont Stakes. That didn't mean too much to his fans. Pleasure was still a great colt.

Probably the only person who had an idea which one of us was faster was Jacinto Vasquez. He had ridden us both. In fact, Jacinto was up on Pleasure when he won the Derby, and he'd ridden the colt in a lot of other races. Therefore, Jacinto had his choice of mounts. He could ride me, but he was also offered Foolish Pleasure.

Jacinto chose me. Does that tell you something? A very good jock named Braulio Baeza went aboard Pleasure.

Slips was at Belmont when Ruffian broke down. Evidently he was at the rail, not far from the spot where the tragic incident occurred. His notes recorded the event in detail.

It was raining a little the day of the race, but not enough to amount to anything. It was a pretty good track. Maybe fifty thousand fans came to see Ruffian go off the favorite. Everyplace you looked there were television cameramen.

Ruffian came out of the gate on the inside and veered even more toward the rail. Foolish Pleasure took a small lead, but coming into the chute they were about even, and at the three-eighths pole the filly started to pass the colt.

Then, Jacinto told me later, there was this loud POP like a twig snapped off the branch of a tree. Ruffian kept running a couple of steps and then began to hobble. Her head was bobbing up and down, out of control, she was in *agony,* scared. When Jacinto heard the sound, he was off Ruffian's back like a shot, grabbing at the reins, calling out to the filly. He was crying like a baby.

Ruffian's front hoof was turned up like the shoe on a fairy-tale elf; the leg was covered with her blood and dirt from the track. Pieces of shattered bone were sticking through her skin. She had run those final few strides *on her leg bone!*

People came running from everywhere. A horse ambulance drove onto the track. The fans were so quiet you could almost hear them breathing. A vet slipped a cast over the filly's leg, the kind that fills with air. Ruffian was pushed and shoved and muscled into the ambulance. The air cast filled with blood and a new one was slipped in place. The vet managed to sedate the filly.

X rays showed that Ruffian had broken both sesamoid bones in the leg. It was a delicate, complicated operation the vets performed, because bits of jagged bone had to be pulled out of the joint and tendons. A new kind of cast was fitted for the leg.

A crowd hung around the parking lot outside the hospital. There was only one way to know if the operation was a success, and that was to get Ruffian up on her legs. Finally, we learned, Ruffian came out of the anesthetic. She began to struggle, and she kicked out blindly in a panic. The cast on her leg slipped down and the bleeding began again.

On July 7, at 2:20 in the morning, a vet injected Ruffian with a massive dose of phenobarbital. She drifted away into peaceful sleep.

Ruffian lies buried near a flagpole at Belmont Park. When she was buried, her head was pointed toward the finish line.

AFFIRMED

I must have been a beautiful baby because I grew up to be such a gorgeous adult. That's not bragging, it's true. A horse is judged by its *conformation,* which, I guess, is about the same as "built." I've heard the grooms and stableboys talking when a very classy human filly passes by, and they all say, "Now there is somebody with a *build.*" Of course I'm not a filly, I'm a colt, but colts can be good-looking too. A very smart artist named Richard Stone Reeves is supposed to be some kind of judge of good-looking horses, and he said I was in a class with Buckpasser and Secretariat. He even painted my picture.

However, racing fans do not judge a horse by its great beauty, because beauty contest winners do not always pay off at the mutuel windows, only winners of races do. I paid off plenty.

Let's get my background out of the way first. I was born in 1975; my sire and dam were Exclusive Dancer and Won't Tell You. My owners are Mr. and Mrs. Louis Wolfson of Harbor View Farm, which is located in Florida. My trainer was Lazaro Barrera. My groom—why should I call him a groom when he was really my best pal, my buddy?—was Juan Alaniz. Once we got to know each other Juan and I were never apart. Some-

A sleek Affirmed getting ready for the Youthful event. Cordero is up.

times we even took an afternoon nap together in my stall. You might say we were *muy simpático.*

Even as a weanling and yearling I knew I was fast. Along with the other young horses at the farm I'd have some fun with short sprints, and I always ran away from them. I always loved to run. When I was taking my afternoon nap, the grooms said I would paw around in my sleep and wiggle my ears. Maybe I was dreaming I was in a race.

Basically I was a good kid, very neat and tidy. For instance, I never could stand to have saliva wetting my mouth, so after a workout I'd amble over to Juan and wipe my lips on his pants. Juan wasn't exactly thrilled the first few times I used his pants as a napkin, but after a while he got used to it, in fact he expected it. We considered that little ritual standard operating procedure, especially after a race. I'd meander into the winner's circle, look around for Juan, go right over to him, poke him in the belly with my muzzle and wipe my mouth on his pants. That's how it always was with Juan and me. He wouldn't let anybody else near me.

Then I was ready for racing as a two-year-old. I took my maiden race at Belmont Park, and then, at the same track, I won the five-and-a-half-furlong Hopeful Stakes. There was another entry in that race and I beat him. They said the horse wasn't feeling too well and that was why he didn't win. His name was Alydar. I didn't know it then, but I found out soon enough, that guy could run like he was spooked by a real ghost.

He caught up with me next time out, in the Great American Stakes. He beat me by plenty. It was only my third race and already I knew what it was to lose. And I had no excuse, either. Alydar ran faster than I did. I had to get even with him, because as good as Alydar was, I knew I was better.

They say there's nothing like a change of scenery to cure the blues. I was shipped to California and entered in the Hollywood Juvenile. I won by seven lengths. It was easy to see I was feeling better, so they sent me back east to run in the

Sanford Stakes at Saratoga. That was where I met Stevie Cauthen.

So far I had run with different jockeys—Bernie Gonzalez, Angel Cordero and, in California, Laffit Pincay. Cordero was supposed to ride me, but he promised to get aboard a good new colt named Darby Creek Road, so there was Cauthen ready to go.

It was a little surprising at first. Cauthen had made a rep for himself as a young "pheenom." He was still a raw teenager, yet that boy really knew how to ride. He wasn't too sure how to

Affirmed showing off his magnificent conformation, just prior to winning the Sanford Stakes. Cauthen is high in the saddle.

handle me at first, but he caught on fast. In that race Stevie got squared away, and took me right down the middle of the track for a win by almost three lengths. A pretty good horse named Tilt Up chased me home.

But we weren't about to leave Saratoga just yet. The Hopeful Stakes were coming up and Alydar was among the entries. I had a score to settle with him. So far I had beaten him one time and he had one win over me.

It wasn't so easy. Alydar gave me all the fight I could handle. We were both laying back and Stevie was giving me a beautiful ride. Going into the homestretch I took a small lead, but Alydar made his move too, and we battled it out stride for stride. At the end I was ahead by half a length, and nobody could say that Alydar wasn't up to par.

So now I had a one-win edge over Alydar. We bumped heads again in the seven-furlong Futurity Stakes at Belmont. Nobody at the track will ever forget that race.

Out of the gate a long shot named Rough Sea took the lead, but I was right on his tail along the rail, and Alydar was there too on the outside. As we went into the far turn Stevie nudged me into the lead, still on the rail, but Alydar was right alongside me, so close our bodies were almost touching. We fought it out into the stretch and then Alydar began to move ahead. When two horses are so close, the one on the outside might have a little better chance. I guess it's because most jocks are right-handed and that's the whip hand. I was too close to the rail, so Stevie couldn't transfer the whip to his other hand, and besides, Stevie never was one for belting a horse on the flank. But I knew what had to be done and so did Stevie. He tapped me a few on the neck and I began to win back the lead, inch by inch, until I was ahead by a head. But even one or two strides from the line, Alydar wouldn't quit. He gave one more lunge forward, but I hung on, and I won by a nose, although I wasn't sure of the outcome until the tote board said so.

Now it was Affirmed leading Alydar, three wins to one, but I didn't have time to gloat. A month later we were both geared up for the one-mile

Champagne Stakes, again at Belmont. Alydar had a new rider, although the reason was a mystery. Eddie Maple had done all any rider could do, but maybe Alydar's trainer thought it was time for a change because I'd beaten Alydar twice in a row. His new jockey was Jorge Velasquez, as smart a horse handler as ever shoved a boot into a stirrup.

I lost that race and it was my own fault. It looked to me like Darby Creek Road was the one to beat. Alydar wasn't around for the moment and I like to run against a horse no matter what his name is. Maybe I was fooling around too much. Out of nowhere Alydar came shooting by on the outside and blasted home to win by a length and a quarter. Stevie knew what happened. He said, "My horse had plenty left, but he was so busy playing games with Darby Creek Road he never even saw Alydar until it was too late."

So now the count read Affirmed three wins, Alydar two, with the eight-and-one-half-furlong Laurel Futurity coming up for another go-round. By that time everybody who had ever consulted a form chart was talking about us, the pair of two-year-olds who kept beating each other. The older geezers recalled the duels between Equipoise and Twenty Grand more than forty years earlier, and the battles between Nashua and Summer Tan over twenty years ago. They also remembered individual thrillers, like the Woodbine Stakes when Kelso and Gun Bow had it out almost like it was a private race, and the gut-busting showdown between Jaipur and Ridan in the Travers. Alydar and I each had loyal fans, but both sides agreed that when we ran, we put on a hell of a show.

Alydar's trainer, a crafty gent named John Veitch, said he knew how his horse would win. "You don't want to dog him and wear him down," he said. "You want to sneak up on Affirmed."

Barrera must have thought Veitch was pretty shrewd, because what he said made sense. "Alydar won't sneak up on my horse again," Barrera said. "In the Champagne, Stevie was between horses when Alydar made his move. After Alydar took the lead, he didn't gain any more ground."

Stevie Cauthen had been to the wars too, and he had a good memory. He knew what happened when he took me inside and Alydar almost crowded me off the track. He knew Alydar could come with a rush, especially when I wasn't looking. He said, "I won't be between horses this time. Affirmed will run where he can see Alydar all the time. I've got the outside position and I plan to keep it that way."

It was a dandy race. When we broke from the gate, a horse named Star de Naskra jumped out in front, but I took the lead away at the far turn, and Star began to fade. Like everybody figured, it was a two-horse race, me and Alydar, and maybe I had the lead, but it wasn't by much. I couldn't shake Alydar and I was running my heart out. But so was he. At the eighth pole we were still driving, and my lead was never the same two strides in a row; first it might be a neck, then a nose. But that was it. Alydar never did catch me. I won by a neck. The third horse was ten lengths back.

Stevie was smiling. He said, "He always had a little bit more up his sleeve. He just likes running with Alydar." Sure, maybe I did like it, but later I kept thinking there must be easier ways to make a living than running against that horse. And I was sure I hadn't seen the last of him.

All in all it had been a pretty good year for this two-year-old. I'd run nine times and won seven, with both my losses in races against Alydar. Now it was time to rest and have a few siestas with Juan.

Laz Barrera wanted me to begin my three-year-old running in California, so that's where I was shipped. In a way his plans backfired at first. California always brags about nice, sunny weather, but when it came time for me to start training, I never saw so much rain in my life. The track was fine if you happen to like big oval swimming pools, which I do not. Laz was afraid I'd step out on the track and sink down in the mud up to my surcingle, so a lot of my time was spent in the barn, where it was reasonably dry. Laz planned on about sixty days to get me ready

for my first race, but now he had to cut training time down to forty-five days. He was worried sick that I might become overtrained, so when I did run—and I did win—he backed me down just a little bit. It was very confusing, and I don't confuse very easily.

I started out at Santa Anita, and the race was just six and a half furlongs, which was practically a sprint. No problem there. But then my training eased off, and in the mile-and-a-sixteenth San Felipe Handicap, it was all I could do to come out ahead, and the opposition wasn't that great. The truth is, I didn't know how I felt, except that there was a job to be done and I did it.

To make matters worse, I had to go into the Santa Anita Derby without Stevie. The kid got himself suspended for what they called "careless riding." Well, at least I didn't have to be introduced to a total stranger, because it was Laffit Pincay up, and I always liked him. It was a very nice run. I beat a horse named Balzac by eight lengths.

My final California outing was the Hollywood Derby, and a lot of people began to wonder if Laz Barrera had lost his marbles. After that would come the Kentucky Derby, and the superstitious horseplayers (are there any other kind?) couldn't understand what Laz was doing. Because, since the Hollywood Derby was started, no horse in history had ever won both the Hollywood and Kentucky.

You want tradition? Before Churchill Downs the horse goes into the Blue Grass Stakes at Keeneland, or maybe the Wood Memorial. Alydar won the Blue Grass by more than thirteen lengths, and a horse named Believe It took the Wood.

But maybe Laz wasn't so dumb. He explained his thinking: "I don't like to take chances shipping the horse around the country. And there was a very good chance to win $250,000 in the Hollywood Derby."

Still, I couldn't understand the instructions he gave Stevie. Laz figured we stood to win easy, unless I got blocked out or I fell down. He wanted Stevie to take me up front and stay there. And then he said something to Stevie that made me sad and angry. He told the kid, "I think we've been babying him too much. Today let him get used to being whipped."

I did take the lead. I almost ran a horse named Radar Ahead into the ground. I don't run a good race without a horse to challenge, and there wasn't anybody even close, but Stevie had to follow orders even if he didn't enjoy going to the whip. He hit me some smart shots. He hit me an even dozen times. What the hell was the point? I had the race won, and I wasn't about to break a leg setting a new Hollywood Derby record. So I didn't pour it on, and I won by only two lengths.

Stevie thought I was only playing. I suppose I was, a little, but I don't think he had to tap me so hard or so often, not when I was ahead. Come to think of it, I did deserve better treatment. By then I had earned more than $700,000 which, at the time, was more money than any horse ever earned before the Kentucky Derby.

But there was always the shadow of Alydar staring at me. That son of a gun was running wild, and he was doing it in races that seemed to matter more to the public than mine did. He opened his season with a win at Hialeah, and then he won again in the Flamingo Stakes. In the Florida Derby at Gulfstream, Alydar had to fight off a charge from Believe It, and he did, and Believe It won the Wood Memorial later. Alydar topped it off with the Keeneland win and he was ready for Churchill Downs.

It rained off and on for a few days before the Derby, but by race time the track was fast. Someone said later that Alydar didn't like the track, but the way that colt ran, the track could have been paved with cement or under a foot of water, it wouldn't have made that much difference. Give the horse his due, he knew how to run.

There were no surprises. Raymond Earl took the early lead and Sensitive Prince came up too, but there are always front-runners, pace setters to kill off the late chargers—if they can. I was running a nice third. It stayed that way for a while, with Alydar far back, but trust that horse to drive when the race is pounding down. He began to edge up on the field.

Going into the top of the final turn it was a newcomer forging ahead, Believe It—naturally!—and I was dogging his heels, with Alydar coming fast. I know Believe It gave the race all he had, but he got tired, and Alydar closed in on him. Then it happened.

Alydar bumped Believe It. Not a hard bump, maybe not even enough to throw any horse off stride, but when something like that happens there's a swerve and maybe a fraction of a second is lost. Stevie must have sensed we had the race won because he hit me a couple of times to make sure, and I copped the Duke by a length and a half.

So now the score between second-place Alydar and first-place Affirmed stood five wins to two.

The Preakness was next. You know how some movie actors play the same kinds of parts again and again? That's how it was with all the races Alydar and I ever ran against each other. It was like somebody wrote out a script and we ran the way the director wanted us to. It might just as well have been a match race as far as the other entries were concerned. At the head of the stretch I was leading, but that didn't mean anything, because Alydar began cutting into my margin. I wasn't about to give up the whole lead without a fight, but that horse kept coming, and I did just edge him out at the wire by a neck. Wow, that was close! But not as close as the Belmont turned out to be.

I'd beaten Alydar six out of eight, and maybe he should have lost heart by Belmont time, because a lot of other horses would have been sick of the sight of me. But not Alydar. I suppose with him each time out was a new day, and no matter how often I looked at him, he didn't get the message. Still, I wasn't feeling up to par for the race. I'd been running for a long time since I got back in action, six hard races in about four months. I'm sure Alydar also felt the strain, he hadn't been loafing around mooching into his dinner bucket. I think Stevie knew how we felt. He was afraid I might not have it left to give at the finish.

And yet, when we left the gate for that long

mile-and-a-half run, we were following the script after just four furlongs. There we were in a two-horse race, running almost side by side like we were buddies instead of rivals. By the time we were into the turn for home we were both laboring, but neither one of us would give in to the other. Alydar kept charging and charging, and he went into the lead just past the quarter pole. I was so tired I felt like dropping in my tracks, but something inside said I didn't dare quit. It looked like he had me at last. But there was an eighteen-year-old kid named Stevie Cauthen on my back, and he wouldn't let me lie down. He's not a whip boy, but he really let me have it—*slash!*

slash! slash! three times on my left hindquarter. He was talking to me, clicking his tongue, and Velasquez was yelling at Alydar, and we were dead even again. I could feel my ears flicker, just like in my dreams, and now we were less than fifty yards from the finish. Somehow I got my head out in front, and I kept it there as we went under the wire.

Stevie said, "He was so tired I almost felt him take a huge breath at the top of the stretch when we switched leads. He has amazing determination."

Amen and thanks, Stevie. And the same to you.

Victory at Belmont, and the Triple Crown! The charging Alydar almost caught Affirmed at the finish. The photo shows how close they were. Cauthen is Affirmed's rider.

Beating Sensitive Prince by a long nose in the Jim Dandy Stakes at Saratoga. It was a come-from-behind win for Affirmed and Cauthen.

I took a little rest after my Triple Crown. How long can any horse run after seven straight wins with no time out for a breather? My next outing was the Jim Dandy Stakes at Saratoga, and Alydar wouldn't be around for it. That was probably just as well. We'd both had enough of each other, at least for the time being. The horse I had to look for was Sensitive Prince, mostly I guess because I was giving away nine pounds.

I wasn't too thrilled with the track. It was still a little mushy from old rains, and I didn't get my sea legs until we were coming around the turn. By then I was in full stride, but I was also seven lengths behind.

Everybody hears about horses that come from behind and win by an edge. It's nothing new in racing, but the folks who line the rail enjoy the sight, even if they've seen that kind of finish a hundred times. At the furlong pole I was still four lengths out, but I knew I could catch Sensitive Prince. I sure did, by half a length. That was my eighth straight win.

Alydar did show up for the Travers Stakes, and everybody was expecting another nail biter, but it didn't turn out that way. First, Stevie wasn't running with me. He was still getting over a fall earlier in the month and he wasn't up to it. It was okay with me that Pincay took the leg up, because we always got along, but nobody ever handled me the way Stevie did. The race was a letdown. I had been forced far to the outside, and when Pincay tried to cut back in I gave Alydar a bump that was so hard Velasquez was almost knocked out of the saddle. I crossed by two lengths, but track officials aren't dummies, they have eyes, and I was disqualified. All I can say is, sorry about that. It gets close working inside, outside, and between horses, and bumps come with the territory, but it wasn't intentional. What was the point, especially when Pincay and I both knew we'd lose.

I didn't know it then, but that was the last time Alydar and I ever went head to head in a race. The final count read Affirmed seven wins and Alydar three. Hey, I'm not saying I was that much better than him, only that I was better. Just look at the way he beat me:

The first time, in my third race, he won fair and square; he surprised the hell out of me with his speed and guts. The next time he won I was lollygagging after Darby Creek Road and Alydar just plain outsmarted me. That was strictly legit and I should have known better. The last time it was a bump, and there are no excuses. The race might have been one of those usual thrillers, but it didn't happen.

The Marlboro Cup at Belmont was next, and in that one I was scheduled to run against Seattle Slew among others. The Slew had won the Triple the year before, and hadn't run too much since. Was I afraid of him? Hell, no! I just wasn't feeling too well the day of the race. Not just tired from racing eight times, but sort of sick. It was a peculiar feeling because I'd never had a sick day in my life. My throat was sore, like I'd swallowed a rosebush, thorns and all.

The race was over right after the gates opened. Slew took a lead of three lengths and that was the way it ended. Slew didn't break any records, he didn't have to.

They found out the trouble the next day. I'd picked up a virus somewhere which left my throat full of blisters. It wasn't a dangerous thing, just uncomfortable. The same thing happened to a lot of horses in England, and it took them three months to get well.

Now I knew what it was to lose two in a row. Juan and I weren't happy. I remember the two of us lying down in my stall. It was dark and I had my head on his shoulder; he didn't say anything at all.

I still had another crack at Seattle Slew in the Jockey Club Gold Cup, and maybe I could have

won it, only my luck was even worse that time out. Know what happened? My saddle slipped. It was all but sitting on my ribs and Stevie was almost on the track, but he got off in a hurry. It happened going into the stretch, and there were three of us who might have won it: Slew, Exceller, or me. It turned out that Exceller took it at the wire. That was the only time in my life I finished out of the money. Nobody could put the blame on me. I have never heard of a horse who tightened a saddle on his own back.

My season was over, and so was my status as a three-year-old. I should have been happy because I was voted Horse of the Year, but I wasn't. Too many people were saying that the "other" Triple Crown champion, Seattle Slew, was a better horse.

I don't know what came over me then. I was bigger, I felt stronger, and I even felt smarter. Maybe it was experience, or it could be that I didn't know if I was good, better, or best. I'd finished as a three-year-old on a downer with three straight losses, although it could be said that all three were flukes. One loss was on a bump, the other because I just plain felt sick, and the third was a slipped saddle.

Even Stevie and I felt differently toward each other. I used to love Stevie—I still did—but it wasn't quite the same thing anymore. I wasn't his "kid brother," I'd grown up. It's like you leave your friends of childhood behind. Was Stevie too easygoing for me now? I wasn't sure. He went to the whip only when he had to, and I liked that in him, but I began to realize love of running wasn't enough anymore. Maybe I had to be motivated.

That could be the reason I returned to action and lost the Malibu Stakes. In fact I was third behind Little Reb and Radar Ahead, and they were very fast horses. I could have beaten them the year before, but now I just didn't run. The same thing happened in the San Fernando Stakes. I finished three lengths behind Radar Ahead.

My owners had a hard decision to make, and they did it, but they were sad. Stevie Cauthen was out as my rider and Laffit Pincay was in. Five straight losses said so.

Pincay turned me around, all right. It was in

Victory in the two-mile Jockey Club Gold Cup. Affirmed held off charges by Spectacular Bid and Coastal. A mud-splotched Pincay was aboard.

the Charles H. Strub Stakes at Santa Anita, and I was leading by two lengths approaching the turn for home. Pincay went to the whip, and he fetched me a crack that stung like a hornet had broken ground in my hide to build a new nest. Talk about motivation, that was enough for me. I bolted ahead and won by ten lengths.

The Santa Anita Handicap came up next, and Pincay did it all over again, same place on the track with almost the same results. I broke the track record, 1:58³/₅ for the ten furlongs. I practically ran away from a great horse named Tiller;

it was a win by four and a half lengths. Funny, but tied for fourth was Exceller, the horse that beat Seattle Slew in the Jockey Club Gold Cup.

Pincay had found the right road with me. In the California Stakes I led all the way and won by five lengths. Upcoming was the Hollywood Gold Cup, and if I won that I'd make my owners multimillionaires, the very first in racing.

It wasn't going to be as easy as a morning workout. The horse I figure I had to beat was Sirlad, a tough *paisano* who won the Italian Derby, and I've heard European horses also know what to do on a track. Some students of horses said he was the very best horse to come from Italy since Ribot, and I've heard of Ribot but had never seen him run. On the other hand there wasn't much point in seeing Ribot run. He went to the post sixteen times and he won sixteen times. That's about as good as any horse can get. Even being compared with Ribot showed that Sirlad wasn't just a bowl of pasta.

Now that was a tough grind. I had to carry 132 pounds, and also, everything they said about Sirlad was true. It wasn't just a matter of running faster, I had to break that tourist's spirit, and I doubt that I did. Pincay damned near tore my hide with his whip, and like it or not, that's how it had to be. He belted me eight times, and that wasn't too often, because it was all I could do to win by three-quarters of a length.

You think the New York crowd was impressed? In a pig's potato! The last time they had seen me I was a loser, and people from New York are worse than people from Missouri, you've always got to prove things to them. Everybody was talking about a horse named Spectacular Bid, who had won the Derby and Preakness, but lost the Belmont to another speedster, named Coastal.

In a way the attitude of a horseman named Grover "Buddy" Delp was understandable. He owned Spectacular Bid, and that was one good horse. When a colt can win the Derby and Preakness, it's not like you're talking about a horse who pulls a hansom cab in Central Park. Delp was looking forward to the Marlboro Cup, where his entry would knock the stuffing out of me. Laz Barrera was too smart for Buddy. He scratched me from the Marlboro. Delp demanded to know why.

Laz's answer was simple. Why run me in the Marlboro over nine furlongs and give Spectacular Bid nine pounds when we could meet in either the Woodward Stakes or the Jockey Club Gold Cup over twelve furlongs at weight-for-age? Sure, the handicappers liked my chances, or they wouldn't have saddled me with nine extra pounds, but Spectacular Bid wouldn't be facing Affirmed in the Marlboro.

So Spectacular Bid did win the Marlboro by five lengths, and that only added fuel to the fire that Delp started. Delp sure was a rare one. He tried everything but a duel with swords to get me together with Spectacular Bid. He said things like, "I'd love my horse to meet up with Affirmed—if only I could get Affirmed out of the barn." And he called Laz "coward" when Barrera walked into the paddock area.

That was why the Woodward was so important for me. If I lost, Delp could say I was a plater, because his horse had won his race. And I was going to meet some horses who—like they say—left the issue in doubt.

First there was a three-year-old named Czaravich, who won five of his last six starts including the Jerome Handicap. Czaravich was the son of Nijinsky, who didn't run in America but had won eleven of thirteen overseas. Another contender was Coastal, who beat Spectacular in the Belmont. Also, there was a threat from a nice horse named Mister Brea. To cap off everything, the track was a little muddy.

The gates were sprung and we went at it. Mister Brea took the early lead, I was second, Czaravich was third, and in fourth spot was Coastal. So far it was according to form.

We held position along the backstretch and went into the turn. Suddenly Czaravich moved past me and I was third, and then Coastal charged ahead and I was fourth. The mud was flying all over everybody, but I still hadn't made my run. Coming out of the turn the time had come, and damned if I didn't show everybody who was boss! I shot in between Czaravich and Mister Brea and now only Coastal was up front. He was no problem, I knew that. I ran away from the Belmont winner and took the Woodward by two and a half lengths.

Finally came the race Buddy Delp—and racing fans too—were looking for. Okay, Mr. Delp, I will meet your pride and joy in the Jockey Club run, and after that maybe you'll shut up.

Delp did everything possible to make sure of a win—not that Spectacular Bid needed much done, because, I'll say it now, maybe his owner did brag, but he had a lot to brag about. Any-

Just an exhibition race before retiring to stud.

way, Delp called in Willie Shoemaker to ride him, and from what I understand, jocks don't come better than Willie the Shoe. Laz stuck with Pincay.

We came out of the gate in good shape, and I made for the lead around the first turn. I was ahead in the backstretch, and Spectacular Bid made his move then. I held him off.

Later, I heard what Laz said when we passed the half-mile mark: "When Affirmed breaks like that you can put the beans on the fire because you are going to eat for sure." I do like the way

141

Laz turns a phrase, but there was still a race to run, and I was entered, not my trainer.

In the backstretch Shoe gave Bid another shot at taking the lead, but I beat him back again. And yet Willie wouldn't give in; neither would Spectacular Bid. At the three-eighths pole they came at me again and he even almost tied me, but Pincay got me ahead into the lead. We almost got careless. Maybe Pincay and I thought Delp's horse had run his race. No way—not just yet.

Now, close to the rail, Coastal arrived. Hello, where did he come from? I had to get him off my tail, and I did. We were at the eighth pole, and Spectacular Bid took his last, best shot at me. Shoemaker took his mount to within half a length of me. Only now, for the first time in the race, Pincay went to the baton and he cracked me a smart one. That did it. I finished first by three-quarters of a length.

Make no mistake, that was a rough race. I had beaten back five separate challenges—four by Spectacular Bid and one by Coastal—and they were two of the best three-year-olds in the country. Pincay said it best though, when he told somebody, "Affirmed cannot be beaten. I don't know why they keep trying."

Buddy Delp was still hollering for a rematch, but the Wolfsons didn't care to bother with any more racing for me. I had nothing left to prove, even to the doubting Thomases from New York. I had won exactly $2,393,818. I had been syndicated for $400,000 a share, which now looked like a real bargain. I had won twenty-two out of twenty-nine races and finished out of the money only once, when my saddle slipped down. What I could look forward to now was going to stud at Spendthrift Farm.

That's how it ended. But the grooms say that when I'm taking my nap I sometimes wiggle my ears, almost like I was back on the tracks. Could be. Maybe I've been dreaming about running against Alydar again.

In another winner's circle in New York in 1979, Affirmed looks bug-eyed at the camera while his owners, Mr. and Mrs. Louis Wolfson, look pleased.

SEATTLE SLEW

Baby Huey! How I hated that name when I was growing up. Hated Mr. and Mrs. Turner, too, when they were breaking me in. They'd hit me, spur me, yell at me, "Not that way, Baby Huey, not that way!"

Baby Huey! I was a stumblebum and a joke. I would get my legs snarled up when I tried to do the simplest things—like getting out of a starting gate. I remember hearing a stablehand say, "What do you expect from a horse that cost only $17,500—Man o' War?"

My clumsiness wasn't all my fault. I was born with what some people call a slew foot. It wasn't really a slew foot and the word "slew," as you also must know, has nothing to do with my being named Seattle Slew. What I really had was a right front foot that curved slightly outward, not inward, like a true slew foot. I'm not a doctor, but that's what I've been told. Anyway, with my right front foot curving outward like that, I swayed toward the outside as I ran. My feet got tangled up and sometimes I fell down.

Once, after I took a tumble, all the grooms and exercise boys were laughing. I heard Mr. Turner say, "Well, at least he's big enough to pull a milk truck." At that time I would have been happy to pull anything to get away from training to be a

After winning the Belmont and the Triple Crown, Jean Cruguet smiles and Slew romps.

racehorse, because who likes people laughing at him? And I knew I could never be much of a racer.

All this happened on a farm in Maryland where Mr. and Mrs. Turner trained horses. I was sent to the farm by my owners, Karen and Mickey Taylor, who maybe you've met. I was born in 1974 in Kentucky and sold at an auction at Keeneland about a year later. Most of the people who came to Keeneland are millionaires, or at least that was what I heard from the other yearlings, but you know how little they know. Karen and Mickey came from way out in the state of Washington. Karen used to be a stewardess on planes. Mickey was in the lumber business, turning trees into sticks of wood, I have heard, but I don't think he was a millionaire until I came along.

With them at the Keeneland auction was a friend, Dr. Jim Hill, who is a vet. As the horses paraded by, Dr. Hill pointed at me and said to Mickey and Karen, "Buy that one." I don't know why he said it, and years later he told people he just liked my looks, even though I was sold for only $17,500 at an auction where other horses went for $200,000 and up.

That was the original Slew Crew, as they later called themselves. Mickey always said they were just lucky. But when they began to hear from Mr. and Mrs. Turner about what a stumblebum they had bought, they must have thought they were $17,500-unlucky.

A little while after I arrived at the farm in Maryland, I heard grooms laugh when I stepped out of my stall for a morning workout. I didn't understand at first why they laughed. Now I do. I looked funny. Years later I heard Mr. Turner tell a reporter: "He didn't look like a racehorse at all. There was a piece of him here and a piece of him there. He had a big body and a little pony's tail. His mind hadn't caught up with his body. We called him Baby Huey after the cartoon character who is always doing everything wrong."

That curved right foot was one reason the Taylors, Mickey and Karen, got me so cheap. I had a well-known sire, Bold Reasoning, who won eight of twelve races. His dad was Bold Ruler, who sired Secretariat, a horse I heard too much about during my career. My mom, My Charmer, wasn't well known, to be as kind as I can, and that brought down my price. I didn't look like much—my coat was a muddy brown, my feet so huge that I heard Mickey say they could use my shoes as anchors for battleships.

Many people think I got the last half of my name because of the so-called slew foot. I got the first half of my name because Mickey and Karen Taylor come from near Seattle. The Taylors wanted to give me a Florida name because Dr. Hill comes from there. A swamp in Florida is called a slew. Seattle Swamp didn't sound so sexy, I heard Karen say, so they decided to name me Seattle Slew.

By early 1976, when I was two years old, Mr. and Mrs. Turner began to think I might amount to something after all. My Baby Huey days were behind me.

Mr. Turner often rode me. Before Billy Turner got so tall and thin—he's built like an eighth pole and comes up to my ears—he rode those jumping horses in steeplechase races. He knew how to teach a frisky horse like me how to run under control, to jump through the hoops, as he once said to another rider. He told people I was a headstrong horse who liked to run.

Mr. Turner often rode me toward a big stone wall that towered over me. My heart pounded with fright. I feared he wanted me to jump over it like I was one of his old steeplechasers. I tried to veer away as we galloped closer and closer to the wall. When I veered, Mr. Turner rapped me

across my snout with a stick. That got my attention, let me tell you. My nose stung for days. I rode toward that wall, shaking a little, but I rode straight up to it.

Mr. Turner told people what he was doing to me. He said you should pick out something a horse doesn't want to do, then just make him do it. Then he knows who's boss. And I remember him saying often, "You'd rather have them hate the farm—discipline them there—but love the racetrack."

That spring of 1976 Mr. Turner took me up to the Belmont track in New York City. Right from my first gallop, I loved the track—its long turns, its pretty straightaways. Later on, Mr. Turner called it my "gym" and he said I had the home-court advantage whenever I ran at Belmont. The home-court advantage, I think, has something to do with that game of basketball I see the stable-hands play, right?

We worked out at Belmont in the mornings all that summer, me and Mike Kennedy, my exercise boy. Mr. Turner told Mike that I was so eager to run, I might hurt myself. He said that my biggest problem was learning how to relax. "He's just a hell of a lot of horse who wants to run," he said to Mike. That gave Mike an idea.

Mike would walk me slowly out of the stall before the workout. He'd stop me and he'd talk to people at the other stables. He'd walk me slowly around the paddock. And all the while, I'm straining to get out on that track and just fly.

And when we were flying, it would be for no more than a quarter of a mile. Then Mike would rein me in and we'd go from a breeze to a light gallop. They took no chances on my hurting my young legs.

Mike walked me back to my stall on a different route than the one we'd taken to the track. Mike told a friend of his that Mr. Turner thought I got too rambunctious and playful when I knew exactly what was going on around me. He said they tried to keep me confused.

That Mr. Turner, he knew us racehorses better than we knew ourselves. Once I heard him tell Mike that about once a month he walks through his shed row of horses, the ones he's training.

They see him coming, they snort and rear, these horses he's been hitting on the nose for the last month. They lunge at him, they bite him on his leather jacket as he goes by. "All they want," he told Mike, "is a bite out of the boss." He said it made them feel cockier and braver.

He was right. Whenever I chewed on that thick jacket of his, I always felt a lot less the Baby Huey, a lot more the horse that could be a champion.

I had yet to run a race when we went north to Saratoga. But I hurt my leg being playful in my stall one morning, and never did race there. I had some fast workouts, though. After one workout, I heard later, a writer named Red Smith said I'd put every stopwatch in upstate New York out of whack.

At Saratoga I met Jean Cruguet, who would be my rider for nearly all my races. He once watched me run during a workout, then went back to the jocks' room. He heard a bunch of riders talk about a horse named For the Moment, who'd won a string of races. Jean said, "There's a horse who hasn't even run yet who's a better horse than For the Moment." Now that's what I call a horse picker.

Back we went to Belmont. By now so many people had heard of my Saratoga workouts that I went off in my first race, in a field of twelve, as the favorite. I won by five lengths.

Coming up at Belmont was the big race for two-year-olds—the Champagne Stakes. I'd raced twice by now, won twice. Mr. Turner decided to enter me in the Champagne, which was unusual. "How often does a horse win the Champagne after only two starts?" Mr. Turner said. Still, he said, it was time for me to start to run against the big boys.

For the Moment started in the Champagne against me. For the Moment had won four of six races. I won by nine lengths. That was my last race as a two-year-old. I'd won all three and I must have looked good winning them—I was picked as the two-year-old Horse of the Year.

Mr. Turner took me to Florida where, he said, I could roll in the sand if I wanted to. He told Mickey, Karen, and Dr. Hill that he wanted me to take it easy. He believed that two-year-olds have to be babied along for the three-year-old Triple Crown. He was willing to risk that I'd come to Churchill Downs as a short horse—a horse that couldn't weather the Derby distance of a mile and an eighth. He said he'd rather see me short for the Derby than long. Sure, he said, a horse could win the Triple Crown but then be so worn out he'd break down and never win again. He said that happened to more good three-year-olds than a lot of trainers were willing to admit. They couldn't admit it because then they'd get into trouble with owners anxious to win Triple Crowns.

Come the spring of 1977, though I had raced only twice in Florida, winning both times, I was the favorite to win the Derby. Mr. Turner said I would race only one more time before the Derby—in the Wood Memorial at Belmont.

Boy, did he hear the hoots! How could I go the Derby distance after only three races? For sure, I was a short horse.

I won the Wood by three and a half lengths. I had won six straight races. I went to Churchill Downs as the first undefeated horse since Majestic Prince arrived there in 1969 and got beat.

Was anyone impressed? Not so you'd notice. I heard one groom say to another, "What do you think will happen when someone catches up with Slew and asks him the question?"

My groom didn't answer. I knew what the question was. We've both run a mile. There's an eighth to go. We're both exhausted. Which one of us will quit first? That's the question.

I heard a jockey, Angel Cordero, put the question another way. He said one day to Jean Cruguet, "Seattle Slew is like a boxer who has never been hit hard. You have to wonder what will happen when someone throws hard punches at him."

At Churchill Downs Mr. Turner heard ten times a day that he had a short horse. He shrugged. He told Karen and Mickey not to worry, that he knew what he was doing. But I could see from the way that they looked at each other, they were worried. Mr. Turner was worried. He'd always been tall and thin. Now he had the look of

Slew, magnificently slick, comes onto the track at Aqueduct for a workout in 1976, when he was named the two-year-old Horse of the Year.

someone who hadn't slept well. I was his first Derby horse. He knew people would say he'd botched the job if I didn't win.

People expected me to win, despite all the talk about my being short. I heard later that more money was bet on me at the track [slightly more than $1 million] than on any horse in the previous 102 Derbys.

I had heard grooms say that the Derby was like a circus. I have never been to a circus, but they must be noisy affairs if they're anything like a Derby. When we got to the paddock area, people swarmed around me. They grabbed at me, patted my flanks, and flashed light bulbs in my face. When we came out for the post parade, the band blared so loud my ears rang. I couldn't hear Jean, in the saddle, as he shouted to a rider next to him.

I was the fourth horse into the gate. I had to stand for about two minutes while the handlers got everyone else in. The wait turned me jittery. When the bell went off and the gate shot up, I was startled. My head jerked sideways and glanced off the side of the stall door. The knock cut my mouth and blood flowed from it all during the race.

For a moment the blow stunned me. I lunged out of the gate and stumbled, almost heaving Jean out of the saddle. The thirteen other starters flew away from me while my brain spun.

148

Jean steadied me. I took off after that long line of horses. I stampeded by two horses and side-swiped Bob's Dusty, bouncing him a half-dozen yards to his right. And amid all the screaming of the jocks, the whinnying of the horses, the roar of the hooves, and the clods of track bouncing off my head, do you know what crazy thought ran around my head? It was this: Mr. Turner saw me stumble and I knew he's thinking—Baby Huey's messed up again.

As we came to the first turn, I had broken through the wave of horses. I saw For the Moment lean into the curve, ahead of me by a couple of lengths. We stayed that way through the turn and into the backstretch. Jean had a good hold on me. If he ever lets go, I told myself, I can go by For the Moment whenever I like.

Jean thought the same thing. Later I heard him say that he looked back, saw nothing coming up, and decided to bide his time in passing For the Moment until the stretch.

We came around the far turn and Jean let loose his hold. I shot right by For the Moment, who I could see and hear was laboring. A moment later I heard hooves coming closer and so did Jean. Run Dusty Run and Sanhedrin roared by For the Moment and set their sights on me.

Jean rapped me with the stick a half-dozen times to let me know something was coming. I don't mind that kind of message. I don't have eyes in the back of my head. And a jock can't send you a letter to let you know of trouble coming from behind.

But I had heard this trouble. I drove for the wire and went under a length and a half ahead of Run Dusty Run.

I had won seven straight races. I had won the first crown of the Triple Crown. Were racing people shouting out my greatness? Nope. They were saying—the Kentucky crowd anyway—that I wasn't as good as Secretariat.

Secretariat had been the last horse to win the Triple Crown [in 1973]. A guy named Eddie Arcaro—I had never heard of him but I heard Jean say that he'd once been a great jockey—this Arcaro, on TV, said that Secretariat was a great horse, while I was just one of the best of an or-

dinary bunch. Someone else wrote that the year's three-year-olds were a bunch of fat men racing each other at a company picnic.

I know why I heard all those knocks. Secretariat had just been sold to a syndicate for about $6 million and retired to stud. That was the most money ever spent up to then to buy a horse. Secretariat had been owned by Kentucky people. Now they saw this young Seattle couple, Mickey and Karen, buy a horse at auction and the horse looked like he might outshine Secretariat. How could people who weren't from Kentucky pick up a bargain-basement horse and say their horse was better than the horse the Kentucky people had just unloaded for $6 million? That wouldn't do. What would the people who paid the $6 million think? The Kentucky people had to put me down.

Mickey and Karen, though, got their time on TV. Karen had that shiny smile that airline people seem to be born with. She'd get in front of the cameras and tell some cute Baby Huey story about me. She told how she and Mickey had dug into their pockets for the $17,500 to buy me. Soon the newspapers called the Taylors and Dr. Hill the Slew Crew and the "people's owners." I was the "people's horse." That got the Kentucky people even madder.

We went to Pimlico to get ready for the Preakness. Mr. Turner still looked worried, but Karen, Mickey, and Dr. Hill were having a good old time, which was the way Mickey often put it. So far they had won a lot of money for their $17,500 [$376,000]. One morning I heard Mickey say to someone, "Did anyone get the license plate of that bottle of Jack Daniels that knocked me down last night?" I didn't know there were license plates on bottles, but all the stablehands thought what he said was very funny, although one said he couldn't afford Jack Daniels, whoever he is.

I got off with a sane and healthy start in the Preakness and ran away from the field. I liked what one writer put down in that magazine the grooms are always reading [*Sports Illustrated*]. The writer said that the closest horses to me were Iron Constitution, Run Dusty Run, Cormorant, and an English horse, J.O. Tobin, and I made them all took like Dasher, Prancer, and Vixen.

Later on, I heard from Mr. Turner that Mrs. Turner began to cry as I came down the stretch far in front. She was remembering the colt with the big head and the pony's tail and all those clumsy starts. "Baby Huey," she kept saying as she cried, "Baby Huey, my goodness, you turned beautiful."

Even a few Kentucky people said that maybe I just might be talked about with some respect. Jimmy Jones, the trainer at Calumet, which had saddled more Kentucky Derby winners than any other stable, came by one day to talk to Mr. Turner. He knew that people said I hadn't beaten anybody. "Well, they're right about that," Mr. Jones said. "He hasn't beaten anybody, he's beaten everybody."

We went up to New York and my home court for the Belmont Stakes. One day I heard a groom read from a newspaper the list of horses that had won the Triple Crown. There were nine—Sir Barton, Gallant Fox, Omaha, War Admiral, Whirlaway, Count Fleet, Assault, Citation, and Secretariat. I could become the tenth—and the only one that had never been beaten.

I had never seen so many people in my life when I came onto the track for the Belmont [more than seventy thousand]. Again, just as in the Preakness, I got away first and stayed there. In the backstretch, Run Dusty Run, who was all heart whenever I raced him, dashed up and came almost even. I lengthened my stride and he fell back, all done for the afternoon. Then came Sanhedrin and again I drew away.

The track was filled with the loudest roaring I had ever heard as I came down the stretch, all alone. Someone said later that I ran away from the pack as though the other horses were running in place. About a hundred yards from the wire, Jean stood up and whirled his stick and the roar grew louder. Why not? Nobody had done what I had done—gone unbeaten to win the Triple Crown.

Seattle Slew runs away from the field, Jean Cruguet's whip at rest, to win the 1977 Belmont Stakes.

In the winner's circle, Seattle Slew looks unusually humble as the crowd salutes the tenth winner of the Triple Crown. Jean Cruguet flashes a triumphant salute, but the lanky trainer, Billy Turner, simply looks relieved.

I was the first auction-bought horse to win the Triple. People began to push money at Karen and Mickey Taylor, telling them to cash in their profit on that $17,500 they'd paid for me. Some Texans offered $14 million.

Racetracks sent offers of $100,000 purses. Mr. Turner said he didn't know when I would race again, but certainly not until the fall. I heard him tell one of the grooms, "Pull the shoes off him and let him roll in the sand. He's earned a long break from racing."

They never took the shoes off me and I raced within two weeks. Mickey got a call from Hollywood Park offering a $100,000 first prize in the Swaps Stakes. Meanwhile, Mickey had been making deals to turn out Seattle Slew T-shirts, cocktail glasses, and even something called Slew Rings. A Las Vegas hotel wanted to have a Seattle Slew Suite. And a big company [Xerox] would pay for me to pose for photos next to their machines.

Mr. Turner had tried to nurse me along to win the Triple Crown. He had risked that I might be short for those three races. Instead, I had come to each race in perfect shape. Now he wanted to do the same thing—take it easy on me—so I'd be fit for the fall. I heard from a groom that I'd be flying west.

I climbed up a ramp into a big room in the belly of a big plane. It was for me and my crew only. A groom gave me a pill. He said it would keep me calm during the flight, which he said would take about five hours.

I came off the plane to stare at the lights of TV crews. They shot more commercials for deals that Mickey had arranged. When Mr. Turner saw me—he'd come on another flight—I saw a worried look on his face when he heard how I'd been given stuff to make me quiet during the flight and during the TV shootings.

At Hollywood Park I heard that Mickey was talking about me setting a track record or even a world record. That talk upset me. I knew that Mickey was pulling in all that money because I had never lost. I worried about what he would think when I lost—even Man o' War lost once.

For the first time in my life, I worried about the other horses. Mr. Turner told Jean that I'd see a lot of speed in this race. The fastest was the English sprinter, J.O. Tobin, the horse I beat in the Preakness. Mr. Turner told Jean I had to stay close to J.O. or he might build up a lead that I couldn't make up.

The third biggest crowd in Hollywood Park's history, I heard later, came to see the race. They chanted "Slew! Slew! Slew!" as I trotted to the gate. The California horses glared at me, jealous, of course.

My heart thumped. I'd never been as nervous. My knees seemed like jelly under me, not like springs, which was the way they'd always felt before this.

J.O. Tobin bolted out of the gate and took the lead. I bounded after him and tucked myself in along the rail in second place, about three lengths behind, as we entered the first turn. I still hung about as close halfway down the backstretch when Jean asked me to move up. I did what I always did, took off with my rear legs for one long bounce—the first of a series of bounces that lengthened my stride and added the speed for passing.

I felt no spring in those rear legs as I summoned up strength for that first bounce. I came down from the bounce still three lengths behind J.O. I tried again, now feeling panic in my gut. This time, when I landed, I saw J.O. going away from me.

And now, coming to the far turn, I felt the ache of tiredness and a new sense of panic knifed into me—*I wanted to stop!* I had heard other horses talk about the nightmarish feeling—that suddenly you are just standing there, a laughing-stock, ears down, while a jockey beats you with a whip. Was this about to happen to the proud Seattle Slew who had never lost?

We came around the turn and I saw J.O. Tobin run away from me while I felt frozen in ice. I didn't care. I just wanted to go under that wire and stop. In about thirty seconds I had learned all I ever want to know about being a loser.

I finished fourth, sixteen lengths behind J.O. Tobin. Willie Shoemaker rode J.O. toward the winner's circle. As I panted toward the shed row I heard the crowd chanting "Shoe! Shoe! Shoe!" I had learned something else—how quickly they forget.

Mickey had tried to win $100,000 and had lost $7 million, reporters wrote. My value had dropped by half, they said. They asked him why I had seemed to stop running. He said he didn't know. One magazine wrote that it was too bad there wasn't a machine that could peer into the heads of horses. I thought it was too bad there wasn't a machine to look into the heads of owners.

We flew back to the East. Mr. Turner told reporters that I should never have been sent to California, that I needed to be rested. That got Mickey and Dr. Hill upset. They got rid of Mr. Turner.

You can imagine how bad I felt. He'd given pride to a Baby Huey. Soon I was feeling bad all over. I came down with a bad cough. I missed all of the 1977 fall races. I went to Florida and seemed to get better. By January of 1978 I was turning in swift workouts—maybe too swift.

I stopped eating. I don't really remember much of what happened during the next few weeks. Later I heard the grooms say I broke into sweats that lasted for hours. I'd try to stand up and I'd fall down.

Dr. Hill discovered that I had some kind of blood disease. For about a week in February, he and Mickey thought several times that I had died, I lay so still after pitching over. Even after I came to, I tossed and groaned so bad they began to think they might have to put me out of my misery.

Slowly, I got well. Mickey and Dr. Hill, by this time, had learned to bring a horse along slowly. I didn't race until June. We went up to Saratoga and I beat a bunch of crows—as they call bad runners in the stable. It was my first race since the

Coming back from the illness that almost killed him the previous winter, Slew preps at Aqueduct on a sloppy track for his 1978 showdown with Affirmed.

loss to J.O. Tobin some eleven months earlier. But I felt after the race like the undefeated Seattle Slew of 1977.

A big brown horse, Affirmed, had just won the 1978 Triple Crown. Never before had two Triple Crown winners raced against each other—so naturally there was talk of a match race between me and Affirmed.

Mickey and Dr. Hill knew that the only way to get my price back up to $14 million, what I was worth a year earlier, was for me to beat Affirmed. I liked the idea, too. People still said, "Who did Slew ever beat?" If I beat the best of 1977's three-year-olds and I beat the 1978 three-year-old champ, what else could I prove?

Affirmed entered the $300,000 mile-and-an-

eighth Marlboro Cup at Belmont Park, a September race. My new trainer, Doug Peterson, began to get me ready for that race. As a tune-up, I ran in the Patterson Handicap at the Meadowlands in New Jersey. I got the top weight of 128 pounds and lost by a neck to a tough little guy, Dr. Patches, who carried only 116 pounds. I'd lost for only the second time in thirteen starts, but again you know what I heard: "Who did Seattle Slew ever beat?"

After the race Jean Cruguet said I wasn't ready for a big race like the Marlboro. That angered Dr. Hill and Mickey and they fired Jean, the only rider I'd ever carried. That pretty much finished the bust-up of the Slew Crew.

Mickey hired Angel Cordero, a guy whose

flashing eyes and big smile I liked. But I worried about a new jock who didn't know me. And I missed Mr. Turner, who used to come around to the stable and say, "Slew, you are some kind of horse." Even when you are a winner, you need people who tell you how good you are. When you've just lost, you need that pat a lot more.

I noticed that nobody asked who Affirmed had beaten. He'd won the Triple Crown and lost only once in nine starts so far in 1978. That loss happened in the Travers Stakes when he finished first but was disqualified, with Alydar declared the winner. Other horses asked me about Affirmed. I said, "Look at his record—he's the best. I just wish that horses and people had said the same thing about me last year when I was undefeated."

Mickey Taylor saw the glint in my eyes as a groom saddled me for the Marlboro. He and I were never too close. I got along much better with Karen, his wife, who was crazy about horses. But Mickey saw how badly I wanted to win this Marlboro and beat Affirmed. I wanted the Marlboro more than I had wanted to win the Triple Crown. My Triple Crown had proved nothing to people. They still asked who did I ever beat? If I beat Affirmed, I knew I'd never again hear that question.

I felt my hindquarters tremble as I stepped into the starting gate. But I had no jitters, I was quivering to break out of there and run.

I broke on top and swept into the first turn at the head of the pack. Behind me I heard the squeaky shouts of Stevie Cauthen, the "Kid" to the other jocks, so I knew Affirmed was pounding at my heels.

We stayed that way—me in front, Affirmed three lengths back—as we ran the backstretch, leaned into the turn, and came out of the turn into the homestretch.

The Slew Crew: Sally and Jim Hill (left) and Karen and Mickey Taylor.

I felt strong, my legs full of spring. I knew I had this race won. I just knew it. So I had to be playful. After all, I thought, this could be your last race—go out with a bang.

I swung wide to the outside. That flung open a wide door for Affirmed, galloping on the inside, to dart through and come even with me. What I was saying to Affirmed and the world was this: I won the first part of this race. Now let's start even Stephen and I'll win the second part.

That's what happened. As soon as I saw, from the outside, that Affirmed had come abreast of me, I called on all the speed I had in me. Up on top, meanwhile, Angel Cordero wondered what was going on. He'd never ridden me before, so he hadn't expected that sudden swerve to the outside. Later on he said he thought we'd blown the race.

I shot right through that stretch. I beat Affirmed by three lengths. My time [1:45⁴/₅] was only two-fifths of a second off the track record set five years earlier by Secretariat.

I listened to the grooms when they read the papers the next day. I liked best what one reporter wrote—that few comebacks in recent sports history could equal my rising up from what seemed my deathbed to beat a Triple Crown champion. Another reporter wrote that no longer could the critics ask who did I beat. I beat Affirmed, that's who.

A few months later Dr. Hill and the Taylors sold me to the Spendthrift Farm people for about $12 million. It's a nice life here [near Lexington, Kentucky]. I earn my keep, though. I'm told the Spendthrift people get $100,000 for each mare I date—is that the word humans use?

You've been to what the grooms here call the Romance Room, haven't you? It's a shed that's all white so that it looks like one of those hospitals I see in the afternoons on TV. They lead me in, where I meet the mare. This morning it was Allez France, who won a lot of races in Europe. I am told she was one of Europe's two all-time money winners.

We got in a little chit-chat between us. I told her I hoped the colt or filly would be a winner. She said she hoped that for all her foals. I was embarrassed. I said, "Sure, yes, I did too."

The actual affair, "covering the mare," as the people around here refer to it, took no more than a minute or so. As she left, Allez said she hoped we could do this again, and I said I really hoped so. Yes, it's true, I say that to all the mares. They're all nice, but you like to leave them thinking that they were the nicest.

My stall here is one of the best I've ever had. Look at that view of the farm. That TV camera watches me all the time to make sure nothing's wrong. I get everything I need. But, as crazy as it seems, there's one thing I'd like. Just once, I wish someone would again call me Baby Huey.

SPEND A BUCK

 There are no guarantees in mating Thoroughbred horses. A breeder can put together a champion sire and a stakes-winning mare, but all he gets out of it is just another horse. Or he can pair off a stud and a female who are not top-of-the-line, and out comes a champion. It's like a crapshoot.

Take me for instance. My pop was a horse named Buckaroo, and not a lot of people ever heard of him, although his sire was very much in the news once. That was Buckpasser, Horse of the Year in 1966. Buckaroo won a couple of stakes races, but never made it big. My mom was Belle de Jour, a nice lady, but the closest she ever came to becoming a household name was when she won a $5,000 claiming race. You might say they were both good horses, but not part of high society. More like middle-class citizens.

As a kid my home was Irish Hill Farms in Kentucky. The people there are businessmen. They put up a big cash outlay before they see a return on investment. They hire grooms, vets, and stableboys; the young horses are watered, walked, watched, fed, curried, and fretted over. God forbid one of us should get sick, or (don't even think of it!) bust a foreleg. There goes the investment down the drain.

Cordero waves his hand in victory signal as the new Churchill Downs champ eases up.

Then most of us are sold. It's all part of the business; it's time to move out, just like a human tells his sonny boy, "Go out and get a job, kid, you can't hang around the house anymore." Along with a lot of other horses I was put up for sale. I didn't expect anybody to hock the family silver to buy me, but gee, what with inflation, the $12,500 price tag was like grabbing a suit off the rack at Gimbel's basement. I was picked up by a gentleman named Dennis Diaz. Let me tell you a little about him.

Dennis represents all the dreams of horse owners who dip a toe into the Thoroughbred business and hope to make a quick killing. He used to own other businesses—insurance, real estate, things like that. He was a middle-aged respectable guy who got burned out real bad in the rat race and decided to quit. He sold his companies, took a vacation, traveled around, and then began looking for something to keep him occupied. Somebody suggested he buy racehorses. He did. I was one of them.

It was Dennis who named me Spend a Buck. The way he explained it, it was partly because of my sire's name and partly because he wanted to identify me with all the little guys in racing. Listen, Calumet Farm he certainly wasn't. His motto was. "Spend a buck. Who knows, lightning might strike."

Down in Ocala, Florida, they have a select sale for young horses in training. A vet came around to examine me. He poked and pried into parts of my body I didn't even know I had. He didn't

157

say anything, but he wouldn't let me be put up for sale, either.

Poor Dennis, he didn't know then that having the door slammed in his face was the best thing that ever happened to him. He moped, he grumbled, he groused. Once while he was passing by he stopped and kicked the wire mesh on my stall. He yelled, "If somebody walked in now and gave me thirty thousand for this horse, he'd be gone."

Dennis was stuck with me, so he figured he might as well give me a shot. As a trainer he hired a guy named Cam Gamboletti, and that was funny all by itself. Cam was even greener as a horse trainer than Dennis was as a horse owner. Cam used to be an assistant to a trainer named Norman St. Leon, until St. Leon went out of business. Cam had his doubts about the horse-racing industry. Once I heard him say, "Nothing can make you consider running a laundromat more than training a barn full of slow horses."

I'll buy that. I only like slow horses when I race against them.

There was a lot Dennis and Cam had to find out about me. All creatures, great and small, have individual characteristics, including dogs, cats, humans, and horses. My bag was simple. When I started running, I wanted to go all out, right from stride one.

I hear quarter horses are like that. They bolt out of the gate, but they can sustain the pace for only maybe a quarter of a mile or so, which must be the reason they're called quarter horses. They're sprinters. So am I. They have no stamina. I do.

I didn't start out in the big time. In the beginning I ran at Calder Race Course in north Florida, an oval that was supposed to be home for second-raters. Not many horses in the super class have come out of Calder after running in the steamy Florida summer. But I did all right. I won my maiden race, won the next one, placed in my third race, and won my fourth. Now that wasn't too shabby a showing. Dennis and Cam thought that maybe they were on to something good and I was ripe for a step up, like a stakes race. I was shipped to River Downs, just outside Cincinnati.

I was entered in the mile-and-a-sixteenth Cradle Stakes.

Was that supposed to be a test? It was like I was running against a herd of horses all named Dobbin. I was out of the gate and moving while the other nags were still looking around and counting the house. At the wire I was fifteen lengths ahead and wondering where the rest of the field had gone. I hate being lonely.

Three weeks later I started in the $622,200 Arlington-Washington Futurity at Arlington Park. I must say the competition was a lot stiffer, but I came through by half a length. Dennis and Cam almost kissed me on the lips.

It was autumn by then. Dennis and Can took me another step ahead, this time the Young America Stakes at the Meadowlands, New Jersey. A lot of things happened there, mostly bad.

After the race I heard talk that I was spooked by tire tracks on the course. Who am I to argue with human psychologists? But I can tell you what did happen.

A horse named Script Ohio was burning up the track and I went after him. Somewhere along the way I felt a twinge in my right knee. Hell, I didn't think too much of it at the time, although there was some pain and it did bother me. I favored the leg. Script Ohio beat me by three-quarters of a length.

Now that it's over, I have to admit that sometimes I can be pretty stupid. The soreness in my knee was still there, but I tried to tough it out. I walked around like it was just a fluke that I lost.

Dennis and Cam still had faith in me. They entered me in a really big event, the $1 million Breeder's Cup Juvenile at Hollywood Park. This time the competition was the absolute best, like Chief's Crown, Tank's Prospect, and a few others who knew how to make it around a track.

I just couldn't cut it. I faded in the stretch. I looked like I was tired at the finish. Tired? How would you feel with an aching right knee, running around with somebody sitting on your back? I finished third behind Crown and Prospect. Well, I was still in the money, and it's no disgrace to be beaten by horses that good.

Now I couldn't hide the knee. Cam and Dennis didn't waste time. After some X rays they hired a vet named Dr. Wayne McElreath out of Colorado State University. Somebody clocked the arthroscopic operation: twelve minutes from the time he stuck the knife into my leg until he reached in and slipped out the piece of bone chip. Come around to my stall sometime, I'll show you my operation.

I had nine weeks of rest and rehab. That means a lot of walking, a little jogging, a couple of gallops, and then some swimming. Swimming is good exercise for anybody, horses included. My body felt buoyant and I could move my legs around easily. Then it was back to training.

It was March, getting close to Derby time, and I ran in the Bay Shore Stakes at Aqueduct, my first time out since I was sliced. The run was only seven furlongs, but I didn't have my wind back yet. The tote board said Spend a Buck was third, which is in the money to be sure, but not where I like to see my name. And that was the third time in a row I wasn't *número uno* at the wire.

But I was ready by then. I knew it and I'm sure Dennis and Cam knew it. We all took a trip to New Jersey. On April 6, 1985, the guys I worked for decided to give the new Garden State track a little class by entering me in the Cherry Hills Mile. The horses there didn't figure to be a whole lot of competition. That's how it turned out.

When the gate was sprung I took off like I was anxious to get to my supper bucket. Before the crowd could focus field glasses I was ahead by two lengths. I didn't hear anybody chasing me, but just for the hell of it I opened the lead to six lengths, and then eight. At the end I was ten and a half lengths in front and I hadn't even worked up a sweat.

We hung around New Jersey, and two weeks later I was back in action for the Garden State Stakes. The date was April 20, 1985, and mark it well. When the sun had set, the touts and tipsters didn't know whether to consult form charts or hold a seance to decide the winner of the Kentucky Derby.

Like always I took the early lead, but I wasn't being challenged. None of the horses were making a move. Well, if that's how they wanted to play, the hell with it. I made up my mind to put in a short day's work and go home early. It was a win by nine and a half lengths.

Meanwhile, some of the other Derby entries were showing fine form. Over at Aqueduct they held the Wood Memorial, a very important pre-Derby outing. One of the horses in that race was a speedster who ran a lot like I did, meaning he liked to grab the lead and hold it. His name was Eternal Prince. One of his owners was a chap named George Steinbrenner, and thereby hangs a tale.

Steinbrenner, who is well known for fisticuffs in elevators, is chief owner of the New York Yankees, which is a baseball team with stalls in the Bronx, New York. George also owns a racetrack and a fleet of freight ships. He had owned Prince before but sold him. His son felt the colt had the goods and asked Papa to buy him back. Big George did that and it cost one million bucks, which only shows that the man is very free with loose cash. Prince had a beautiful run in the Wood Memorial. He won by just under three lengths, beating a couple of very good colts named Proud Truth and Rhoman Rule.

Meanwhile, down at Oaklawn Park, another colt was making hash of the field. His name was Tank's Prospect, and I knew him from the Breeder's Cup. I make it a point never to forget a horse that beats me in a stakes race. Prospect won the nine-furlong Arkansas Derby in 1:48$^{1}/_{2}$, which was thrilling time for his owners.

Five days later, the previous year's two-year-old champ, Chief's Crown, tuned up for the Derby in the nine-furlong Blue Grass Stakes at Keeneland. Sure, I remembered Crown too. He also beat me in the Juvenile Cup. He beat a lot of horses, and he did it again at Oaklawn. In fact he practically ran away and hid from the opposition. The Crown took it by five and a half lengths. His time was 1:47$^{3}/_{5}$, just a fifth of a second off the track record. Now that's one hell of a horse. He should be, considering his grandfather was Secretariat.

I heard that until I copped the Duke in both New Jersey races—Cherry Hills Mile and Garden State Stakes—Dennis and Cam weren't too eager to enter me in the Kentucky Derby. They were aiming for the Jersey Derby, just a few weeks away.

The sovereign state of New Jersey had come up with its own version of the Triple Crown. They wanted horse fanciers to forget about the traditional Derby-Preakness-Belmont series, so they put a lot more money into the pot. The New Jersey version of the Triple Crown included the Cherry Hills Mile, the Garden State Stakes, and the Jersey Derby. I already had two legs up on the Jersey Triple Crown. If I won the Jersey Derby, the big cash-in was one million bucks.

Aha! But wait!

Suppose I won the Kentucky Derby, then went on to win the Jersey Derby also? Then it became a *bonus* situation. I would be the winner of the Kentucky Derby, *plus* the winner of the Jersey Triple Crown. For winning all four of those races, the management offered a bonus of *two* million bucks, *plus* the purse for winning the Jersey Derby, which was around $600,000.

And I—Spend a Buck—was the only horse who qualified to bring home the jackpot.

So what did Dennis and Cam have to lose by entering me in the Kentucky Derby? A little luster maybe, if I lost at Churchill Downs, but even so, I could still compete for the single million. Dennis and Cam decided to give it a shot. I went to Kentucky, which, after all, is the state where I was born.

As long as I live I'll always get a chuckle out of listening to the words of wisdom coming from the mouths of the bookies, the form players, and the Off-Track-Betting geniuses. They and the stock market mavens have one thing in common: none of them knows what in hell he's talking about. There was a lot of soul-searching, and it all boiled down to this:

Spend a Buck and Eternal Prince are fast front-runners. They could go head to head for maybe the first mile, burn each other out. Then a couple of horses come out of the pack and charge down the homestretch. And who might the lucky winner be? It could be Chief's Crown, or Tank's Prospect, or Rhoman Rule, or Proud Truth. And there was always Stephen's Odyssey. That colt

had bloodlines that included Danzig and Gallant Man, but nobody could figure out that horse, not even me.

But there was another way to puzzle out who *might* walk into the winner's circle, although it wasn't a hard-and-fast rule. Just take a look at the purse earnings before the Derby is run. How many big stakes races did the horse win? Isn't that the bottom line in this game? How much loot the horse gave his owner?

Even before I put a shoe on the Churchill Downs track I had won a total of $991,709 for Dennis Diaz. You can look it up. Only one Kentucky Derby entry took home a bigger overall paycheck: Chief's Crown, who earned $1,229,422. I'm not quibbling, mind you, because money is where you find it, but a lot of Crown's earnings came from one race, the Breeder's Cup Juvenile, and good luck to him. Tank's Prospect earned maybe $50,000 less than I did, and Stephen's Odyssey was right up there with around $750,000. Gee, no wonder we're treated like royalty.

Speaking of royalty, you want to know how much Eternal Prince earned before the Kentucky Derby? I'll tell you. Exactly $389,362. I agree, those are nice numbers, but not in the same league with Crown, Prospect, Odyssey, and me. Yet Steinbrenner let himself get talked into unloading a million for Prince. No doubt he'll get it all back when Prince quits running and starts making out with the fillies.

Not many people knew that before the race I was given a drug. Hey, don't go running to the Kentucky track stewards, they knew all about it, everything was legal. Cam had noticed that after I won the Garden Stakes, I "blew out" some blood. Cam dosed me with Lasix, which is a diuretic to control respiratory bleeding.

As we walked out on the track I noticed Dennis. He looked like a guy practicing how to hold his breath for a couple of minutes. I was used to that. When I began winning again there was a touch of wonder in his eyes. After one race he said, "We don't know what to make of it. That horse scares me. I don't know what we've got."

Now, with the strains of "My Old Kentucky

The anatomy of a Kentucky Derby victory. A relaxed Spend a Buck goes to the starting gate for the 1985 Derby. That's Angel Cordero aboard.

Home" in his ears, he said, "There's nothing more to do. It's up to the colt. It's up to Angel Cordero. And it's up to God."

I walked into my slot, tenth position. There were three other horses even farther from the rail than I was, and one of them was Proud Truth. The inside horse was Irish Fighter, but he didn't figure to do much. The Irishman still hadn't won a 1985 stakes race.

The gate went aside and I broke well. So did the horse most people were looking at, Chief's Crown. But Crown never was a front-runner. He liked to lay back—not too far back, mind you— then make his move maybe into the third quar-

ter. So there I was, all alone, with Cordero slanting me slightly toward the inside.

Where in hell was Eternal Prince? He was supposed to be coming right with me, but he wasn't. I heard later that Prince didn't get off right, and by the time his jockey got him squared away he was back in the pack.

I ran the first quarter in 23 seconds, leading Crown by a length and a half. Into the second quarter I started pulling away and opened the lead to six lengths. I ran that leg in :22²/₅. I wasn't looking over my shoulder, but it seemed time for Prince to start moving up. He did try but got boxed in and for him the race was over early.

Just breezing along, leading by almost six lengths . . .

The third quarter-mile took 23⁴/₅ seconds, and Crown couldn't get closer than the same six lengths. I'd covered the first three-quarters of a mile in 1:9³/₅, and nobody had to tell me it was good, I could feel it. At the mile pole Chief's Crown was still chasing me. The lead was the same. Time for the mile, 1:34⁴/₅.

You like trivia? I'll tell you something you can surprise all your sports fan friends with. That was the Kentucky Derby record for the first mile of the race. Sure, I know, the race is longer than a mile, but that's not what I'm talking about. The old record for the first mile was 1:35 flat, set by Kauai King when he won the Derby in 1966.

And then the race was over. Cordero stood up in the stirrups and eased me down to a canter. Meanwhile Stephan's Odyssey came on and just did manage to squeak past Chief's Crown for place money.

I took the Run for the Roses by five and a half lengths. My time was 2:00¹/₅, third fastest in Kentucky Derby history. In 1973 Secretariat covered the oval in 1:59²/₅. Next came Northern Dancer in 1964 at 2:00 flat. Not to keep patting myself on the rump, but that was the first time a Derby winner had led wire to wire since Bold Forbes did it in 1976. Also, my five-and-a-half-length lead over a second-place finisher was the

Over the finish line. Cordero begins to rise in the stirrups.

And it's on to the winner's circle for the ring of roses.

biggest since 1946 when Assault won by eight lengths. I always did like to be in good company.

Let me put in a good word for Eternal Prince, the colt who was supposed to break out with early foot. He's a good horse, he just didn't get off well, and that could happen to any horse, even me. So what if he finished way back? What's Steinbrenner going to do, fire Prince and race Billy Martin? Still, good old George ran true-to-form. After the race he fired the jockey.

The guys I ran for said right after the race that I wouldn't show up for the Preakness, because I was headed for the Jersey Derby. That seemed to put a lot of noses out of joint. The gossip and the backbiting started. You'd think Dennis had stolen his grandmother's life savings, and the only thing I was good for was to give kids a ride around an amusement park. For instance:

They said Dennis was breaking tradition by not going after the Preakness and Belmont after the Derby win. Baloney! A lot of horses copped the Derby and skipped the Preakness. Gato del Sol did that just a few years ago.

They said Dennis was only out for the money when he went after the Jersey Derby. Now *that* is a real horse laugh! Investing in Thoroughbreds is a business, just like buying stock in General Motors, only horses are a very handy tax dodge. You want to talk money? Let's do that. I was the only horse in the country who had a chance for the biggest payoff in racing history. If I won in Jersey, the first-place purse was $600,000, but any other winning entry could get that. Nobody else could wind up with the $2-million bonus. And isn't that a hell of a payoff for a few minutes' work?

Then putdowns shifted to me. They said I was bound to win in Jersey because there was no opposition. So who was stopping them from joining me?

They said the only reason I won at Churchill Downs was the hard track, that I couldn't beat a turtle in the mud. Maybe. Some horses are mudders, some aren't. I like a hard track. Is that a crime?

They said I couldn't run in some states like New York because Cam dosed me with Lasix and that's not allowed. I guess they won't be happy until I hemorrhage going around the first turn. Lasix is not an upper, it won't make me run any faster, it simply prevents bleeding.

And are they—whoever the hell "they" are—so smart that they can predict what's going to happen? It could rain on Jersey Derby day and I might get licked. In late spring a shower can come up out of nowhere, and in fifteen minutes the track could be a playground for kids making mud pies.

Dammit, how does anybody know who can win a race? The horses don't know and we're running in it. A colt can go great one day and not so great a couple of weeks later. Take the Peter Pan Stakes race at Belmont, for instance. Proud Truth won it, but in the Kentucky Derby he finished seventh. Stephan's Odyssey ran second in the Derby but he was fourth in the Peter Pan. Go figure horse racing.

So I went to the Jersey Derby aiming for the big purse—and I damned near blew it.

I didn't break well. In fact I stumbled slightly and cut my tongue, so the blood was there anyway, only thank the Lord it wasn't coming from my respiratory system. I got the lead and held on for dear life. Coming around the turn a horse name Creme Fraiche pulled alongside, and that horse was steaming. In fact Fraiche pulled ahead for a few strides. Then my new jockey, Laffit Pincay, went to the whip. He hit my flank exactly three times. That did it. I pulled even, then went ahead by a nose, then by a neck, and I was inching away even more at the wire.

What a payoff—$2.6 million! In one outing I had almost tripled my earnings. Let them sneer at Dennis, he was chuckling all the way to the bank. Sure, I didn't expect to work so hard. The funny thing is, neither Creme Fraiche nor El Bosco, who finished third, were entered in the Kentucky Derby. The trainers of both horses didn't think they were good enough.

Then I took a two-month vacation, which is not always the best thing. Sometimes a Thoroughbred can lose the fine edge after an eight-week layoff. It happened to me at the Haskell Invitational in Oceanport. A horse named Skip Trial beat me by three and three-quarter lengths. Skip went off at 35 to 1, but he had the speed that day. I have no alibis. But, if I wanted to, I could point to the weights. I carried 127 pounds, Skip Trial carried 116. The third-place horse was Creme Fraiche, carrying 126 pounds.

Let me tell you something. Even though I lost, I felt good about beating Fraiche. He's a good horse, make no mistake. You want to know who won the Belmont in 1985? Creme Fraiche, that's who.

By the way, I was bleeding after the Haskell. But Dennis and Cam decided to run me again soon, and not wait two months. They picked the Monmouth Handicap, which is a race run against older horses. That was really taking a chance.

A three-year-old horse does not usually beat a four-year-old horse. That's the way it is, even with the best colts that ever galloped. Take 1978, for instance. Two Triple Crown winners went at it: three-year-old Affirmed and four-year-old Seattle Slew. The Slew won. I learned the hard way how tough a four-year-old can be.

Going into the homestretch, a track burner named Carr de Naskra started coming on. He wasn't just sprinting; if he had had wings he'd been off the ground. I took him on—what else could I do? We strained and we drove and I beat him by just a nose. Wow, what a tussle! But it was worth every stride. I set a track record. I think Carr de Naskra did too.

I don't know what Dennis had planned for me after that. Maybe another outing or two somewhere, and the Breeder's Cup probably, but none of it happened. On September 12, I wrenched my ankle. Damn, that hurt. My bosses took one look at the fetlock and called it a career for Spend a Buck. I was now a syndicated horse standing at stud.

To some people I'll never be a top-grade horse, and I'd like to know what I have to do to convince them I'm for real. Maybe if we looked at the record and compared me with the best that ever ran, they might change their minds.

I went to the post fifteen times. *I never finished out of the money.* Of all the horses that earned over $1 million, I am the *only one* who can make that statement. Let's drop some names: Secretariat, Seattle Slew, Affirmed, Buckpasser, Swale, Spectacular Bid, and the old-timers like Citation and Damascus—all have one thing in common. All of them finished out of the money one time. Not me. I won ten, placed three times, and showed twice.

I earned more money in one year than any other horse in history, $3,552,704 to be exact. And here we go again—I got most of it in one race. Strictly speaking, that's not true at all. I had to win four races in a row to hit that jackpot: Cherry Hills, Garden State Stakes, Kentucky Derby, and Jersey Derby. I took on all comers. Chief's Crown, Juvenile Horse of the Year as a two-year-old—I beat him in Kentucky. Tank's Prospect, who won the Preakness—I beat him too at Churchill Downs. Creme Fraiche won the Belmont, but I was faster than he was twice. I beat Proud Truth in Kentucky, and that's the colt who won the Peter Pan Stakes at Belmont. I raced against the best and I beat the best.

Only one horse has won more money than I have, and that's John Henry. Hey, I'm not jealous, Big John is about as good a horse as ever was. He earned a total of $6,597,947, to my total of $4,220,689. But don't forget, John Henry raced more than twice as long as I did. And he's a gelding, so there's no stud fees in his future.

What else is there? Did I set track records? I sure did. I had the third fastest time in the Kentucky Derby, and my critics can play around with that for a while. I have left the opposition in the dust at times, and I also had to run for my life to win a couple of races.

My jockeys know who I am. I heard Angel Cordero tell Dennis that I was faster than Seattle Slew. I heard Laffit Pincay tell Dennis that I was the fastest horse he ever rode.

For a while I thought all the crabbing was finished. I won the Eclipse Award, which is handed out by the combination of racing secretaries of the Thoroughbred Racing Association, *The Daily Racing Form*, and the National Turfwriters Association. It was unanimous. I received first-place votes from each group for a total of 30 points. In second place, with a runner-up vote from each

group, was Proud Truth with 15 points.

Horse of the Year was something else. To win that award, a horse has to beat everybody else, including two-year-olds, three-year-olds, older horses, fillies, and even—for Pete's sake!—steeplechasers. I had a lot of competition, but I won by a comfortable margin. The same parties voted, and this time there was a possible 201 votes. I got 74 votes, Proud Truth got 40. There were others who got some votes here and there. Even Chief's Crown got 10 votes.

I've got a permanent home now. I live at Will Farish's Lane's End Farm in Versailles, Kentucky. No more training, no more starting gates, no more jockeys on my back. All I have to do is run around the field and look out over the hills.

Do I miss the old life? Well, yeah—I guess sometimes I do.

The run for the big bucks: Spend a Buck, Pincay on top, outhustles two pursuers to win the Jersey Derby and $2.6 million.

JOHN HENRY

Sam Rubin once said I could do everything except talk and that it was a good thing I couldn't talk because then I'd ask where all the money I'd won had gone. Sam never tried to talk to me, but if he had I wouldn't have talked about money. I would have talked about the Operation and the Big Needle. I'd mention the French poodles that maybe made him more money than he ever made betting on horses. I mean, I would have talked about *interesting* things.

But that's the way I am. I am always looking for the reasons why things happen. I have always said that I had a lot of good horse sense. Now, let me explain that.

You know how I am. If I see a fan along the rail pointing a camera at me, I'll usually stop so the person can get a good picture of me. I once heard a reporter ask Ron [apparently a reference to trainer Ron McAnally] how I knew enough to pose and Ron said, "He does it all the time, but don't ask me how he knows."

That tells you something about the horse sense of trainers. You see a camera pointing at you, someone's taking a picture of you, right? Why else would they point the camera at you? You're

A "young" John Henry—he was only five—goes to the post for a 1980 race in New York. Laffit Pincay is aboard.

only being polite when you stop so they'll get a good picture.

Which reminds me of another thing. I was always so polite, yet Ron and Sam and other people claimed I was mean and nasty. All right, I did like to step on the toes of my handlers when I was being walked. But that was just plain old horsing around. And occasionally—well, more than occasionally—I'd kick up a ruckus in my stall and chew up any tubs or buckets I could sink my teeth into. As someone once said of me, "One end bites and the other end kicks." But I say: You show me a horse who'll stand all day while cooped up in a stall, I'll show you a loser. Nasty? I was just being frisky.

Now this is true: Once, in the winner's circle, I swung my head into the face of a jockey's wife. But that was an accident. I liked to bob my head in the winner's circle because the TV guys loved it, and the jockey's wife got her head in the way.

Oh, I have bitten a few hands, including those belonging to the people who feed me. Once, when Sam came into my stall late at night while I was sleeping, I charged out, reared up, front hooves flailing the air above Sam's bald head. Later I heard Sam say, "He doesn't know me from anyone else. The horse knew only one thing—he wants to race."

First of all, I knew who Sam Rubin is. He paid $25,000 for me and I made him more than $6 million, more than any horse ever won. That doesn't mean he can wander into my stall when I'm asleep. What would you do if your boss stepped into your bedroom when you were asleep?

Secondly, Sam is right when he says that all I want to do is run and race. Lots of horses don't like to race—the whips, the bits, the sweat, the lungs afire coming down the stretch. I love it all. I go crazy when I'm cooped up in the stall. To me, it's like being in one of those prisons I hear the stablehands talk about, looking from behind bars. Maybe I really will go crazy when Sam retires me and I can't go out on a track and run wild and free.

Even now, after all the money I've made, Sam and Ron think I'm some kind of a nut. They tell the story of how I once finished fourth in a race, came back and tried to turn into the winner's circle. I bit and kicked when Ron and a groom tried to lead me away. Sam yelled, "Hey, John, you lost!"

Well, of course, by then I knew I had lost. I had turned into the winner's circle so often that I had forgotten I was fourth.

I have always been a little forgetful. In my first race I forgot that you are supposed to run when the starting gate pops up. The gate flew up and I *walked* out.

The jockey, of course, was whacking me with his whip. That reminded me about what they had been telling me: The time to run is when the gate springs open. We caught up with the rear-enders at the first turn. I hung second from last as we turned into the homestretch. I passed everybody to win by a nose.

Still, few people thought I'd amount to much. My mother, Once Double, never won anything, and Pop, Ole Bob Bowers, won only one stakes race, the Tanforan Handicap. In an otherwise very nice book, *John Henry*, that Sam wrote about me, he said of Mom and Pop, "a homelier pair you couldn't find." Sometimes I wish I had stomped him when he came into my stall.

He told the awful truth, though, when he wrote I was "an ungainly creature," a turkey nobody wanted. I was built small and low to the ground, but my chest bulged. Vets shook their heads when they looked at my knees, which bent backward. I banged my head on the stall's walls

almost every day. That got me a reputation for being crazy.

The vets said my "calf knees," as they called them, were so bad I'd break down in training and never race. They told the owners of the Golden Chance Farm in Kentucky, where I was born in March of 1975, to get rid of me. My knees are still bent backward, as you can see, but they never gave me any trouble and I am still running when lots of horses my age—I'm nine this year—are dead. So much for what vets tell you.

In January of 1976, I am told—I don't remember a lot of this early stuff too well—I was put up for sale at an auction. Sam says it was like a "fire sale," meaning that all the horses were sold cheap.

A horse owner named John Callaway took me for about as cheap as horses get—$1,100. I know some owners who spend that much money in a week on lunch.

Mr. Callaway bought me sight unseen. Later he told Sam Rubin that he'd bought me right out of the catalog because he'd liked my breeding on my mother's side. But when he saw the calf knees, he decided he wouldn't even try to put a saddle on me. And when I began to tear buckets off the walls of my stall, he decided I was retarded. "The only thing I thought he was good at," he told Sam, "was stomping on buckets." Now, when he reads about me winning those millions of dollars, he says he feels kind of sick, or so he told Sam in that book Sam wrote.

Before he got rid of me, though, Mr. Callaway gave me my name. He got the name from that song "John Henry." By now I know most of the words:

John Henry was a steel-drivin' man
He carried his hammer all the time
Fore he let the steam drill beat him down
Die with his hammer in his hand.

It's a weird story, that song. It seems this John Henry got into a race with a machine called a steam drill. He tried to beat the steam drill. Naturally, with only a hammer, he couldn't—and he died trying. And you people think I'm crazy!

Callaway sold me at an auction to a Kentucky trainer named Harold Snowden. Harold frowned—I remember that frown—the first time I tried to kick down a stall door and barge onto the track that I could see through my rear window. Snowden decided the Operation would calm me down. The Operation made me a gelding. Sam once asked, "What color is a gelding?" And he said that after he bought me!

Trainers will tell you that gelding calms down horses and keeps their minds on the business of racing. Don't you believe them. I think as much about mares as the next stallion. But unlike them, I can't do much about what I am thinking. And the Operation was supposed to calm me down.

A trainer came up from Louisiana to Lexington to look at some of Snowden's horses. His name was Phil Marino. A slim, dark-haired man with a swooping black mustache, Phil trained for a group of Louisiana people, including a woman who owned a shop that clipped French poodles.

When Marino came into the stable, I was—as usual—trying to kick the place down. A handler said to Phil, "The horse just wants to get out and gallop." Smart man.

They put the tack on me and Phil climbed into the saddle. We blew around the track for half a mile. When Phil got off I heard him say to the handler, "He's the best-movin' horse I've ever been on." Right then Phil fell in love with me and me with him.

He paid $10,000 of the Louisiana money and off I went by truck to Baton Rouge. I was only two, but I figured that going from $1,100 to $10,000 in a year had to be good news.

Yet I also knew I had to start making money for the owners. I had learned what they did to horses who didn't win. Handlers came around at night with the Big Needle and put you to sleep. You don't wake up from the sleep of the Big Needle.

I ran for the first time at Jefferson Downs in a place called Kenner, Louisiana, in May of 1977. I already told you how I walked out of the starting gate. But I came on in the stretch to win my first purse—$2,200.

I ran third and second in my next two races. I wasn't unhappy about not winning. I figured if the owners could cash place or show tickets on you, the men with the Big Needle wouldn't prowl for you in the night. You can talk all you want about the "heart" of a racehorse. I think it's knowing what the Big Needle can do to your future . . . that's what makes most of us strain to cross under that wire first.

The Lafayette Futurity, a rich race for two-year-olds, was coming up. Phil told everyone I would win. I saw other trainers make twirling motions with their fingers pointed to their heads when Phil turned his back. They thought he was as crazy as me.

A hurricane drenched the track, Evangeline Downs in Baton Rouge, on the morning of the Futurity. Good old Phil, he told reporters I loved a sloppy track. That wasn't true. I dread slipping and taking a header in mushy mud. I have always liked the firmness of grass tracks to the softness of dirt ones.

My jock was a cheerful, mop-haired fellow, Angel Guajardo, and he steered me smartly. We ran most of the race along the rail. As we turned for home, he saw a hole and we shot through it to pass three horses. Ahead were Sound Note, unbeaten as a two-year-old, and a filly, Lil' Liza Jane. I charged right by both of them to win by a head.

Mud dripped from my sides as we got to the winner's circle. I sneezed and knew I had a cold coming on. Only Phil noticed. The owners jumped up and down and hugged and kissed each other. I had just brought home $86,000.

That night I slept soundly for the first time in months. I was enjoying doing what I loved—running and racing. I had just licked one of the country's best two-year-olds. And I knew I was safe from the Big Needle.

During the next six months, however, I didn't win a race—my best a couple of thirds. Phil said I ran well at Evangeline Downs in the mornings, when the track was firm. In the afternoons, racing time, horses had churned up the dirt and I didn't like mushing my way through the deep footing.

Phil told the owners I should be shipped to another track. They agreed. But one of the owners, the lady who clipped French poodles, said she wanted to go with me to the new track. She couldn't go right away, though—you guessed it, some poodles needed clipping.

Well, sir, the upshot of all this was that the owners sold me back to Harold Snowden in Kentucky. I was happy to get out of that Louisiana muck and delighted to hear that I went for $25,000—$15,000 more than the Louisiana people paid for me.

But I felt an ache in my innards when Phil said goodbye. I could see in his eyes that he also felt bad. Years later he told Sam, "God brought me and John Henry together. Hardly an hour goes by that I don't think of him."

And because some French poodles needed clipping, big and burly Sam Rubin came into my life. I've heard him tell the story of how he bought me at least a hundred times—Sam is a good talker.

Sam owned a company on Manhattan's Fifth Avenue that sells bicycles. But he had always been much more interested in horses—and betting on them—than in bikes. One spring day in 1978, he decided, as he often did, to go to the track. Along the way he decided to do what he and his wife, Dorothy, had talked about doing for months—buy a racehorse.

At the track he met a friend, Joe Taub, and asked, "Hey Joe, know anybody that's got a couple of good $25,000 horses for sale, or a good $50,000 horse?"

Within minutes an agent stopped at Sam's table in the track's restaurant. "Joe Taub tells me you're looking for a horse," the agent said as he sat down. "Now we've got just the horse for you in Kentucky. The price is $25,000 plus a ten percent commission for me."

The horse was me. Harold Snowden still didn't think much of me, apparently. He sold me for the $25,000 he paid to the people in Louisiana.

A truck took me up to New York. I became the first and only horse in the new Dotsam Stable (Dorothy and Sam, get it?). The Dotsam trainer was a former cop, Bob Donato, a friend of

Sam's. I got to New York one night in late April of 1978 and bedded down at Aqueduct.

I hadn't won a race since back in September when I was a two-year-old. In six races so far as a three-year-old, my best had been one show.

Donato entered me in a six-furlong claimer at Aqueduct on May 2. I came out of the gate third and felt like I was running on pavement after wading through the mush at Evangeline. I popped into the lead about the halfway point and edged away to win by two and a half lengths.

I carried the Dotsam brown and blue silks into the winner's circle. Sam wore a wide grin on his face. He had a pocketful of $50 tickets on me to win—and each of those tickets was now worth about $300.

That summer of 1978 I stepped up to the handicap class with the big boys. I went to Arlington Park in Chicago for the Round Table Handicap. They put 121 pounds on me, which made me grimace. Later I'd be delighted to carry only 121. I won by twelve lengths and the two horses swallowing my dust carried only 111 and 109.

As we came down the stretch, my jockey batted me with the whip. I guess he wanted to win by thirty lengths. After the race Sam fired the jock.

"The horse was winning by fourteen lengths," Sam told people, "and he was beating his brains out coming down the stretch."

I knew then that I would never again have to fear the Big Needle. Sam, I now knew, was a friend for life.

Bob Donato had come to know what Phil Marino had known—that I was a better runner on firm grass than on mushy dirt. In 1979, I ran eleven times, mostly on grass, and won four. I finished second in five others, and out of the money only twice. So far, in about a year and a half of racing for Sam, I'd won about a quarter of a million dollars for him. And I was only four years old. Neither Sam nor me realized how many more good years stretched ahead. If I had known, I would have been delighted. I told other horses, "When you're a gelding, what else do you have to look forward to except the next walk into the winner's circle?''

Sam changed trainers—owners have a way of hiring and firing trainers—and I ended up with a dark-haired, quiet fellow, Ron McAnally, who worked closely with a California trainer, Lefty Nickerson. I saw more of Ron than I ever did of Lefty, but I always had a special place—it was in my taste buds, to be truthful—for Lefty. I don't think I have tried to stomp him more than once or twice. Whenever I arrive at track, there is always a big pile of apples, carrots, and escarole in my stall—a welcoming gift from Lefty. "He loves this stuff," Lefty tells people. He's right. If you bring carrots, apples, or escarole around when you visit me, you see the side of me that's like the purring of a pussycat.

At the start of the 1980 season I had a new rider. His name was Darrel McHargue, a young and easygoing fellow who I knew didn't have to be boss all the time, the way some jocks are. Darrel brought apples to my stall to get on my best side. When I nipped at him, he knew I was only being playful.

Racing on grass at Santa Anita and then in Florida, I won my first six races. The streak stopped when I went north to Belmont. In the Bowling Green Handicap, Sten beat me by a neck. Sten carried 117 pounds. I lugged 128.

"You're getting old," Sten told me when we met the next morning after our walks. By now I was five, a year or two older than most of the handicap horses. I got a lot of kidding about being an old man in a young man's game. I told Sten, "If they put one hundred and twenty-eight pounds on you, my young fellow, they'd have to send the meat wagon to cart you home."

Sten didn't like that. He told another horse I was getting grumpy in my old age. The amount of backbiting that goes on among horses in the stables—sometimes it makes me ashamed I am equine.

McHargue got hurt and, to my regret, never rode me again. My new regular rider was Laffit Pincay. The railbirds shouted at him, "Lafayette, you are here, but the winner's circle is over there!" That got lots of laughs but I never did get the joke, do you? Most people around a track, I have found, don't know what a really good horse laugh is.

Laffit and I won my last race of 1980, the Oak Tree, at Santa Anita. My record for the year stood at eight victories, three seconds, and one third in twelve starts, so I never dropped out of the money. The newspapers hailed me as the "people's horse," meaning that I won for the $2 and $5 bettors. For Sam Rubin I won something like $900,000 [$925,217].

I took off on another streak, winning my first four races of 1981. I finally got beat in the Gold Cup Handicap at Hollywood Park when I ran fourth behind something called Super Moment. I carried 130 pounds, he was carrying 117. I said to another horse after the race as we puffed back to the shed row, "I don't know why they don't just put a refrigerator on my back and then they could see how far I would go before I collapsed." People will tell you: "Handicappers make all the horses even at the start and that's what makes horse races." I say all that handicappers do is make sore backs.

By now Sam Rubin wanted only the best for me—and that meant the winningest jock of them all, Willie "the Shoe" Shoemaker. Willie agreed to ride me. We won three straight races in 1981, including the Sword Dancer at Belmont and the Jockey Club's Gold Cup, also at Belmont. We went to Arlington Park in Chicago for the Arlington Million.

Rain poured down on the track all morning long. I stared out from my stall at that rain and imagined myself skidding in all that mud.

At the starting gate, the Shoe patted me to calm down. He knew I dreaded what I faced—that strip of slippery mud in front of us.

We broke and I think I skidded left, right, frontways, and sideways. Later I heard Willie tell a reporter, "He was slipping and sliding on that messy turf and it took him three-eighths of a mile to get his feet under him. But he finally did get a hold of it."

I got a hold of the track coming down the backstretch to move from eighth to fifth. As we turned for home, I passed two wheezers and now held third. Ahead—a long way ahead—pounded

Left forefoot leading, John Henry goes for the wire in the 1981 Sword Dancer in New York. Willie Shoemaker urges a drivin' horse to keep on drivin'.

Key to Consent, who trailed The Bart by about a length.

I could hear Key to Consent's lungs roaring and guessed that he was through. But up ahead The Bart had his ears pinned down, his body flat. He's still got it all, I thought. He's sprinting like he just came out of the gate.

Key to Consent came back to me fast. I went by him with *my* ears pinned back, *my* body stretched like a lion in pursuit of dinner.

Some $600,000 waited at the wire for the winner, only $200,000 for the one who came by second. For $400,000, I told myself, you can kill yourself for the next five seconds.

The man who would pocket the $600,000, big Sam Rubin, measured the distance between The Bart and me—and then the distance between me and the wire.

No way, he told himself, no way my horse is gonna catch that other horse.

I never came as fast down a stretch. In two or three strides I had come even with The Bart's flank. I hear his jockey screaming in Spanish. Willie is screaming his head off—something like "Come on, come on!—but it came out across the air as one long screech.

The Bart and I lunged together for the finish line. People said later that we went across as one horse.

An NBC announcer, I was told later, said that The Bart had won. His happy owners ran, laughing, to the winner's circle. As they got there, they saw the official finish come up on the board—I was the photo-finish winner.

I ended 1981 with eight victories in ten starts. I came in out of the money only twice. For the year, I had won almost $2 million for Sam, who still tried to kiss me whenever he talked about

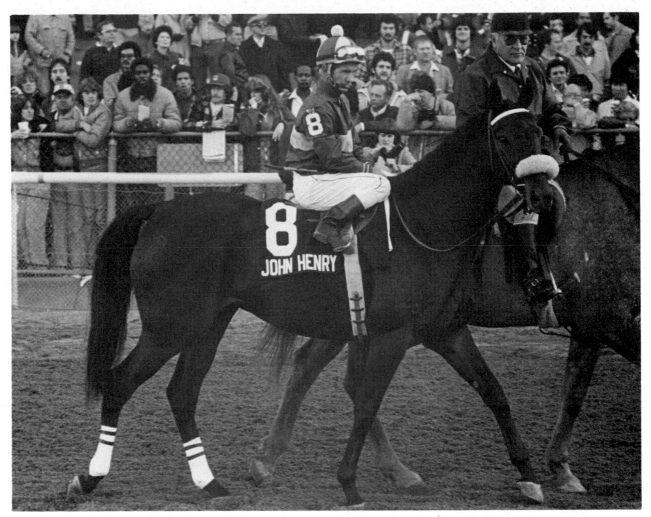

The Shoe and John Henry parade to the post for the 1981 Jockey Club Gold Cup at Belmont (above). The Shoe has only to show the stick to John Henry (below) in a race for the wire won by the horse that won more money than any horse ever—more than $6 million.

that photo with The Bart. When he came closer I nipped him on the arm and he stopped the sissy stuff. So far, I heard from a groom, Sam's $27,500 purchase of me had earned him almost $3 million. I was named the 1981 Horse of the Year.

A wrenched ankle kept me off the tracks from March until October of 1982. Being seven years old, I heard all the bad jokes from the other horses that "Grandpa," as they called me, even though that was an anatomical impossibility, should be put out to pasture. When I heard that talk, I tried to kick down a stall door, making such a ruckus that the other horses in the shed row couldn't sleep. You'd be surprised how one ruckus of mine shushed that talk.

I went to the post only six times in 1982. I won twice, finished third twice, and twice I ran out of the money. Those two firsts paid handsomely: one, the Santa Anita Handicap; the other, the Oak Tree, also at Santa Anita. That big California money fattened my earnings for the year to about a half-million dollars [$586,387].

By now I had passed the $3-million level for total winnings. To give you an idea how much money that is, keep in mind that the previous two great money-winning geldings—Kelso and Forego—had not earned as much as $2 million.

Now, as 1983 began, I turned the ripe age of eight, twice the age of some of the "veteran" horses. People shook their heads and said I should retire because aches and pains kept me from racing until that summer. Ron and Sam picked the July Fourth running of the American Handicap at Hollywood Park for what the papers called "John Henry's attempted comeback."

The Shoe had swung atop me for my last eleven races, and I'd won six of them. But while I had been out of action, Willie had taken another horse, called The Wonder. I met The Wonder once or twice and never saw anything at all wonderful about him. But maybe I'm being what they say all geldings become—a bitch.

Willie—I forgave him for this later—had the choice of me or The Wonder for the American Handicap and he picked The Wonder.

Ron had been eyeing a new jock, Chris McCarron, and decided to put young Chris on me for the American. This was a critical race for me—the last chance maybe to prove I wasn't washed up—so I wasn't all that happy having a kid on me.

Chris, though, was smart enough to let this old man run his own race. We broke cleanly out of the gate and as I passed The Wonder and the Shoe just before we came to the first turn, I told myself I didn't want to see them in this race again—and I didn't. I hung back in third place for the first mile of this mile-and-an-eighth race. Coming down the stretch I picked off the second horse, then swept by the leader to win by a length and a half. What I liked almost as much as the winning was hearing the track announcer shout, as I trotted into the winner's circle:

"The old man is back!"

By the end of 1983 I had a record for the year of two wins and two seconds in eight races. For the year I had won almost a half million [$652,100, to be exact]. In seven years of racing I had won almost $4 million. I was easily the biggest money winner ever. Nearest to me stood Spend a Buck, who had collected about $2 million. I used to tell other horses that, compared to me, Spend a Buck was middle class.

People asked how long I could go on as 1984 began and I automatically became nine years old. One day, another trainer, Charles Whittingham, came by our stable and I heard him tell one of our hands, as he stared at me, "He beat Balzac when I had Balzac, and now I've got a two-year-old in the barn sired by Balzac and John Henry's still running. They say he's nine years old, but he is better now than when he was four or five. The son of a bitches I have chasing him—they won't even live to be nine!"

I could imagine some glum looks on the faces of the horses in his stable that night.

Ron told people, when they asked, why I had lasted so long. He said I knew how to relax. Other horses, he said, charged out of the stable to the practice track. I ambled out, stopped, looked around, then ambled on some more. And in a race, he said, I had a fluid motion that reduced the pounding on bones and muscles. The way I bobbed my head, he said, gave me more time to breathe in and out—and that got more oxygen to my blood and muscles.

I listened and he may have been right about everything he said. Frankly, I just did everything the way I had always done it—pure instinct, I suppose.

Who knows about racing? When 1984 began, I lost my first race. In a mile-and-a-half event, the San Luis Rey, at Santa Anita, I came home third and gasping. The stablehands said a mile and a half was too long for an old geezer like me—and I thought, panting for maybe a half hour after that race, that probably they were right. When we came to the stretch in that San Luis Rey, two young horses shot by me—they were Interco and Gato del Sol—while all I wanted to do was stop and sit awhile.

Ron and Sam said no—what I needed was work to give me "more legs," as they say around the stables. They were right. A month and a half later I won a mile-and-an-eighth race and then I won the mile-and-a-half Hollywood Invitational Handicap. I carried the top weight of 126 pounds.

That summer of 1984 Chris and I won a flock of heavy-paying races, including the Arlington Million in Chicago and the Belmont Turf Classic in New York.

After I won the Belmont, I heard nothing but talk about the Ballantine Scotch Classic Handicap. It was being held three weeks later over in New Jersey at the Meadowlands. For some out-

In his next to last race, John Henry pounds home first to win the 1984 Belmont Turf Classic. He was the oldest horse, at nine, to be named Horse of the Year.

Sam Rubin leads John Henry, Chris McCarron in the saddle, to the winner's circle after John Henry won the 1984 Belmont Turf Classic.

landish reason—I guess maybe Scotch drinkers stay up late—the start was set at eleven o'clock at night.

I knew I was going west to Jersey. The Ballantine promoters promised a half-million-dollars bonus, on top of the first-prize money of $240,000, to any horse who won the Belmont and the Ballantine back to back.

I had already put more than a million and a half dollars into Sam's deep pockets so far in 1984 and my account with him showed winnings of almost $6 million for my career, but I knew Sam couldn't turn his back on the chance to win about three-quarters of a million dollars for one race. All he asked from me was about two minutes of my time. Even though I thought it strange to be running under the moon, I was glad to do it.

I'd beaten a horse named Win in the Belmont. Win went over to Jersey for the Ballantine and my friends the handicappers give what weight to Win? He almost beat me a few weeks earlier and he has to carry only 120. I have to carry 126. I heard Win laughing for hours after the grooms came by and mentioned the weights we each had to carry.

We lined up under the stars and the moon. I guess I may have dozed off in the gate. I got off slowly—seventh or eighth at the first turn, some nine lengths back. As we went around the first turn, I thought I heard the crowd suddenly go quiet—all the noise going out of the place like air hissing out of a punctured balloon.

I guessed why. The crowd had made me the heavy favorite—and I guess lots of them suddenly thought they'd be going home broke. I wondered if they'd boo me if I lost.

Maybe that woke me up. I went by horses down the backstretch and around the turn. But

as I swung into the homestretch, I saw four horses in front of me.

I was on the outside—nothing ahead of me but track. I took off like the finish line was the last bus out of Jersey. I pounded by Who's for Dinner, Four Base, Win—I had to flash him a nasty grin—and then Hero's Honor. I went under the wire at 2:13, matching the track record.

A few weeks later, at nine, I became the oldest horse to be named Horse of the Year.

That was my thirty-ninth victory in 85 starts. I finished second in 15 races, third in 9. I finished out of the money only 22 times in 85 starts. Talk about a people's horse, like the Seattle Crew people said their horse was. What is better for racing people than a horse who finishes in the money about three out of every four times he runs?

Slips's notes on John Henry end here. In the spring of 1985, John Henry was dogged by a series of leg ailments. Finally, doctors diagnosed the trouble as a "filling," a weakness in those knees so long thought incapable of allowing John Henry to be a racer. On July 21, 1985, a Sunday, Sam Rubin announced to a crowd in Hollywood Park that "the time has come. We want his fans to remember him as a champion."

John Henry traveled to the Kentucky Horse Park in Lexington, where he joined other great champions like Forego and Spend a Buck in what was supposed to be happy retirement.

But John Henry kicked up a fuss, predictably, when he had to stand in a stall and face a track on which he loved to run. "We tried to

take him out of the stall to show him off during special events at various tracks around the country," Sam Rubin told us in the spring of 1986. "But John just went crazy—the handlers couldn't control him—whenever he came into sight of a track. That horse, even at the age of eleven, wanted to do only one thing—race."

Sam permitted John Henry to attempt a comeback by working out in California during the summer of 1986. But the eleven-year-old, two-time Horse of the Year, had run his distance. Late that summer, as it must to all champions, retirement came to the horse who—if you count only the money he won—could be said to have been the greatest of them all.

INDEX